TROUBLED JOURNEY

TROUBLED JOURNEY

From Pearl Harbor to Ronald Reagan

FREDERICK F. SIEGEL

Consulting Editor: Eric Foner

AMERICAN CENTURY SERIES

Hill and Wang   New York

A DIVISION OF FARRAR, STRAUS AND GIROUX

Copyright © 1984 by Frederick F. Siegel
ALL RIGHTS RESERVED
Printed in the United States of America
Published simultaneously in Canada by Collins Publishers, Toronto
Designed by Tere LoPrete
Second printing, 1986
ISBN: 0-8090-9443-6 (cloth); 0-8090-0155-1 (paper)

Library of Congress Cataloging in Publication Data
Siegel, Frederick F.
   Troubled journey.
   (American century series)
   Bibliography: p.
   Includes index.
   1. United States—History—1945-   . 2. World War,
1939-1945—United States. I. Title. II. Series.
E741.S48   1984   973.9   83-26547

To Al and Selma Siegel

Acknowledgments

THIS BOOK HAD ITS ORIGINS in the many discussions on American life and politics I've had with friends over the years. I'd like to thank Leon Fink, Sue Levine, Lynn Garafola, Louie Menashe, Mark Naison, Mike Harrington, Liz Phillips, Chris Alilunas, and Larry Funsten for either reading or listening to my "dramatic" readings of parts of the manuscript. I owe a special debt to Jan Rosenberg and Eric Foner, who have been kind enough to tolerate my eccentricities while making invaluable comments on the entire manuscript. And finally I'd like to thank my publisher, Arthur Wang, whose time, editorial skills, and good judgment have no doubt made this a better book than it would have been.

Portions of Chapter 13 appeared in a different form in my article "Race: The Missing Issue of 1980," *Dissent* (1982).

F. F. S.

Contents

INTRODUCTION   *xi*

1. The Crucible of World War II   *3*
2. 1946: The Crucial Year   *20*
3. Isolationist Revenge   *48*
4. Truman, Eisenhower, and the
   Politics of Prosperity   *86*
5. From Utopia to Dystopia   *105*
6. The Sputnik Years   *116*
7. The New Frontier in Power   *130*
8. From the Great Society to
   Black Power   *152*
9. Vietnam at Home and Abroad   *171*
10. Kulturkampf   *198*
11. Nixon and Kissinger: Deception,
    Dollars, and Détente   *216*
12. Coup and Counter-coup   *244*
13. Jimmy Carter, Ronald Reagan, and
    the Legacy of George Wallace   *261*

EPILOGUE: *The End of American Exceptionalism*   *271*

BIBLIOGRAPHY   *275*

INDEX   *285*

Introduction

Troubled Journey IS A FRANKLY reinterpretive work that views American social and cultural life over the past forty years through the prism of foreign and domestic politics. Politics, broadly understood, is the essential framework for comprehending American life, because in the absence of a common mystique of blood and soil, it is the political creed of the Declaration of Independence that holds the nation together. America's national identity and its political principles are inseparable. "It is our fate as a nation," wrote Oliver Wendell Holmes, "not to have ideologies but to be one." Or as Carl Friedrich put it: "To be an American is an ideal while to be a Frenchman is a fact." The ideal was a society freed of both secular and religious officialdom. "Society," said Tom Paine, "performs for itself everything which is ascribed to government." This time-honored vision of a largely stateless society of self-regulating individuals unsullied by the corrupting hand of bureaucracy was shattered, first, by the New Deal and then by intervention in World War II. For the Protestant Republicans who had governed the country for most of the seventy years after the Civil War and viewed themselves as the hereditary rulers of the land, the New Deal was a sacrilege, and in their reaction to Roosevelt's policies they intensified what Dennis Wrong calls the rhythm of democratic politics, producing a cycle of action and reaction that still endures.

American politics since 1941 can best be understood as a running duel between the shifting coalitions that comprise the heirs and enemies of the "Roosevelt Revolution." The conflicts over the New Deal—like other "great" American conflicts from the Jacksonian war on the National Bank, to slavery, free silver, and prohibition, and on to intervention, containment, welfare, affirmative action, ERA, and abortion—are, as James Q. Wilson has pointed out, fights over what principles government should follow.

The 1980 election, for instance, can be seen as part of a forty-year political/cultural war fought in large measure over the role of government in American life. Seen in this light, Ronald Reagan's victory in 1980 was but the latest round in the continuing cycle of revenge and repression set off by the trauma, for Republicanism, of the New Deal. McCarthyism, to oversimplify, was the revenge of isolationist "true" Republicanism on Roosevelt's foreign and domestic policy, while in the 1960s the political losers of the 1950s and their children got a chance to wreak havoc on their former tormentors. In the course of these forty years, alliances have been altered and reshaped by the social and economic transformation of, first, mass consumption and then post-industrialism but nonetheless remained tied to the past through "conflicting chains of emotional symbols."

Unlike most books on recent American history, this one begins with 1941, because it is impossible to understand either McCarthyism or the contours of postwar American diplomacy without first understanding the divisions created by America's entrance into the European war and the dilemmas produced by Roosevelt's foreign policy choices. The three chapters which cover American foreign policy between 1941 and 1954 pay close attention to the interplay of public opinion, the policy makers' perceptions of Soviet intentions, and the actions of America's allies and adversaries. And contrary to such respected revisionists as Walter LaFeber, I argue that the turning point in the Cold War comes in 1946, a year whose momentous but often overlooked developments are given close scrutiny.

Chapters 4 through 6 analyze domestic life between 1945 and 1960. The emphasis is on the development and significance of mass production, suburbanization, and the changes in the occupational structure which prefigure the development of "New Class politics in the 1960s." Chapter 6 describes the fears on the part of the elite generated by Sputnik and the convergence of conservative and liberal critiques of affluence which paved the way for Kennedyism.

Vietnam and the civil rights movements in the Kennedy and Johnson administrations are the focus of Chapters 7 through 9. Vietnam is discussed in the context of both America's postwar efforts to revive Europe and the Kennedy administration's technocratic vision of regaining the postwar promise of an American century. The indispensable contribution of American radicals and the unintended consequences of Black Power for the Great Society are the distinguishing features of the discussion on civil rights.

Chapters 10 through 13 describe the Nixon years, beginning with a discussion of how the civil rights movement and the creation of a "new class" of college-educated professionals transformed the political parties and generated in the 1960s and 1970s a new and even more intense version of the cultural civil war fought out during the McCarthy era. Chapters 11 and 12 analyze the way the cultural clash was worked out in American foreign policy and the failed attempt by Nixon to capture control of the federal bureaucracy in order to roll back the Great Society. The last chapter carries these earlier developments through to the "last election of the 1960s," Ronald Reagan's victory in 1980. Finally, the Epilogue suggests that the cycle of political conflict begun by the New Deal may be drawing to a close as the reorganization of the American economy wrought by high technology and international competition transforms the American class and occupational structure.

TROUBLED JOURNEY

1

The Crucible of World War II

More than half the world is ruled by men who despise the American idea and have sworn to destroy it. . . . It is not hysterical to think that democracy and liberty are threatened.
—WILLIAM ALLEN WHITE, in support of America's entry into World War II

Foreign Politics demands scarcely any of those qualities which are peculiar to democracy; they require, on the contrary, the perfect use of almost all those in which it is deficient . . . a democracy can only with great difficulty regulate the details of an important undertaking, persevere in a fixed design, and work out its execution in spite of serious obstacles. It cannot combine its measures with secrecy or await their consequence with patience.
—ALEXIS DE TOCQUEVILLE

PUT ASIDE YOUR MOVIE MEMORIES of World War II—pictures of GIs (usually an Italian, an Irishman, and a Jew, with an occasional black)—united in a camaraderie born of a determination to stamp out fascism. Wartime surveys taken by the Army revealed that troop morale was dangerously low. Most soldiers had little idea of why they were fighting and few cared about the political meaning of the war. They were there because they had to be, and they fought for their own lives and those of their buddies, not for some higher principles.

Morale at home wasn't much better. The public was uncertain about the war's objectives and it was hesitant about supporting a total war against Germany. Americans felt a great distaste for Hitler, but, according to an Office of War Information survey, nearly half the public had positive feelings toward Germany. Of those who had an opinion, about one in five thought Hitler's policies toward the Jews were probably justified and more than half thought that Jews had too much power in America. While New Deal writers, labor leaders, and intellectuals saw the war as a fight for democracy, the American people as a whole shared few convictions regarding Germany. Their strongest feelings were reserved for Japan and a desire to "pay back" the "dirty Japs" for their December 1941 sneak attack on Pearl Harbor. It was only after the fact that our blood sacrifice and subsequent knowledge of the Holocaust broadly sanctified the war.

Among the public at large, feelings about the war ran strongest among those who had fervently opposed American involvement. The isolationist critics of President Roosevelt's policies who called themselves "America Firsters" were convinced that war was more likely to bring fascism to America than democracy to the rest of the world. Their opposition ran so deep that the "Japanese attack on Pearl Harbor brought war but not unity to the American people."

Stunned by the Japanese attack, Roosevelt's Republican critics temporarily abandoned their public posture of isolationism. With the nation at war Republicans turned to criticism of how the President was directing the fight. Republican isolationists like Ohio's Senator Robert Taft called for an investigation of American unpreparedness at Pearl; privately many were convinced that the attack had been part of a plot by FDR to push the country into war.

The 1942 congressional elections were a sharp setback for the President. Supporters of Roosevelt's policies had targeted 115 isolationists for defeat in the general election; 110 were reelected. The voting returns gave the Republicans 44 more seats in the House and 9 in the Senate. Surveying the election results, a writer for the party organ *The Republican* crowed, "It would be absurd to say that 'isolationism' was not a factor in the election." The Administration was left with a razor-thin margin of 7 votes in the House. Like Woodrow Wilson before him, FDR was threatened with an isolationist revolt.

Isolationism was a deep and abiding tendency in American life. Temporarily forced below the surface by Pearl Harbor, it continued as a powerful current. Typically, America Firsters, or members of the "peace bloc" as some styled themselves, were fiercely hostile to Roosevelt's foreign as well as domestic policies. Fiercely anti-Communist, they were convinced that a devilishly clever Roosevelt had maneuvered the country into an unnecessary war against the wrong foe just as he had used his wiles at home to foist the alien measures of the New Deal's "creeping socialism" on an unsuspecting nation. They were more likely than their fellow citizens to believe that we could "do business with Hitler" and they saw Japan and particularly Russia as America's real enemies. The isolationists were able to withstand the pressure to support the war wholeheartedly because they based their dissent on a time-honored American tradition of noninvolvement in European affairs. They felt themselves the "true" Americans; it was the rest of the country that had strayed.

Isolationism reflected Protestant America's view that the United States was God's chosen nation, a land which had been divinely set apart from the wickedness of the Old World to serve as a beacon of righteousness unto all the nations. Seeded intellectually by Puritanism, the isolationist impulse took political form with George Washington's Farewell Address warning America to steer clear of decadent Europe. Bordered by militarily weak neighbors to the north and south, and shielded by vast oceans to the east and west, Americans enjoyed free security and a sense of invulnerability. This knowledge led young Abe Lincoln to boast that "all the armies of Europe, Asia and Africa, combined with all the treasure of the earth (our own excepted) in their military chest, with a Buonaparte for commander, could not by force take a drink from the Ohio or make track on the Blue Ridge, in the trial of a thousand years." But Lincoln warned, in lines often quoted by isolationists, that "danger" could "spring up amongst us." If America were imperiled, the threat would come from within.

American involvement in World War I inspired broad opposition and served to heighten isolationism. Wilson pushed for war because he feared the consequences of one power, in this case Imperial Germany, dominating the continent of Europe. It was in America's interest to see that a balance of power was maintained. But Wilson, moralist that he was, never discussed such considerations; instead he explained American participation almost exclusively in terms of German wickedness and American morality. It was to be a war to end all wars, a war for democracy. Wilson sincerely believed that if democracy and capitalism were brought to the world the different nations would be too busy creating wealth to bother fighting one another. When World War I ended, not in a triumph for democracy, but in an orgy of squabbling over the remains of the German Empire, it seemed clear that a great deal of American blood had been shed for naught.

In the 1930s the rise of Hitler and Mussolini forced Americans once again to look across the ocean. Isolationists, replaying America's entry into World War I, responded with a devil theory of war. Munitions makers and bankers, greedy cosmopolitan capitalists aided by the masterminds of British finance, they argued, had placed self-interest above patriotism and insidiously drawn the innocent American lamb into the European slaughter. By the late 1930s the collective devil of the cosmopolitan bankers and munitions makers were replaced by a single figure, Franklin Delano Roosevelt, at once the most loved and the most hated man in America. "The 1930s produced an enormous number of people with a special mission—a mission to warn America that the President had treason in his soul." FDR, they would insist, was a Communist who would betray America, a Judas who would ruin America with a kiss.

The wellborn Roosevelt was hated both in the corporate boardrooms, where he was considered a traitor to his class, and in the heart of the country, in small-town Protestant America, where his support of labor unions, social welfare programs, and government regulation was seen as an expression of the social forces threatening to destroy the nineteenth-century world of a self-reliant people and a self-regulating economy. A popular nativist ditty of the period read:

> God Bless America
> The Jews Own It
> The Catholics Run It
> The Negroes Enjoy It
> The Protestants Founded It
> But
> The Communists Will Destroy It.

For New Deal loyalists such doggerel was yet another example of the fascist forces that threatened America from within and without. If Republican diehards insisted that Roosevelt was "that Bolshevik in the White House," ideological New Dealers returned the favor by denouncing conservative Republicans as fascists. Henry Wallace, the point man for the New Dealers, fought the 1940 election with the slogan "Keep Hitler out of the White House." Wallace conceded that "every Republican is not an appeaser. But you can be sure that every Nazi, every Hitlerite, and every appeaser is a Republican." Wallace glossed over the isolationism of leading Democrats like Burton Wheeler who were left-leaning at home yet impassioned appeasers. Reflecting public sentiment, the Democratic Party's 1940 platform contained a tougher anti-war pledge than the Republicans'. At their harshest, fervent New Dealers dropped the qualifiers and pronounced Wendell Willkie, Roosevelt's middle-of-the-road Republican opponent, "the man Hitler wants elected President." Willkie, a devout internationalist, or "One Worlder" as they were then called, became a strong supporter of New Deal foreign policy after his defeat.

The New Dealers' rhetoric was exaggerated; their fear of fascism was not. The twentieth century had brought democracy under unprecedented attack. In the wake of the senseless slaughter in World War I, many writers and social scientists emphasized the irrational nature of politics. The free choice necessary for democracy was, they said, a pleasant myth, out of place in a world where mass sentiment and public opinion could be manufactured like bicycles. The "masses," it was concluded, were incapable of managing their own affairs. The distinguished isolationist Harry Elmer Barnes announced that "differential psychology has proven the inferiority of the masses," by which he meant the new immigrants, thus confirming, he claimed, "the old Aristotelian dogma that some men are made to rule and others to serve."

If anyone doubted that dictatorship was the wave of the future they had only to look around. In the years after World War I, first Portugal, then Spain, Italy, Greece, Japan, Turkey, Russia, Poland, Czechoslovakia, followed by Austria, Germany, Hungary, Yugoslavia, and a host of Latin American countries, had turned to dictatorship. Americans, with their traditional faith in progress, had believed that they were the future, that democracy would spread around the globe. Now it seemed probable to many that democratic institutions had outlived their usefulness. With the onset of the Great Depression an optimist was a man who thought the future was uncertain.

In a nation ravaged by depression and doubt, Roosevelt, through word and deed, made democracy a fighting faith again. By his vocal opposition to what he called the "economic royalists" and his insistence that Nazi Germany was more than just another great power, Roosevelt created a climate in which a broad range of immigrant, labor, liberal, and left-wing groups began to reconstitute a sense of national purpose. Some evoked Jefferson and the Founding Fathers to proclaim that Communism was twentieth-century Americanism, while a far larger group of liberals saw in the social engineering of the New Deal a middle way between Soviet authoritarianism and the tyranny of the market.

The New Dealers saw foreign policy as a chance to extend the democratic revival worldwide. "There was a sense that once justice was achieved in America it would be necessary to spread it abroad" so that the tide of dictatorship might be pushed back forever. When the war came, Henry Wallace, who believed America was "the Chosen of the Lord," applauded as the young James Reston insisted that we could not win the war with Germany "until it . . . became a national crusade for America and the American dream." Reston thought the war would be a failure if a single totalitarian state remained. Wallace's America, said a Wallaceite, had "accepted a divine mission to save the world, Roosevelt [was] to be its prophet," World War II was to be "a people's war for worldwide democracy."

Roosevelt, the pragmatist, encouraged these views with his own grandiloquent statements of America's purpose in fighting. Like Wilson before him, he never publicly discussed his overwhelming concern with the balance of power, for fear that it would be divisive. Instead he cloaked his foreign policy in the rhetoric of the Four Freedoms and the Atlantic Charter. To match Hitler's "New Order" Roosevelt proposed a new "moral order." He declined territorial ambitions and projected a reeducation of the world along the lines of Christian morality. This Sermon on the Mount world of self-determination and democracy for all nations was so inspiring that one Catholic cleric was moved to describe democracy as "the nearest thing to God on earth."

Roosevelt was neither a tribune of the new moral order nor a "Red dupe." Critics and admirers alike would have been better served if they had watched what he did rather than listened to what he said. From December 1941 on, the President subordinated all his efforts at home and abroad to the goal of winning the war. He allowed New Deal programs to atrophy as businessmen brought to Washington to build up the arms industries elbowed aside the social reformers who had dominated Washington for a decade. Roosevelt stood back and watched as special interests lobbied ferociously for pork barrel bills to aid farmers or car dealers or some particularly deserving capitalist. In return Roosevelt expected support for the fragile consensus he had built for both winning the war and creating a permanent American international involvement to maintain peace.

Roosevelt was willing to sacrifice some of what he had built at home because he was firmly convinced of the danger abroad. While the isolationists were replaying World War I, Roosevelt was trying to detail a forceful diplomatic response to Nazi imperialism. He understood that international affairs was a game of power subject to its own rules. His task was to play that game within the constraints of American power and domestic politics. To defeat Hitler he was willing to make a deal with the French fascist Admiral Jean Darlan. When he was castigated by liberals and leftists for negotiating with Darlan, he replied with more than a touch of disdain: "My children, you are permitted in time of great danger to walk with the devil until you have crossed the bridge." Later, unleashing his temper, he shouted: "Of course I'm dealing with Darlan, since Darlan is giving me Algiers!" The deal with Darlan was a reflection of the limitations of American power. But when it came to alliance with first Britain and then the Soviet Union, a good many thought that Roosevelt had indeed made a deal with the devil; Britain and Russia were cordially hated by many of his countrymen.

Roosevelt saw Britain as America's first line of defense. But for many Irish- and German-Americans, the nation's two largest white ethnic groups, and particularly the Irish, a hatred for England came with their mother's milk. Both steadfastly denied that any moral distinction could be drawn between British and German imperialism. For the Irish, German sins in Czechoslovakia were not nearly so odious as Britain's in Ireland. For some German-Americans the suffering they experienced during World War I blinded them to Nazism. They simply didn't want to see America go to war against Germany again. Others, like the nation's most prominent isolationist, aviator-hero Charles Lindbergh, and Joseph Kennedy, the American Ambassador to Britain, had a soft spot for the New Germany. They saw England as old and effeminate, while Germany, like America, was young and virile. "Civilization," Lindbergh intoned, "depends on [Hitler's] wisdom far more than on the action of the democracies."

Almost all isolationists hostile to Britain were deeply suspicious of the U.S.S.R. as well, but the strongest opposition to American aid for the Soviet Union came from American Catholics. Catholics and particularly Catholic intellectuals applauded when one of Roosevelt's most effective critics, Robert Taft, warned that "the victory of Communism in the world would be far more dangerous to the U.S. than the victory of fascism." For Catholics isolationism was a matter of anti-Communism. Catholics and Communists had been at war for nearly a quarter of a century, battling over Soviet persecution of religion and the future of Spain, when FDR tried to convince American Catholics that an alliance with Russia was in America's best interest. Roosevelt feared that without millions of Russian soldiers to absorb the brunt of the fighting, the U.S. casualties required to defeat Hitler would far exceed what the American public would tolerate. Catholic leaders were unmoved. They described an alliance with the Soviets as a "covenant with hell." Pointing to the Soviet conquest of part of Poland and the Baltic states, they warned that cooperation with Stalin could only destroy the moral position of the United States. Anti-Soviet feeling was so intense that one bishop declared: ". . . rather than serve as an ally of a communistic government, young Catholic men should refuse to join the armed services of this country."

Catholics found powerful allies within the Administration. The professional diplomats at the State Department shared their anti-Communist sentiments; State experts on Europe were cultured, conservative aristocrats with warm feelings for the highly cultivated pre-Nazi Germans they had known. Russia, by contrast, evoked disgust. They saw it as a land of barbarism and bad manners, a threat to the traditional order of Western civilization. George F. Kennan, in the late forties a prime mover in the postwar hard line toward the Soviets, wrote: "Never . . . did I consider the Soviet Union a fit ally or associate, actual or potential, of the United

States." Sharing the Germans' anti-Semitism, many diplomats saw Bolshevism as a Jewish disease, and like the Catholics they feared above all that war against Hitler would leave Russia in control of Eastern Europe. Aware of these fears and the pro-German feelings of some of his diplomatic advisers, Roosevelt is said to have joked shortly after Pearl Harbor that his "State Department was neutral in this war and he hoped it would remain that way." The President, I. F. Stone has argued, was "torn between the rival claims of Stalin and the Vatican. To hold his party together, he had to appease Pius XII; to keep his casualties down, he had to appease Stalin." There was no way in principle to resolve the conflict.

To overcome the opposition of his critics, Roosevelt made promises about the Russo-American alliance on which he could not deliver, promises that were to haunt postwar America. Roosevelt allayed the fears of Catholics and isolationists with talk of how the alliance would democratize the Soviet Union, which would forgo its position as the center of world Communism to become a nation-state like any other. Ironically, it was because Roosevelt and his advisers saw important similarities between Germany and the Soviet Union, similarities confirmed by the Nazi-Soviet pact of 1939, that they were willing to take a chance on such a transformation.

Stalin's policies throughout the 1930s—his pledge to build "socialism in one country," his expulsion of Trotsky, the prophet of permanent revolution, his brutal liquidation of the old Bolsheviks, and his deemphasis of Marxist ideology—seemed to indicate to FDR that Russia was becoming an ordinary nation-state, which could be dealt with in conventional terms. Stalin's national Bolshevism looked very much like Hitler's national socialism—the standard quip being that the principal difference between the two was that Moscow was colder than Berlin—with two very important differences. First and most significant was the belief that the Soviet Union lacked the diabolism and dynamism which made Germany so dangerous. Hitler was a genuinely popular leader who galvanized the masses with a pornography of violence alien to the bloody but bureaucratic Stalin. So that while Soviet Marxism promised salvation in a long-deferred future, Hitler was promising an Aryan heaven now by way of immediate conquest and racial "purification." Secondly, the Soviets, despite their reign of terror, and unlike the Nazis, still spoke the language of Western humanism. They killed in the name of freedom and a better future, so it was possible to argue, as many did, that "the methods were deficient but the basic idea was good." Or as Harold Ickes, FDR's close adviser, put it, "I hate Communism, but it is founded on a belief in the control of government, including the economic system, by the people themselves." It was the very antithesis, he thought, of Nazism.

Roosevelt gambled that, in the course of an alliance, American influence would begin subtly to shape the Soviet Union into a civilized nation by Western standards. He hoped, in effect, that the forced alliance of war would spawn the true friendship of peace, which over the long run might further modify the regime. During the war, there was some reason to believe that just such a modification was taking place. Stalin, aware of the need to rally popular support, eased up on government control of religious and personal life. And as a gesture of his newfound nationalism, Stalin officially dissolved the Communist International, the supposed general staff of the world revolution. Encouraged by these developments, Roosevelt privately told New York's Cardinal Spellman that the Anglo-Americans would not be willing to fight the Soviets for control of Eastern Europe once Hitler was defeated, that the European countries would have to undergo a great change to adapt to the military power of the backward Russians, and that in ten or twenty years European influence would civilize the Russian barbarians. The Europeans, FDR explained, could not expect America to rescue them from Russia as well as Germany. Thus the great need to exert a moderating influence on Russia by paying sympathetic attention to Stalin's claims to Eastern Europe.

Here lay the great, and perhaps unavoidable, contradiction in Roosevelt's policies. If he were to keep the Soviets happy and draw them into a postwar alliance to keep the peace, he would have to acknowledge Soviet control over Eastern Europe. But a Soviet Empire in Eastern Europe would be a clear violation of the promises of self-determination embodied in the Atlantic Charter for which Americans were supposedly fighting and dying. Roosevelt's announced foreign policy and his actual foreign policy were on a collision course.

The tension between these two policies reverberated within the

United States. Roosevelt, trying to make his wish, a new Russia, father to the fact, joined left, liberal, and labor groups in sometimes effusive praise of Stalin and the Soviet Union. Movies like *Mission to Moscow*, based on a book by the American Ambassador to the U.S.S.R., Joseph E. Davies, celebrated not only the truly heroic struggle against the Nazi invaders but Stalin's personal virtues as well. It was all laid on so thick that James Agee, writing in the pro-Soviet *Nation*, called the movie "a great, glad two-million-dollar bowl of canned borscht, eminently approvable by the Institute of Good Housekeeping." Davies was effusive in praise of Stalin but he wasn't alone in hyperbole; the middle-of-the-road *Life* magazine proclaimed Lenin "perhaps the greatest man of modern times" and the Russians "one hell of a people . . . [who] to a remarkable degree . . . look like Americans, dress like Americans and think like Americans."

In a few years *Life* would be fervently anti-Soviet, but even at the height of the war such views elicited a hostile reaction. Max Eastman, Trotsky's former confidant in America, attacked the "mushheads and muddleheads" who "are doing us in" by carpeting the country with admiring accounts of "Uncle Joe." America's Russophiles, concluded Eastman, who had turned conservative, were a danger "to the survival of free institutions *within* America." Catholic leaders echoed Eastman. Prelates sympathetic to FDR urged him to prove his good faith by purging and prosecuting American Communists to atone for the Soviet-American alliance. A failure to root out Communists at home, warned Edmund Walsh, later a key figure in launching Joe McCarthy's anti-Communist crusade, would constitute proof that FDR's support of Russia in the war against Hitler was based as much on ideological sympathy as practical necessity.

Victories in North Africa and Italy in 1943 and the invasion of Normandy temporarily quieted isolationist and anti-Communist sentiment. Gearing up for the 1944 presidential election, FDR secured his right flank by throwing his outspokenly reformist and pro-Soviet Vice-President Henry Wallace to the political wolves. He replaced Wallace with Senator Harry Truman, a Missouri Democrat acceptable to both New Dealers and the growing number of conservative Democrats. Their Republican opponents, Thomas E. Dewey, a crusading New York district attorney with close ties to Wall Street internationalists, and his running mate, Governor John Bricker, an Ohio isolationist, gave the Democratic ticket a close race. Sensing that for the first time in a dozen years a Republican victory was within grasp, Dewey and Bricker tried to capitalize on a mixture of growing anti-labor and anti-Communist sentiment. They taunted the Democrats with cries of "Clear it with Sidney," referring to the hold the "pink" CIO chieftain was supposed to have over FDR. For all his alleged power, however, Sidney Hillman had failed to keep his choice for Vice-President, Henry Wallace, on the Democratic ticket. The Republican mudslinging was undercut by the well-publicized Soviet role in the Allied victories. And the Democrats replied to Republican charges with a gleeful chorus of "The Old Red Scare Ain't What She Used to Be."

FDR the campaigner went out of his way to reassure the solidly Democratic Polish and Catholic voters about the future of Poland. He posed with a map of the old Poland prominently displayed, proclaiming that "Poland must be reconstituted as a great nation." He assured the voters that once Hitler was defeated he would know how to deal with Stalin on Poland's behalf. The ploy worked. Despite grumbling, Poles and Catholics stayed with the New Deal coalition that had brought them into the mainstream of American life. Roosevelt was buoyed by the defeat of numerous isolationists in the House and Senate, but the joy was short-lived.

With the successful Anglo-American landings on the beaches of France on D-Day, June 6, 1944, it became clear that the Allies would win the war. The question became when, and with which victor getting what part of the spoils. Britain and the Soviets were clear about their ambitions. As far back as 1939 British-Soviet negotiations for an alliance against Germany broke down, in part because of the Russian desire to reconstitute the boundaries of the old Czarist empire by taking Latvia, Lithuania, and Estonia, the Baltic republics which had broken away from the old Russian empire during World War I. When the two negotiated in 1941, Stalin, with Hitler at his throat, insisted that at war's end Russia would retain the territories acquired in the Nazi-Soviet pact plus Rumania. Churchill recognized that Russian success would have to be rewarded at the expense of Eastern Europeans. He was willing to leave Eastern Europe in Soviet hands if in return he could preserve the British Empire and its influence in Western Europe. Churchill knew that at war's end the Americans would withdraw their troops from the Continent. He feared above all that unless the Soviets were locked into a clearly defined set of borders and spheres of influence, the massive Russian armies would dominate Europe. Stalin, for his part, was more than willing to acknowledge a free hand for the Anglo-Americans in Western Europe if he was given similar freedom in the East.

On October 9, 1944, Stalin and Churchill sat down in a business-like manner to divide up Europe. "Churchill, stating that London and Moscow must not go at cross purposes in the Balkans, pushed across the table to Stalin a simple stark list giving Russia 90% predominance in Rumania, and 75% in Bulgaria, Britain 90% in Greece and dividing Yugoslavia and Hungary 50/50 between Russia and the West. Stalin paused only a moment, then with his blue pencil made a large tick on the paper and passed it back to Churchill."

FDR and his Secretary of State, Cordell Hull, denounced the "percentages deal." Roosevelt was willing to concede Eastern Europe to the Soviet sphere of influence. Roosevelt, American Ambassador to Moscow Averell Harriman recorded, "consistently show[ed] very little interest in Eastern European matters except as they affect[ed] sentiment in America." But that was the rub; discussing Poland, presidential pollster Hadley Cantril made it clear that public support for FDR's policies was "unusually sensitive to events." Roosevelt could never acknowledge that American blood had been shed to exchange German imperialism for a Russian variety. Even internationalist papers like the influential New York *Herald Tribune* were already warning against "selling out" Poland and the Baltic states to Soviet imperialism.

Roosevelt rejected the percentages agreement but refused to spell out what he wanted the future map of Europe to look like. As one reporter correctly put it, the President seemed to be "long on ideals, short on plans." If he wasn't sure of what he wanted, though, Roosevelt knew what he didn't want. When he was urged to demand Russia's agreement to an independent Poland, he responded testily, "Do you want me to go to war with Russia?" Filled with a self-confidence that exuded the optimism his country-men had learned to love during the dark years of the Depression,

Roosevelt's style was to play up the positive and ignore the darker possibilities. Explaining his interpretation of Russia to the Advertising War Council Conference in 1944, Roosevelt exclaimed, "They didn't know us, that's the really fundamental difference." And he went on: "They are friendly people. They haven't got any crazy ideas of conquest and so forth; and now they have gotten to know us, they are much more willing to accept us." "His technique of government was always to leave questions open and hope that events would play into his hands [as they did at Pearl Harbor], but as they conspicuously failed to do after 1944."

Roosevelt had an enormous faith in his powers of personal persuasion. It was a style that served him extremely well in American domestic politics and he tried to extend this personal touch, what Isaiah Berlin has called "royal cousin diplomacy," to foreign affairs. In 1936, for instance, he thought Hitler might be curbed if he could ask the Führer "personally and secretly . . . to outline the limits of German objectives"—something he failed to do with Stalin. He made a great effort to win Stalin's confidence, even to the point of making jokes at Churchill's expense to win the Marshal's confidence. After they got chummy, he told aides that "I can personally handle Stalin better" than anyone else. Through man-to-man, personal diplomacy he expected to ease some of the tensions between his public and his private foreign policies. He hoped that by drawing Stalin into a web of mutually interlocking relationships, culminating in a big power consortium (the Four Policemen) at the UN, he could moderate Stalin's aims. Roosevelt the realist saw that despite America's vast military muscle, the war's end would produce irresistible pressures to demobilize quickly; so if he was to secure the peace, he would have to do it while the military alliance still bought Russian goodwill.

The Yalta Conference of the Big Three—Roosevelt, Churchill, and Stalin—took place in February 1945, two months before FDR's death and three months before the German surrender. It was the Indian summer of Allied cooperation. The President accepted the reality of Soviet domination in Eastern Europe. His problem was how to tell a public that thought it had been fighting the war for an Atlantic Charter promising freedom to oppressed peoples that Polish independence was to be at Stalin's sufferance. When FDR explained to Stalin his difficulties in getting these policies across at home, Stalin replied that "some propaganda work should be done." But Roosevelt would have to return home to face the likes of Congressman John Dingell of Michigan, representative of a large Polish-American constituency, who had warned that "we Americans are not sacrificing, fighting and dying to . . . make Joseph Stalin a dictator over the liberated countries of Europe."

Since Stalin, his troops in place in Eastern Europe, had the power to act while Roosevelt could only argue, what he needed and got was a face-saving formula. Roosevelt proposed and Stalin acceded to a Polish government whose core would be attached to Moscow but which would also include Polish nationalists. The agreement gave FDR some breathing space at home, cleared the way for sorely needed Russian aid in the war against Japan (this was before the bomb), and secured Russian support for creating the UN. The American delegation left Yalta elated. The exception was Admiral William Leahy, later a key Truman adviser; he grumbled that the accords were so elastic that the "Russians can stretch it all the way from Yalta to Washington without breaking it."

Though he knew of the historic hostility between the Poles and the Russians, FDR thought he had squared the circle of the Polish question. But in July 1944 Polish partisans in Warsaw rose up against the Nazi occupation. For eight weeks they fought valiantly even as Soviet troops perched on the edge of the city refused to come to their aid. The official Russian position was that the uprising was unleashed by "a group of criminals to seize power." Upset, FDR wrote plaintively to Stalin: "We must think of the reaction of world opinion, if the anti-fascists in Warsaw are left to their own devices." When the Nazis had crushed the rebellion, the Soviets marched into Warsaw. Roosevelt averted his gaze; he continued to hope, on the basis of some significant gestures of goodwill from the Russians and extensive conversations with Stalin, that Soviet recognition of the need for good relations with the United States—who else had the money to help rebuild the war-ravaged Soviet economy?—would lead to the measure of Polish freedom needed to satisfy American sentiments. In effect, his wish was for an open rather than closed sphere of Soviet influence in Eastern Europe.

A few weeks before his death, FDR, on March 1, 1945, made an extraordinary effort to forestall the growth of isolationist sentiment in Congress. Forgoing the dignity and reserve afforded a speaker at the podium, he had himself wheeled into the well of the Senate chamber. "There," as *The New Republic*'s columnist TRB described it, "for the first time in living history a President sat literally on the same level with Congress . . . and for the first time [FDR] referred publicly to his paralyzed legs," as he tried to calm and cajole the Congress with his anecdotal account of how Yalta would turn out all right.

Roosevelt put the best possible face on things for Congress, but he too was worried about Russian unwillingness to make even the cosmetic changes agreed on at Yalta. He feared that the fragile domestic consensus he had worked so hard to build was in peril. In late March 1945, less than two weeks before his death, he cabled Stalin explaining that the Polish question had "aroused the greatest popular interest so that it was urgently necessary for the Russians to provide for something more than a 'thinly disguised continuation of the [Soviet-backed] Warsaw regime' or America would come to regard the Yalta agreement as having failed . . ." A few days later, FDR explained with some exaggeration that "the American people make up their own mind and no exertions of the government can change their judgment . . ." He concluded ominously: "I have been forced to wonder whether you fully realize this fact." It's unlikely that Stalin did understand. He responded by accusing Roosevelt of trying to rewrite the Yalta accords while steadfastly refusing to put an acceptable face on the Polish government. Comments at the Yalta meetings suggest that he viewed the question of American public opinion as little more than a dodge. "When for the nth time at Yalta Harry Hopkins [Roosevelt's aide] brought up the question of American public opinion," Stalin responded testily, "I will not hide behind Soviet public opinion." Yet another mention of public sentiment led Deputy Foreign Minister Andrei Vishinsky to carp that the American people should obey their rulers.

Roosevelt was disappointed with Stalin's response but unwilling to risk an open break. Faced, as Walter Lippmann explained it, with the problem of "how to make good our principles in territories Stalin held," Roosevelt realized there was no alternative to persuasion. On the last day of his life he wrote to Churchill, who had been pushing for a tougher stand: "I would minimize the general

Russian problem as much as possible . . . our course thus far is correct."

Roosevelt's death was to spare him the hard choices that lay ahead. As FDR told Stalin, "Genuine popular support in the United States is required to carry out a government policy foreign or domestic." But in the wake of the intense Catholic and isolationist response to Yalta it was no longer possible to maintain both a consensus at home and an understanding with Russia. FDR was like a fantastically skilled juggler who thrilled the crowd by juggling dynamite only to toss up one stick too many. When the sticks of dynamite began to fall, FDR was gone and Harry S. Truman was sitting in the White House.

"What an enviable death was his," mourned Winston Churchill, who lived to see what followed.

2

1946: The Crucial Year

We are the pioneers of the world . . . the political messiah has come . . . he has come in us.

—HERMAN MELVILLE

IN THE YEAR BETWEEN FDR'S DEATH in April 1945 and March 1946, the Russo-American alliance, that misbegotten child of wartime necessity, was crushed under the glacial pressures of what came to be known as the Cold War. By year's end, the rivalry between the two great powers had begun to freeze into the mold which we have lived within ever since. Thoughtful people who take the long view of things argue that since World War II destroyed the power of all but the two giants, it was inevitable that they would fight over the spoils. Citing Thomas Hobbes, they explain that there is a "general inclination of all mankind toward a perpetual and restless desire of power after power, that ceaseth only with death." With much of the world in ruins then, it seemed only natural that two such drastically different societies, each with a messianic sense of its own mission in the world, should come to blows. That is all well and good, but it doesn't tell us why the conflict took the form and intensity that it did. For that we have to look closely at the men and policies that guided the two nations during the crucial year of 1946.

FDR died on April 12, 1945, from a massive cerebral hemorrhage. The man who stepped into his oversized shoes was Harry S. Truman, a middle-sized man from Missouri, "the average man's average man."

The facts of Truman's life are plain enough. He was a typical son of the middle border, a farm boy who served in World War I and then returned home to fail as the owner of a men's haberdashery. A lifelong Democrat, he turned to the party machine run by Kansas City "boss" Tom Prendergast. A loyal but honest party worker, Truman was a "joiner without peer." He belonged to 218 organizations from the Shriners to the Baker Street Irregulars. "He would don a silly hat" or join in a club ceremony without having to be asked twice. Truman was the sort of politician who knew that "the Masonic handshake could cash checks anywhere." Truman parlayed his flair for "friends and neighbors" politics into a county judgeship and eventually a seat in the U.S. Senate. As a senator he was a faithful but largely undistinguished Roosevelt supporter. His one moment of Senate glory came when he forcefully led a committee that cracked down on wartime profiteering. In 1944 he was the beneficiary of a conservative tide which knocked the left-leaning Henry Wallace off the ticket, something for which Truman was never forgiven by more ardent New Dealers. As Vice-President he was a self-described "political eunuch." Barred from Roosevelt's inner circle, he was regarded by FDR's intimates with barely disguised disdain as a provincial, a "small-bore politician of county courthouse caliber." The new President and Commander in Chief had scant knowledge of foreign policy. He was neither aware of the plans for an atomic bomb nor privy to any of the unwritten understandings Roosevelt had achieved with Stalin.

The public came to know him as a direct and uncomplicated man who spoke his mind with homespun honesty. Though he was often cocky, his humility could be endearing. Upon learning of Roosevelt's death, he told reporters: "Boys, if you ever pray, pray for me now. I don't know if you fellas ever had a load of hay fall on you. But when they told me what happened yesterday, I felt like the moon, the stars and all the planets had fallen on me." His life history passed for the embodiment of the "great American dream . . . the country boy who worked reasonably hard, made friends, didn't get into any serious trouble, and grew up to be President.

It was as simple as that," wrote one of his first biographers in 1947. Or so it seemed. To be sure, there was a great deal of substance to the image of Truman as a successful Willy Loman, a lifelong striver and glad-hander who finally made it.

Truman's father had spent a life pursuing get-rich-quick rainbows to no avail. The son, blessed with all the virtues of small-town life, seemed doomed to a similar fate when his business failure left him with a staggering debt and a populist hatred for bankers. But true to the story line, Truman, through hard work and self-sacrifice, paid off every cent he owed. Despite his slight stature and thick glasses he did not lack physical and moral courage. In the 1920s the Ku Klux Klan was a powerful and menacing presence in Missouri. When his kind words for blacks led the Klan to threaten his life, Truman went to a Klan meeting and dared them to carry through.

Truman's strength was his willingness to face up to a problem with his no-nonsense, take-the-bull-by-the-horns style. He was fond of homilies; a plaque in his office read: "The buck stops here." And he liked to reply brusquely to the timid: "If you can't stand the heat, get out of the kitchen." But his abrupt style was also his weakness. "His mind," said his future Secretary of State Dean Acheson, "was not as quick as his tongue." Because he seemed to think only in primary colors Truman could make quick decisions or loud pronouncements about complex issues without studying them carefully. At times he was so forceful in presenting those decisions that he didn't leave room for compromise.

There was another, less heroic Harry Truman, a man who in his personal life bore a resemblance to the harassed comic figures made famous by W. C. Fields and Rodney Dangerfield. Thirty-five when he married his childhood sweetheart Bess Wallace, he half seriously referred to her as "the boss." With his wife Truman inherited a mother-in-law, straight out of a 1920s comedy, who was free with her criticism and demands and certain that her daughter had married beneath her station. Sensitive about his lack of a college education, Truman endured his mother-in-law's carping, only to react ferociously, as he would later with political critics, in private. In letters or in comments to friends he would give vent to his resentments, lashing out at the "high-hats" and "counterfeits" who were given to pretension. When Roosevelt brain trusters mocked his friends and political hangers-on in Washington, the so-called moochers of the "Missouri Gang," he told his close adviser Clark Clifford that the New Dealers were "crackpots," an offense to corn-fed common sense. He explained: "I want to keep my feet on the ground; I don't want any experiments, the American people have been through a lot of experiments, and they want a rest." But there was to be neither rest nor an end to experimentation; the sharp cultural divisions among the Democrats and the dilemmas of the foreign policy he had inherited saw to that.

When news of FDR's death reached Hitler and Goebbels in mid-April, they were exultant; this, they thought, was the break they had been waiting for. Without Roosevelt's leadership, they expected the strong anti-Soviet feelings within the United States, of which they were fully aware, to surge to the fore, split the Allies, and create the possibility of a separate anti-Communist peace with the Anglo-Americans. Hitler's "struggle against the Bolshevist flood tide," said the German admiral Karl Doenitz, "was made on behalf of Europe and the entire civilized world. . . . The Anglo-Americans are therefore no longer continuing the war in the interest of their peoples but only in order to promote the spread of Bolshevism in Europe." This tactical appeal and accusation was to find numerous American echoes in the years ahead, but it had no effect on the new President, Harry Truman, who faithfully continued to follow Roosevelt's policy of achieving unconditional German surrender as quickly as possible with the fewest American casualties. Nor, despite some pique with earlier Russian flirtations with offers of a separate peace, did Truman try to use Germany's impending collapse for American political advantage. Had they chosen, the Americans, with only a moderate increase in casualties, could have gained postwar leverage by reaching Berlin, Prague, and perhaps even Vienna before the Russians. But Truman and his commanding general, Dwight Eisenhower, passed up the opportunity. They were unwilling to jeopardize what were widely expected to be harmonious postwar relations with Russia.

With the victory over Germany assured, Truman and America's entire political class, the officials, journalists, and academics who mold foreign policy, were forced to take a new look at their

Russian allies. The mood, reported the closely observant British Embassy, was one of "nervous perplexity, a search for motives, an attempt to put fairest interpretation upon [Russian] behavior." They asked themselves two crucial questions regarding the character of the Soviet Union: Did Marxist/Leninist ideology determine Russian foreign policy? Does a totalitarian domestic system necessarily produce an expansionist foreign policy?

Truman, and most of those who thought about these questions with the exception of the isolationists, answered as Roosevelt had: they said no to both. During the war Stalin had asked the Russian people to fight for the Fatherland, not for Marxism-Leninism. To Truman, Stalin was one of the new czars, not a revolutionary dedicated to spreading his brand of Communism around the globe. "Communism, the Russian variety," Truman wrote in his diary, "isn't Communism at all but just police government pure and simple." "Moscow Communism," he went on, was "no different in its methods and actions toward the common man than the czars and Russian noblemen (so-called they were anything but noble men)." For Truman, the old-fashioned Democrat, Russia was nothing but a "hotbed of special privilege."

Truman's emphasis on Russian nationalism was broadly shared by the nation's political and business leaders. Henry Wallace foresaw a gradual political democratization of Russia joining with the economic socialization of the United States to produce a harmonious convergence between the two societies. Case-hardened businessmen who were anti-Communist to the bone at home had high hopes for trade with Russia, a land, they noted gleefully, where there was no trouble from trade unions and higher production was the primary goal. Dale Carnegie, the American apostle of success, went so far as to include Stalin in his *Biographical Roundup* of 1946, a collection of inspirational profiles providing examples of "getting ahead" for the rising businessman. Carnegie quoted Stalin as saying: "The main thing is to have the courage to admit one's errors and to have the strength to correct them in the shortest possible time!"

The American State Department's model for an accommodation in Eastern Europe was based on U.S. relations with Latin America. There, the United States had an "open sphere of power" where it was dominant without directly controlling individual governments.

State looked upon the Russian-Czech agreement of 1943, in which the Czechs were bound diplomatically and militarily to the Russians yet had a considerable degree of internal freedom, as the basis for a similarly "open" Russian sphere of influence in Eastern Europe.

Domestic politics aside, American concern for Eastern Europe was derivative. For most Americans, Eastern Europe was a collection of "Merry Widow principalities, colorful peasant pawns on the edge of the European chessboard." If Hitler had been content with conquering Eastern Europe, it is highly unlikely America would have entered World War II in Europe. American trade with the area was so limited that during the war officials dismissed Eastern Europe as "perhaps the least important of all the areas in the world with which the United States has to deal." What made Eastern Europe important was that it was both a test of Russia's good faith and a potential launching pad for the conquest of Western Europe.

Policy makers believed that a Soviet sphere was necessary to placate the Russians and acceptable so long as it was not so closed and tightly tied to Russia as to pose the danger of a divided Europe. An "open" sphere would be assured, they believed, if the constituent states were given a measure of domestic autonomy. The left-wing *Nation* ridiculed the concern for domestic autonomy as a foolish attempt to apply Jeffersonian principles to backward societies. But the concern for democratic government was more than an idealistic fetish. The assumption was that popularly elected democratic governments, most of which would be run by the non-Communist left, would be friendly to the Russian giant without being easily integrated into a military bloc that might threaten the balance of power in Europe. The idea, the *Christian Science Monitor* reported, was "not to challenge a Russian sphere of influence" but "to guide and control its development along lines that would not jolt the world into conflict."

The Russian bear, licking its deep and painful war wounds, would have no choice, it was assumed, but to be so guided. Everyone from the left-wing journalists of *The New Republic* and *The Nation* to conservative businessmen assumed that the Russians, who had suffered an estimated 20 million dead (600,000 starved to death during the siege of Leningrad), 2,000 towns and 70,000 villages destroyed, 25 million homeless, would be forced to concentrate all their energies on the task of internal reconstruction. Liberals and leftists argued that because of the Russian people's courageous struggle against the fascist scourge, America owed them help in rebuilding. Businessmen and their business magazines agreed. They assumed a harmony of Russian needs and American profits. "Let us not forget," the self-made legend, financier Bernard Baruch, told reporters in June 1945, "that it is the productive capacity of America that all countries must rely on for the comforts—even the necessities—that the modern world will demand. Without us the rest of the world cannot recuperate."

To be an American in June 1945 was to have the world at your feet. To be sure, old attitudes persisted. The vast majority of the population assumed, along with the isolationists, that at the war's end American military involvement overseas would be dramatically curtailed. Similarly, there was a popular consensus against using taxpayers' money to have "Uncle Sucker" finance the rebuilding of our shattered wartime allies. But there was also a swelling pride in American might and preeminence. With the Old World in ruins, Europe reduced to being cared for by her American nursemaid, it was the United States that had picked up the baton of civilization. As Walter Lippmann expressed it: "What Rome was to the ancient world, what Great Britain has been to the modern world, America is to be to the world of tomorrow."

America's responsibility, intoned the urbane J. William Fulbright, later chairman of the Senate Foreign Relations Committee, "is to furnish leadership to the world. . . . The civilization," he went on, "to which we must devote our leadership is not, as some suppose, a vague and idealistic formula . . . it is the essence of our way of living, the only way worthy of a free man." Fulbright's statement reflects the extraordinary trajectory whereby America moved from a position of isolationism based on feelings of moral superiority to the outside world to an assertion of international leadership based on the same feeling.

America's victory over fascism was seen as a proof of democracy's transcendent virtue, while the great success of the wartime economy, the vast outpouring of war production that astounded the world and pulled America out of the Depression, was seen as a sign of America's economic grace. Any new American foreign policy would have to be adequate to the material power behind it. Flush with both material and spiritual power, America's business and political elite from left to right took it as self-evident that the world's needs and the expansion of American power were but the opposite sides of the same coin. Americans, the British Ambassador in Washington explained in a confidential dispatch, see their country as a "benevolent giant, who perceiving the world to be out of joint, feels it his duty and opportunity to set it right." But then recognizing that the desire to help and that the desire to control are closely related, this representative of an empire warned of the imperial mood in Washington, a mood of America First—everywhere! It could lead, he said, to an "intransigently patriotic representation of U.S. interests overseas." Liberals, Wall Street, and the isolationists could now join hands in internationalism because "America could now enter the community of nations while remaining indisputably first." America had shed the trappings of America First isolationism only to revive its nationalist assumptions in international garb. "No country," wrote a French observer, "is more convinced" than America "that she is right, or more arrogant in her moral superiority. If she intervenes in the affairs of the world," he concluded, "it will be to impose her ideas, and she will consider her intervention a blessing for lost and suffering humanity." Resistance to such a self-consciously benevolent force could only be interpreted as wickedness.

The first resistance came from the Soviet Union, a country with wickedness to spare.

The new President shared the mood of national assertiveness. He wanted quickly to make it clear both to Roosevelt loyalists at home and to his allies abroad that he was fully in charge. Truman, like Roosevelt, was troubled by the failure of the Russians to cooperate in protecting the Administration's domestic flank on the matter of Eastern Europe. But, unlike Roosevelt, he was determined to force the issue. Within a day of becoming President he told his Secretary of State, "We must stand up to the Russians. We have been too easy with them." Truman's instincts were reinforced by the reports he was getting from his Ambassador to the Soviet Union, W. Averell Harriman, the son of the railroad magnate. Like many newcomers to Moscow, Harriman had difficulty adjusting to the shock of dealing with the Russians. He was deeply frustrated by months of fruitless negotiations over the Polish dilemma and personally offended by the gratuitous discourtesies he had suffered. He warned of a "barbarian invasion" in Eastern Europe whereby Russian dictatorship, secret police, and all were being used to create a closed Russian sphere of power. "We must recognize," he told Truman, "that the terms independent but friendly neighbor"—referring to the language of Yalta—"have entirely different meanings to the Soviets than to us." "Unless we make those differences clear," Harriman counseled, the Soviets will take "as a sign of weakness on our part our continued generous and considerate attitude toward them . . ."

Harriman's charges were buttressed in early May when the Russians arrested sixteen leaders of the Polish anti-Nazi resistance. Promised safe conduct, they were on their way to Moscow to discuss broadening the Soviet government in accord with the Yalta agreements. Disturbed by this and earlier incidents, columnist TRB, writing in the pro-Soviet *New Republic*, admonished the Russians. They would have to play "a slightly more subtle game than in the past few months," he advised, "if the immense store of good will which they have won . . . is not to be frittered away." Worried that the Russians were ignoring the realities of American domestic politics at their own peril, TRB concluded somberly that "at times it has seemed that the Soviet leaders were trying to throw away Washington's good will."

Harriman was criticized by Secretary of War Henry Stimson. Stimson, a Republican Wall Street lawyer, met with Harriman and chastised him for threatening the peace over the question of Polish freedom. Poland, he argued, had never known free elections. What was important, he said, was to let the Russians know that we were supportive of their need for security; after all, it was through Poland that the U.S.S.R. had been twice invaded in twenty-five years.

Stimson was worried about the "perfectionists" like Michigan's Senator Arthur Vandenberg insisting on the letter of the Yalta "law" which had indeed promised free elections. There was no use, he said, in getting the American public all "churned up" over an area where the United States had no power and Stalin was likely to be unyielding. Stimson might have added that many of the perfectionists had been far less scrupulous about the rights of independent nationhood when it was the Germans rather than the Russians who were gobbling up their neighbors.

Harriman carried the day. Eleven days after assuming office the President called Soviet Foreign Minister Vyacheslav Molotov into his office. Molotov (the name means hammer in Russian) was the hard-liner in Russo-American relations. A relentlessly crude and forceful man who slept with a gun under his pillow, Molotov was seen as the evil demon who forced "Uncle Joe" into tougher positions than he would have preferred. Truman, lecturing Molotov in words of one syllable, insisted that the Russians live up to the letter of the Yalta agreements. A new government would have to be formed in Poland. In Truman's own words, he gave Molotov a "straight one-two to the jaw." An angry Molotov replied, with perhaps a touch of sarcasm, that "he had never been talked to like that" in his life. "Carry out your agreements," Truman supposedly replied, "and you won't get talked to like that." The following day, Truman, still trying to get his presidential legs, turned to the Russophile Joseph Davies and asked, "Did I do right?" Davies, upset, tried to tactfully suggest that it had been a mistake.

Stalin may have thought it was more than that.

Stalin was described by a fellow Communist who knew him as a man who possessed "the senselessness of Caligula" along with "the refinement of a Borgia and the brutality of a Czar Ivan the Terrible." While Truman deferred to his wife, Stalin killed his. His social style made Truman's glad-handing look refined. Stalin's misjudgments were numerous; he had aided the rise of Hitler by instructing the German Communists that the Social Democrats and not the Nazis were the "real" enemy and in 1941 he had refused to believe what FDR suspected and his spies had evidence of— namely, that Hitler planned to attack Russia. Indeed, Hitler may have been the only leader Stalin ever trusted. Stalin survived, in part, because his extraordinary suspiciousness helped make him a master of internal bureaucratic politics. What then was this suspicious man to make of Truman and the Americans? During the war, they had delayed opening a second front against the Germans while Russia bled for two horrible years. Many Americans wanted to see the Nazis and the Communists destroy each other. Had FDR secretly shared such feelings? And what of Eastern Europe? Why had the Americans rejected the "percentages agreement"? Why had they refused to draw any clear lines; did they want influence even in Russia's own bailiwick?

I pose these issues as questions because we know so little about the Soviet Union, particularly in this period when Russia was largely closed to travelers by an anxious Stalin evidently fearful that the West would become aware of Russia's true internal weaknesses. The consequence, as one historian has put it, is that we know more about periods of the Middle Ages than we do about postwar Russia. What seems very likely, however, is that Truman's "one-two to the jaw" rhetoric inflamed Stalin's considerable mistrust of the West.

Stalin responded in kind to Truman's toughness. The following day he dismissed the President's demands. Relying on the "spirit" of Yalta rather than the letter of accords, Stalin correctly pointed out that he had refused to interfere in Greece, where the British had put down a Communist rebellion, and he expected a similarly free hand in Poland. He noted sharply that Poland bordered on Russia, and not on the United States or Britain.

In May 1945 a worried Truman wrote in his diary: "I want peace and I am willing to work hard for it." In preparation for the forthcoming summit to be held in Potsdam, Germany, Truman dispatched two advisers friendly to the Russians to patch things up. He sent Joseph Davies of *Mission to Moscow* fame to London and Harry Hopkins, Roosevelt's confidant, to Moscow. Truman told his advisers that he wanted to make it clear to Stalin that despite Anglo-American concerns over Eastern Europe the alliance was still intact.

In 1939 England had gone to war in defense of Polish independence, yet Churchill was now faced with the prospect of Poland losing that independence to an erstwhile ally. He reacted angrily when Davies told him that Truman wanted to meet privately with Stalin before Potsdam to assure the Marshal of America's benign intentions. Tempers flared and Davies accused Churchill of having Goebbels-like views on Communism. An annoyed Churchill understood that Truman, like Roosevelt before him, was not about to sacrifice good relations with Russia on the altar of Polish independence.

In Moscow, Hopkins repeatedly emphasized the Administration's desire to have "a Poland friendly to the Soviet Union" and in fact he added that the United States "hoped to see friendly countries all along the Soviet borders." But in late May and early June 1945, when he met with Stalin, he also informed him that even commentators friendly to the Soviets were growing increasingly doubtful about Soviet policy in occupied Eastern Europe.

What he didn't say is that critics of American policy toward Russia were becoming increasingly vocal. Senator Vandenberg, Republican foreign policy adviser John Foster Dulles, and Harriman had already succeeded in turning the founding convention of the UN into a forum for mobilizing anti-Russian sentiment.

Hopkins' worries about Vandenberg and the fragility of American-Soviet relations echoed an earlier exchange between Roosevelt's Secretary of State, Cordell Hull, and the leading Republican. "Malcontents," warned Hull, referring to the not-so-former isolationists like Vandenberg, "were doing their best to drive Russia out of the international movement by constant attacks and criticisms." Unless it was possible to prevail upon newspaper commentators and columnists to refrain from criticism of the Soviet Union, he feared, "it would be difficult for any international undertaking . . . to succeed." Vandenberg rose to the bait. It was a setup for the Michigan senator, a man with the "gift of complete sincerity." (His hobby was writing short stories about idealistic young people fighting against millionaires and unscrupulous politicians.) In a well-publicized speech, he counterattacked at Hull's and the Administration's weak point. Did friendly relations with Russia, he asked, depend on the suppression of free speech and American ideals? Why weren't Americans free to criticize the Soviets, particularly when Russian violations of the Atlantic Charter called into question the Administration's own justification for the war?

When Vandenberg said that American ideals "sail with our fleets. They fly with our eagles. They sleep with our martyred dead," he was speaking not just for Republicans and "former isolationists," he was speaking for most of the country. He was challenging the Administration to reconcile its foreign policy vis-à-vis the Soviet and British empires with the principles it proclaimed at home. If the Atlantic Charter wasn't implemented, said Montana's Senator Burton K. Wheeler, our boys would "have died in vain." It would mean that we have fought only to substitute "Stalin for

Hitler." The most telling comment on this score came from the internationalist-minded *Christian Science Monitor*, which warned after Yalta that the "concessions won from American Statesmen are far from being won from the United States."

With the message of the *Monitor*'s warning in mind, an ailing Hopkins discussed the Polish situation with a conciliatory Stalin. Stalin had every reason to be tough on this point, for as even a hard-liner like Averell Harriman had pointed out, it must have been difficult to "understand why [the United States] should want to interfere with Soviet policy in a country like Poland, which [Stalin] considers so vital to Russia's security, unless we have some ulterior motives." Stalin refused to yield on allowing the self-determination spoken of at Yalta, but he went out of his way to reassure Hopkins of Russia's limited aims. He assured Hopkins that he had no desire to export Russian Communism to Poland. Disarmingly and correctly, he noted that the Polish national character guaranteed that such an export would have difficulty taking root. He acknowledged the imprisonment of the sixteen Poles but explained their fate in terms of wartime necessities and the lack of democratic freedoms in countries which were not so fortunate as the United States. Graciously he agreed to a face-saving compromise in which a number of non-Communists were given minor cabinet posts in a provisional Polish government of National Unity. Stalin proved accommodating on other matters as well. He renewed his pledge to enter the war against Japan, acceded to the American position on voting procedures for the UN Security Council, despite the strength of Mao Zedong's Communist forces, continued to recognize Chiang Kai-shek as the rightful ruler of China. A satisfied Hopkins made it clear that Truman and Churchill would not meet separately before Potsdam.

Obviously pleased, Truman announced at a press conference that "there has been a very pleasant yielding on the part of the Russians to some of the things in which we are interested." Flush with the possibilities of amity, he concluded: "I think if we keep our heads and be patient, agreement with the Soviets is possible . . . because the Russians are just as anxious to get along with us as we are with them." There may have been a measure of truth in Truman's remarks; circumstantially, it appears that Stalin may have recognized that for the time being his empire had already reached its tolerable limits. Far more concerned with power, his own and that of the Russian state, than ideology, he went out of his way to restrain the Yugoslav and Western European Communists, who, he feared, might both become independent of his control and provoke the British and Americans into strong countermeasures. For their part, the Anglo-Americans began the unconscionable process of repatriating wholesale more than a million Russian soldiers taken prisoner by the Nazis. Tainted by their association with the Germans, these men, some of whom probably had been collaborators, faced certain death on their return.

Truman's kind comments on the Russians led to accusations of his being "pink" or soft on Communism. He was no softer than Roosevelt. FDR had left behind a number of trump cards to be played should the Russians prove recalcitrant. These included financial and technical assistance as well as the atomic bomb which was being prepared at Los Alamos. After the bomb had been used in August to end the war in the Pacific, Truman and Stimson planned to relinquish sole control of the infernal device to an international agency in return for a "settlement of East European and Asian questions on terms favorable to the U.S." Truman, nervously awaiting news of the A-bomb test, first delayed and then reluctantly left for Potsdam without knowing whether the weapon worked.

The Potsdam meetings held in Soviet-occupied eastern Germany were inconclusive. Discussions centered on the future of Germany. At the war's end the three allies plus France occupied separate zones of the Reich. By the time of Potsdam, a bare two months after the German surrender, a war-ravaged Russia had already gone a long way toward stripping their zone of machinery and equipment. Despite Roosevelt's wartime promises, Lend-Lease aid for Russia was cut off by the United States as soon as Germany surrendered. Without Lend-Lease and with future American aid dependent on both a tight-fisted American Congress and unpalatable political concessions to the Americans, Stalin focused his efforts on a united and even non-Communist Germany—he had once remarked that Communism fit Germany like a saddle fits a cow—which might open up the other zones for forced reparations. He was opposed by the British, also economically hard-pressed by the war. They remembered how excessive World War I reparations prepared the way for Hitler and they wanted to ensure that the Western zones would at least be self-supporting. After the deadlock that ensued, supposedly temporary zones would eventually harden into East and West Germany.

There was a visceral anti-Soviet sentiment growing in the American delegation at Potsdam. The Russians, led by Generalissimo Stalin—this was his self-chosen title—frightened as much by their manner as by their words. Many of the Americans were visibly shocked by the obvious widespread looting and the police-state atmosphere of the Russian zone; even the usually even-keeled Stimson was set back by Russian crudity. For this part, Harriman was shaken not only by what he called "oriental barbarism" but what seemed to be confirmation of his worst fears. During a break in the formal discussion he remarked to the Generalissimo that he must be very pleased to have the Red Army in Berlin. Stalin replied, "Czar Alexander got to Paris!"

Truman refused to be put off by the Russians. "Stalin was an S.O.B.," the President told his startled companions on the way home, but then he added affably: "I guess he thinks I'm one too." He still had reason to believe, as he told his aides at the time, that "I can deal with Stalin. He is honest—but smart as hell." Truman went on to describe Stalin as a Russian Tom Prendergast, a political boss you could compromise with. Truman's good feelings came in part from the deal he had struck to get much-needed Russian help in finishing off Japan. The Americans had already taken fearsome losses in taking the island of Okinawa. There the Japanese, fighting with superhuman intensity, sent wave after wave of kamikaze pilots at the American fleet and 45,000 Americans were killed or wounded. If the United States had been willing to allow the Japanese to retain their emperor, the Japanese might have begun negotiating for a settlement, which would have foreclosed the need for Russian help. But that would have raised an outcry. After the humiliation of Pearl Harbor, Americans demanded unconditional surrender.

It was on the last day of Potsdam, after Truman and Stalin had negotiated on when Russia would enter the war in the Pacific, that the American President received news from Los Alamos of a successful A-bomb test. Savoring the information but not yet brandishing it, he told Stalin only that the United States had created "a new weapon of unusual destructive force." Stalin (which in Russian means man of steel) responded impassively. He may have already known of the bomb through Russian espionage. He commented tersely that he hoped the bomb would be put to good use against the Japanese. As Potsdam ended, the United States and Britain issued an ultimatum to Japan. Without specifically describing the bomb, they warned that unless the Japanese surrendered unconditionally there would be extraordinary destruction. The Japanese, who had already suffered great losses, responded with disdain.

The age of atomic diplomacy had begun.

While the bomb ended the hot war with Japan, it helped inaugurate the emerging Cold War with the Russians. Visiting Moscow shortly after V-J Day, General Dwight Eisenhower noted that "before the atom bomb was used I would have said yes, I was sure we could keep the peace with Russia. Now I don't know. People are frightened and disturbed all over. Everyone feels insecure again." Truman told Stimson that the bomb "had given him an entirely new feeling of confidence."

For a brief period the bomb seemed like a diplomatic and military cure-all, a substitute for American troops soon to be demobilized. In the wake of the German surrender the White House was blitzed with calls to "bring the boys back home." GIs, unmindful of America's new "internationalism," chanted their favorite ditties for reporters:

> I'm tired of these Limeys and Frogs.
> I'm fed to the teeth with these gooks, wops, and wogs.
> I want to go back to my chickens and hogs.
> I don't want to leave home anymore.

When they weren't chanting they were rioting; from London to Manila, citizen soldiers, with a fierce hatred for the privileges enjoyed by the officer corps and a desire to return to a United States grown prosperous since they had gone to war, mutinied and rebelled. The brass, said one soldier, "want to keep playing war, that's why they won't let me go home." In Paris, protesting soldiers marched down the Champs Elysées shouting "Scab!" at the men who wouldn't join them. One frustrated colonel, referring to the UAW strike against General Motors which was part of the new wave of labor militancy back home, screamed out: "You men forget you're not working for GM. You're still in the Army!"

Back home right-wing politicians saw a connection between the leftist leaders of some of the "mutinies" and Russian policy; they called them subversives. But the so-called subversives were moved by little more than a desire to make up for lost time. As one angry soldier put it: "When I came home I was even madder. Here these people were, who had sat out the war, they had made money hand over fist while the rest of us were away; they had a big head start and they made the most of it." Conservative and isolationist fears to the contrary, the war and the Army had done little to regiment the minds of the American people.

This "failure" of indoctrination was dramatically projected by the Army's end-of-the-war surveys which revealed that the ordinary soldier had no more political clarity about the war's meaning at the end than he did at the beginning. By and large the soldiers had little good to say about either Jews or labor and their attitude toward blacks was so harsh as to suggest the possibility of racial troubles before the decade's end. One quarter of the returning heroes believed that since Germany was the most efficient country in Europe, it had the right to dominate the Continent. Twenty-five percent felt that Germany had good reason for "being down on the Jews" and a fifth even felt that Germany had "some or more" justification for starting the war. Fully half thought the war hadn't been worth fighting.

Left without an army, Stimson thought that the bomb might be "a badly needed equalizer to the Russian army in Eastern Europe." For two centuries before Pearl Harbor, Americans had enjoyed the free security of two broad oceans; now the bomb promised to take their place and relieve America of having to develop diplomatic skills. "Diplomacy," said one reporter, "is widely regarded as a sort of occult art in which Americans are usually outsmarted" by the fallen and thus wily people of the old world.

The White House elation over the bomb was short-lived. The Russians responded to the new American power with either studied indifference or a renewed truculence. Henry Stimson was on target when he warned: "If we . . . negotiate with [the Russians] hav[ing] this weapon rather ostentatiously on our hip their suspicions of our purposes and motives will increase." When Secretary of State James Byrnes went to London to pick up the negotiations where Potsdam had left off, he found out just how right Stimson was. Molotov proved tougher and more uncompromising than ever. At one point Molotov even mocked him by asking if the Secretary was carrying the bomb around in his pocket. Byrnes told Joseph Davies that Molotov had been so "insufferable" that he was "almost ashamed" for having put up with it.

During these London meetings Molotov played a form of reverse atomic diplomacy. Either he ignored the weapon or when Byrnes proposed to talk about international control of the bomb, he conspicuously pushed that item to the back of the agenda. The bomb, Byrnes soon discovered, was not a decisive weapon. "The impotence of omnipotence" was already clear. If the bomb were used to save Western Europe from a Soviet invasion, it would destroy it in the process. Byrnes backed off from atomic diplomacy, but the dilemma presented by a weapon which destroys what it is designed to preserve remains with us.

A chastened Byrnes returned home, conferred with Truman, and together they decided to abandon atomic diplomacy in favor of an ill-fated plan for the internationalization of atomic energy and a renewed effort to come to terms with the Soviets. Brynes told hard-liner James Forrestal that the Russians were truly afraid that "the rest of the world is ganging up on them." It was time, he insisted, to reach out again. When Byrnes returned to Europe, this time to Moscow, in December 1945 for more than two weeks of talks, he accepted a number of Russian positions on the organization of satellite governments in Eastern Europe and a role for the Russians in the military occupation of Japan; he also made progress on German demilitarization, China, and the international control of atomic energy. He left Moscow optimistic, unprepared for the shift that had taken place in his absence.

While Byrnes was waxing conciliatory in Moscow, Republican criticism of the Administration's foreign policy was reaching levels unseen since before Pearl Harbor. Byrnes's return was greeted with the stentorian pronouncements of Senator Homer Capehart of Indiana, who compared Byrnes's Moscow agreements with "Chamberlain and his umbrella appeasement of Hitler." Freed from the restraint of wartime bipartisanship and with one eye on the 1946 congressional elections, the Republicans were dishing out the kind of tough criticism which suggested the pre-1941 days of bitter fights over American intervention. They were joined by the hard-liners within the Administration. Admiral Leahy called the Moscow agreements a sellout, and he began to wonder privately if Byrnes's suggestion that Chiang Kai-shek should include Communists in his government didn't indicate that Byrnes was under the influence of the Reds in the State Department. At this point the reader, badly confused, may ask: "But wasn't the State Department a hotbed of German sentiment? Yes among the Europeanists, but among the Asian specialists it was a different matter.

Republican hostility came as no surprise to Byrnes. What was new was that Russian activities had brought a new critic to the lists, Truman himself. All through November, December, and early January, each day's State Department cables from Europe seemed to bring fresh evidence of Soviet perfidy. In November, the Soviets intervened in Hungary to reverse the electoral victory of the reformist Smallholders Party. Repression was on the upswing in Poland with a new wave of murders by the secret police. Stalin had repeated his earlier demands on Turkey for unfettered access to the Mediterranean and then added a new one; it called for the entire Turkish Black Sea coast to be turned over to Russia. Most troubling of all was the news from just east of Turkey in Iran. There, contrary to a wartime agreement to remove their troops after V-E Day, the Russians, allied with rebels and Kurdish secessionists, threatened to attach the northern half of oil-rich Iran to the Russian domain.

Truman was in a huff over both the Russian actions and the vulnerable position their moves had left him in at home at a time when he could no longer cloak his conciliatory approach in the garb of a wartime leader. Calling Russian actions in Iran "an outrage if I ever saw one," he was convinced they would soon move on the Turkish straits. Unless Russia was faced with an iron fist and strong language, he told Byrnes, then "another war is in the making. Only one language do they understand: 'How many divisions have you?' . . . I'm tired of babying the Russians."

Truman's anger was born of both frustration and fear. What

were the Russians up to? Why couldn't the most powerful nation on earth get them to play the game according to American rules? One by one Truman had played the cards Roosevelt had left him —cutting American financial aid, withholding recognition of the Soviet satellites, waving the A-bomb—and yet the imperturbable Stalin was not only unmoved, he was increasingly aggressive!

Truman was not alone, although he had yet to publicly criticize the Russians. In the five months since V-J Day public belief in the possibilities of peaceful cooperation with the Soviets had dropped from 54 to 35 percent. The British Foreign Office observers in Washington, closely tracking this change, concluded that public sentiment was out in front of the Administration. The "primitive behavior" shown by the Russian troops in Eastern Europe was widely reported by the press, and the British diplomats believed that "the wartime respect for the Russian armies as the most heroic and relentless opponents of Nazism is largely evaporated."

Then, while this new mood was setting in, the country was hit rapid-fire with three new shocks:

February 9, 1946: A speech by Stalin unnerved the United States. Stalin told the Russian people that the Soviet Fatherland was surrounded by evil "monopoly capitalists" who threatened the very life of the country. These words, said one observer, "had the effect of an electric shock on the nerves of hitherto vaguely optimistic liberal commentators." And there was more. The war against Germany, Stalin proclaimed, was won by the Red Army; there was no mention of the Allies except in the assertion that the war was not an accident, rather it was the "inevitable result . . . of contemporary monopoly capitalism." The message seemed clear: just as the contradictions of capitalism produced fascism and World War II, they would continue to produce those evils unless capitalism was, by dint of Soviet arms, replaced by Communism. It seemed a call to battle in the name of self-defense, a reassertion of the Leninist dogma which had supposedly disappeared with Stalin's victory over Trotsky. Supreme Court Justice William O. Douglas, one of the leading lights of American liberalism, called the speech a "declaration of World War III."

Stalin's motives here, as with so many other things he did, are obscure. The explanations which have been offered center on internal party struggles in the Soviet Union and the need to present a militant face to Western European Communists he was in fact keeping in check, as well as putting the Anglo-Americans on notice. But these suggestions have as much support as the trapeze artist who makes great leaps from point to point, none of which have any visible means of support. As one analyst has put it: "Few gamblers would put their money on a horse if they had as little information as a Kremlinologist."

February 11, 1946: Two weeks after he publicly denied the existence of a secret Yalta protocol on the Far East, Undersecretary of State Dean Acheson was forced by their publication in the Soviet Union to acknowledge them. The Soviet publication of these minimally important agreements undermined the credibility of compromisers like Byrnes and diplomat Charles E. Bohlen, whose reputations stemmed from their relationship with Roosevelt. They fanned the brush fire which had already broken out over accusations that Chiang was being sold down the river by Communists in the State Department. In a matter of months Acheson himself would come under FBI investigation for his supposedly pro-Russian views.

February 16, 1946: The Canadian government announced the arrest of twenty-two individuals accused of spying on American atomic secrets for the Soviet government. The arrests and subsequent discovery that the ring had in fact obtained substantial information was a vindication for anti-Communists and critics of the Administration of all stripes. The House Un-American Activities Committee (HUAC), led by the Mississippi racist and anti-Semite John Rankin, swung into "action." HUAC, which had investigated Hollywood Jews and interventionists before the war, now turned its attention to "Communist front" organizations.

Jostled by unpleasant Soviet or Soviet-related developments, "the average citizen," said a keen British observer, was becoming inured to their occurrence. "Only a few months earlier," said the observer in July 1946, the American press was still saying that the United States and the U.S.S.R. "merely 'misunderstood' each other." But there has been "a radical change in public thinking." Now the American "would feel cheated of familiar sensations if each day did not provide him with fresh evidence in support of his now settled conviction that Soviet Russia is a confirmed troublemaker."

The February shocks pressured Truman to go public with the Administration's new position. But before Truman could signal a shift Vandenberg commanded the Senate's attention with a forceful "What is Russia up to now?" speech: "We ask it in Manchuria. We ask it in Eastern Europe and the Dardanelles. . . . We ask it in the Baltic and the Balkans. We ask it in Poland. . . . We ask it sometimes even in connection with events in our United States. What is Russia up to now?" Vandenberg coupled these "questions" with an attack on the "miserable function[s]" of the "fellow travelers." He was again insisting that the domestic foreign policy and the overseas foreign policy of the United States be placed in tandem after a long period in which first Roosevelt and then Truman had uncoupled them. Above all he demanded that the United States "draw the line" with the Russians. "Where is right? Where is justice?" "There let America take her stand." Vandenberg finished this fiery tirade to standing applause and then a rush of handshakes from his fellow senators. Vandenberg, the isolationist, had insisted before Pearl Harbor that America's moral fiber would be corrupted by intervening in an evil world. The postwar internationalist Vandenberg hadn't changed much; he still proposed to maintain American purity, but now he would do it by imposing a single standard of morality worldwide, with exemptions for friendly but right-wing nations like fascist Spain and Argentina.

The following day, February 28, Byrnes, the object of much of Vandenberg's ire and the most effective compromiser in the Administration, did a public turnabout. He came forth with a speech condemning appeasement which so echoed Vandenberg's it was dubbed "the Second Vandenberg Concerto." Vandenberg took credit for the change, but in fact Truman and his right-wing critics were now running on parallel tracks. The stage was set for the dramatic March 6, 1946, oratory of Winston Churchill.

With Truman, who had read and privately approved of his words, sitting on the platform, Churchill delivered a speech titled "Sinews of Peace." Eloquently he sounded the themes struck by Vandenberg: "Nobody knows what Soviet Russia and its Communist International organization intends to do in the immediate future, or what are the limits if any to their expansive and proselytizing tendencies." "From Strettin in the Baltic to Trieste in the Adriatic," he intoned in a phrase soon to become famous, "an Iron

Curtain has descended across the continent." This, he insisted, echoing the isolationists, was "certainly not the liberated Europe we fought" for. "From what I have seen," he went on, "I am convinced that there is nothing [the Russians] admire so much as strength, and there is nothing for which they have less respect than weakness, especially military weakness." These strong words were but slightly softened by his qualification that the Russians did not want war. "What they desire," he said, "is the fruits of war and the indefinite expansion of their powers and doctrines."

Liberals were outraged by Churchill's speech, for many were still hopeful about the "social experiments" in Eastern Europe; moreover, "Sinews of Peace," they said, sounded more like "Sinews of War." Raising the old isolationist theme, they impugned the British war effort as being primarily aimed at preserving the Empire and hinted darkly of the danger of fascism in Britain and America. Fascism, not Communism, they insisted, was the chief threat to democracy. But they were increasingly alone. By mid-March 1946, 71 percent of Americans polled were critical of Soviet foreign policy; only 7 percent approved.

Stalin's angry response spoke directly to the seemingly fascist tone of Churchill's remarks about the "Iron Curtain" Goebbels had earlier warned about. Was it true, he asked, that it was "God," as Churchill had suggested, who willed that the Americans be the first to possess the A-bomb? And what did Churchill mean when he said the Soviet Union was "a peril to Christian civilization"? These rhetorical points aside, Stalin was angered most by the speech's implied threat to the legitimacy of Soviet domination in Eastern Europe.

Stalin responded with more than words. Within weeks he rejected the terms of a proposed American loan, announced a new Five-Year Plan that aimed at freeing Russia from Western economic pressure, and set in motion what later came to be known as Zhdanovism, an attempt to purify Russia by ridding it of Western influences. Few Americans had ever heard of Andrei Zhdanov, but when Americans ridiculed Soviet claims to have invented everything from the balloon to the telephone, they were referring to his shenanigans. If that was all, Zhdanov's follies would have simply been an embarrassment for America's liberals, still sympathetic to the U.S.S.R., but the Russian cultural commissar also announced that Marxism-Leninism had a transcendent mission "to teach others a new general morality."

The growing hostility between the United States and the U.S.S.R. placed American liberals in a difficult position. They were again and again forced to backpedal as the Soviets, whether in response to American actions or not, imposed exactly the kind of police-state rule which liberals had insisted they would never set up. Hal Lehrman, a self-described pro-Soviet liberal sent to Eastern Europe by *The Nation*, returned to report that Russian brutality had so alienated even potential friends of the Russians that the area now "seethed with hatred" for Moscow. In the face of such reports *Nation* editor Freda Kirchwey was reduced to arguing that because Russia was "socialist," its imperialism was progressive. Such a position did more to weaken the reputation of socialism than support friendship with the Soviets.

The majority of American liberals, though increasingly critical of the Soviets, nonetheless insisted on the need for friendly relations between the two powers. The most prominent left-liberal or "progressive," as he styled himself, was Secretary of Commerce Henry Wallace. Wallace admitted that Russia was ruthlessly authoritarian and that "Communists everywhere want eventually a Communist world," but, he went on, "for the moment I believe they are essentially interested . . . in strengthening the Soviet Union as an example of the kind of socialism they have in mind." Truman, aware of Wallace's support in the Northeast, stayed on good terms with the Secretary despite their obvious differences. Truman, an unelected President, was justifiably worried about how the upcoming congressional elections would reflect on his administration. Their break wouldn't come till early September 1946, when Wallace gave what only a year earlier would have been an unexceptionable Grand Alliance speech.

Wallace, appearing at a Madison Square Garden rally designed as a kickoff for the 1946 congressional election campaign, lambasted the "numerous reactionary elements which had hoped for an Axis victory—and now profess great friendship for the United States." Then turning to the Administration's new "get-tough policy" with Russia, he noted prophetically that it could accomplish little. "The tougher we get," he warned, "the tougher the Russians will get." Wallace, a mystic but by no means a Communist, envisioned a peace based on free and extensive trade with the Russians. Free trade and friendship, he believed, would lead to a prosperous world in which the U.S.S.R. would grow steadily more democratic politically and the United States more democratic economically. This was cheered, but the audience booed and heckled when the forthright Wallace criticized the Russian suppression of civil liberties in Eastern Europe and cited Russian intransigence as one of the sources of the Cold War. The following day the Communist *Daily Worker* roundly criticized Wallace.

The *Daily Worker* attack did little to cheer Truman, however, because in another section of the speech Wallace had, in the name of realism, called for a frank recognition of the Soviet sphere of influence. Wallace wasn't alone here; Walter Lippmann made a similar plea, arguing in effect that while the United States could do very little in the short run to advance the cause of freedom in Eastern Europe, it could do a great deal to harm it. The consequence of increased East-West tension, Lippmann warned, would only be a tighter Russian grip over its satellites.

Harry Truman's patience had been exhausted. Six months earlier Wallace's proposal would have been rejected for domestic political reasons, but now it led to the firing of the Secretary of Commerce and an enraged questioning of his motives. Venting his feelings in his private diary, Truman wrote: "I don't understand a dreamer like that . . . The Reds, phonies and the 'parlor pinks' seem to be banded together and are becoming a national danger. I am afraid they are a sabotage front for Uncle Joe Stalin." Truman's private feelings were increasingly shared by even liberal and middle-of-the-road Democrats. Walter Lippmann, the dean of American political commentators, was the exception to the trend.

Lippmann, in a hard-hitting article for *The Atlantic*, charged that Truman had refused to see the ways in which his own policies had furnished the Russians with a pretext for their iron rule. The Anglo-Americans, he explained, had foolishly chosen to challenge the Russians in the one region considered most vital to Soviet interests, "the very region where the conflict was sharpest and settlement the most difficult." Everywhere else, he pointed out, "Britain and America were supreme. They had Japan, the Mediterranean, Southern Asia, most of China and Germany, all of Africa, command of the seas and the air and the atomic bomb." Given such strength, asked Lippmann, is it odd that the Russians fear for their empire in Eastern Europe?

Truman never replied directly, but his counterarguments were given eloquent justification in the writings of an American foreign service officer, George Frost Kennan. Kennan was a man of nineteenth-century dignities and aristocratic sensibilities. Out of place in the barbaric century of Hitler and Stalin, he described himself as "a guest of [his] own time." He despised Communism for abandoning the "ship of Western Civilization" when it hit the twentieth century's stormy waters. Comparing Communists to a "swarm of rats," Kennan described the Communist rejection of Western tradition as a "sacrilege" which "some day must be punished as all ignorant presumption and egotism must be punished . . ."

Perpetually out of step with FDR's policies, Kennan was content to wait out Nazi rule in Europe, which he thought was sure to be ended by nationalist resistance. A lover of German high culture, he never saw Russia as a fit ally for America. Speaking in the late 1930s while Stalin was systematically liquidating the old Bolsheviks, Kennan described Russia as a backward and barbaric country whose tortured history had produced a modern version of "Oriental despotism." It was, he said, a country in which "extremism was the normal form of rule and foreigners were expected to be mortal enemies." Roosevelt, he would later argue, ignored that expectation at America's peril.

For the first ten months of the Truman administration, the reigning Russian experts in the State Department, led by Charles Bohlen, had argued that the United States needed to avoid not only war but even prolonged antagonism with the Russians by dealing sympathetically with Russia's needs. Truman, believing he had done just that, was at a loss to understand why the Russian bear had not been tamed. Kennan stepped into the breach with the now famous "Long Telegram" of February 22, 1946.

Kennan freed Truman of any responsibility by insisting that conflict with the Russians was inevitable, not because of anything the United States had done, but because of the very nature of the Soviet regime. The old Czars, said Kennan, had shored up their internally weak autocratic regimes by pointing to foreign danger, real or imagined. The Soviets followed suit with the "myth" of capitalist encirclement. In the telegram, Kennan wrote: "A hostile international environment is a breath of life in this country . . . in this dogma . . . [Russia's rulers] found justification for their instinctive fear of the outside world, for the dictatorship without which they did not know how to rule, for the cruelties which they dare not to inflict, for sacrifices they felt bound to demand." Communist ideology was, in this eloquent analysis, in the service of Russian power and not the other way around. "Encirclement was," he later stated, "anchored in the Soviet structure of thought by bonds far greater than those of mere ideology." Rather, the Soviet bureaucracy was "one great vested interest committed to the principle of a hostile outside world."

In a frequently overlooked section of the telegram, Kennan made it clear that the Soviets, unlike Hitler's Germany, were "neither schematic nor adventuristic." They do "not work by fixed plans," he insisted. Kennan later emphasized that it was Russian political and not military power that was a challenge to the United States. But that distinction was lost on policy makers like Clark Clifford, a special assistant to the President, who stressed the military implications of Kennan's argument in presenting it to Truman. Likewise, hard-liner James Forrestal was already arguing that the writings of Marx and Lenin were, like *Mein Kampf*, outlines for world conquest. Forrestal had his own favorite passage, in the most widely quoted section of the telegram, where Kennan seemed to be sounding the tocsin for battle: "We have [in the U.S.S.R.] a political force committed fanatically to the belief that with the United States there can be no permanent modus vivendi; that it is desirable and natural that the internal harmony of our society be disrupted, and our traditional way of life destroyed . . . if Soviet power is to be secured." This section, music to the ears of hawks, read, as Kennan himself was later to admit, "exactly like one of those primers put out by the Daughters of the American Revolution, designed to arouse the citizenry to the dangers of a Communist conspiracy."

The telegram closed what had until then been an open and wide-ranging debate within the State Department about the nature of Soviet motives. Its effects were profound; it produced, as one official recalled, "a universal feeling that 'this was it,' this was the appreciation of the situation that had been needed." One man who was convinced was John Patton Davies, later to be persecuted as a purported Communist because of his criticism of the Chiang dictatorship in China. A year earlier he had been sure that the Russian government was guided by traditional ideas of national interest, but in the wake of Kennan's arguments, Davies wrote that despite appearances of flexibility Soviet Communism was guided by a doctrine "as intolerant and dogmatic as that which motivated the zealots of Islam or the Inquisition of Spain," all for the purpose of creating a "Soviet world."

What was little noticed was that the terms of Kennan's success had been premised on a repudiation of almost all that FDR's public foreign policy had stood for. By successfully arguing that the Soviets were not just a political embarrassment but a true threat, Kennan had handed the isolationists a retrospective yet gigantic victory. Burton Wheeler, it appeared, had been right: we had fought and died in World War II only to substitute one tyrant for another. The Democrats would soon stand naked before their political enemies.

3

Isolationist Revenge

No more Munichs . . . America must behave like the number one
world power, which she is.

—Arthur Vandenberg

For Harry Truman and the vast majority of Americans, FDR's
gamble had failed. It was possible to use Russian manpower to
defeat Germany but it wasn't possible in turn to tame the Russian
bear. This was bound to produce an enormous sense of disappointment. For Americans who yearned for nothing so much as a return
to the pleasures of private life and the chance to get ahead, the
euphoria of victory faded into the anxiety of the Cold War and
McCarthyism. The twentieth century, Trotsky had warned, was
a bad time for people who wanted quiet lives.

Anyone who studies the years between 1946 and 1954 is struck
by the spirit of rancor and revenge that animated political life well
before Senator McCarthy made his way onto the stage in 1950.
The observer notices the disproportion, the sheer imbalance between the various objects of hatred—such as the American Communist Party and Truman's foreign policy—and is puzzled by the
molten passions they evoked. Why should Truman's fervent anti-
Communist pronouncements call up charges of treason and appeasement from Republicans who were also anti-Communists? Why did

the minuscule American Communist Party evoke such fierce hatred and deep fear? Small, impotent, cuckolded by history, drained of its most prestigious supporters, it became the bogeyman which launched a thousand or more denunciations at a time when it was fading into obscurity. Commentators labeled this "the era of the witch-hunt." The sources of the witch-hunt lay in the interplay between Truman's policies and Republican traditions.

In Europe conservatism was based on hereditary classes; in America conservatism was based on hereditary religious, ethnic, and racial groups, overwhelmingly represented outside the Old South by the Republican Party. The GOP looked upon itself as the manifestation of the divine creed revealed to man through the American Revolution. This creed of Americanism, which was central to isolationism, was based on the belief that the United States was conceived in perfection as God's chosen nation. America was, in the words of G. K. Chesterton, the nation with the soul of a church. To be a Republican, then, was to share in a religiously ordained vision of a largely stateless society of self-regulating individuals. The Republican civil religion was shattered by the "American Earthquake," the Great Depression and the usurpation of the government by an alien power, FDR, in league with un-American ideas.

Until the late 1930s the Republicans were frozen in shock by their fall from grace. They were like victims of a natural disaster traumatized by watching their most cherished surroundings slide away while the New Deal reshaped the political landscape. Diminished in place and prestige, ever on the defensive trying to ward off the next social experiment from Washington, they consoled themselves with a time-honored tradition of bizarre conspiracy theories to explain how the devil, FDR, and his minions had come to rule the land. Just as their forefathers had first fought the American Revolution to halt the British conspiracy against American liberty, and just as they had beaten back the "slave-power conspiracy of the Old South," they were prepared to do battle against the new conspirators against liberty. Overwhelmed and resentful, they wanted to be free of New Deal meddling, they wanted to run their towns, their businesses, their workers in the manner to which they had been accustomed. In 1940, just when they thought they were on the verge of political recovery, a war which they fervently opposed revived the Roosevelt presidency, brought the United States into an alliance with Communism, and blocked their return to power, as it was to block them again in 1944. When they were again defeated in 1948 despite widespread expectations of victory, even their most honorable leaders, like Ohio's Robert Taft, were willing to do almost anything to return to power and "restore" the nation.

The literary critic Edmund Wilson once mused that after the Depression the United States was "not a nation but a congeries of warring interests." For the Republicans and others interested in making war on the New Dealers, Truman's turnaround on the Soviet Union proved a godsend. If, as Truman claimed publicly in early 1947, Communism was a mortal threat to the nation, why had we once allied ourselves with that threat? Truman's answer that FDR's policies had been sound but the United States had been betrayed by its former ally, did little to satisfy those who then asked why the Democrats had been so trusting to begin with. For isolationist Republicans weaned on the devil theory of World War I, the answer was obvious. Their worst fears seemed substantiated: the New Deal really was a Trojan horse for Soviet Communism.

Truman's turnabout was an implicit repudiation of the reasons FDR had given for entering World War II. Russia, it seemed, was, as the isolationists had insisted all along, the real enemy. So perhaps it might have been better to have sat back and watched Russia and Germany destroy each other. Conservatives had been shouting since the 1930s that Roosevelt was a Red dupe; now their charges seemed to be confirmed by Roosevelt's handpicked successor. They had been given a retrospective and thus bittersweet victory which they couldn't fully claim because of the martyred war dead. But now they had a golden opportunity to attack the popular New Deal social programs by attributing them to the Communist machinations of the same Roosevelt bureaucrats who had, they thought, sold the country down the river.

Trying to sort out all the players in the anti-Communist crusade is difficult. As in an Agatha Christie murder mystery, almost everyone seems to have had a hand in the dastardly deed. Every group that felt it had been dealt a losing hand by the New Deal hitched its interests to the anti-Communist bandwagon. They included small businessmen squeezed by high taxes, big labor, and big government; Southern planters who needed a new whip to force returning black veterans back into line; German-Americans who had twice watched the Democrats make war on Germany; the newly wealthy oilmen of the Southwest who felt threatened by Truman's Fair Deal extensions of the New Deal; and Catholics of many stripes angered by the Soviet alliance and eager to trumpet their own conversion to the American creed.

In the winter of 1947 Truman was chiefly concerned with the growth of Communist political movements in a Western Europe facing economic and social collapse. The Soviets were not an immediate problem; they had reduced their army from more than 11 million to fewer than 3 million men. "Unless they were completely out of their minds," said Undersecretary of State Dean Acheson, they were unikely to go to war with the United States and its A-bomb. Stalin, said America's spymaster Allen Dulles, "had not the madness of a Hitler," so that the Russians recognized the dangers of "overexpansion." The issue, thought Dulles, was that "three times . . . Russia has been invaded from Western Europe," so while he saw "no reason to believe that Russia contemplated military aggression," he believed that their "historical objective" was to have a Europe "so weakened and so dominated by the Kremlin" that Russia "shall never hereafter be in danger from the West." Dulles concluded that Russia "hopes to absorb 'Western Europe' into her direct sphere of influence without resorting to open warfare."

At war's end, policy makers, acting on the assumption that Russian aggressiveness was at root defensive, a response to weakness, believed that cooperation could be worked out with the Russians. Now Dulles, acting on similar assumptions, had come to a very different conclusion. The shift, as with so many to come, was as much a matter of new perception as new evidence.

The Truman Doctrine, asserting America's right to police the world against Communism, and the Marshall Plan for European economic recovery, which were to become the twin pillars of American foreign policy, had their origins in the Western European crisis. Appropriately enough for what came to be known as the Cold War, the particularly harsh winter of 1947–48 brought the economies of Western Europe to a halt. Britain, a nominal winner in the war, was hit with massive layoffs as the freeze halted the movement of coal and commerce. London, with the famed Big Ben silenced by frozen gears, was within a week of running out of heating coal. The situation was worse across the Channel and there every drop in economic fortunes seemed to produce a rise in Communist political influence. Malnutrition and tuberculosis were rising sharply. The lack of dollars meant that even if war-torn France and Italy wanted to trade with each other they didn't have the means to do so. Reduced to barter, Europe, once ruler of the world, faced a revolt as its colonies in Africa, Vietnam, Indonesia, and India struggled to free themselves.

The crisis in Western Europe, coming on top of the consolidation of Soviet power in Eastern Europe, Russian troops in Iran, and pressure on Turkey, led to panic in Washington. The Truman administration was becoming convinced that each of these developments was part of the general pattern of Soviet imperialism. It was not without evidence for such an interpretation. The highly respected Soviet diplomat Maxim Litvinov had told the American correspondent Richard C. Hottelet that the reason for the Cold War was Moscow's dogmatic insistence that conflict was inevitable between the Communist and capitalist worlds. When Hottelet asked if Soviet suspicions might be eased if the West were more receptive to Russian demands, Litvinov replied no; "he said it would lead to the West's being faced after a period of time with the next series of demands." Learning of the exchange, an alarmed Truman had the report of Litvinov's comments locked in the White House safe. In retrospect it appears, however, that Litvinov may have been referring only to Eastern Europe. For outside that sphere Stalin charted a very different course.

In 1945 he held back from conquering Finland in deference to that country's popularity in America. And when in May 1945 the Yugoslav Communist partisans under the leadership of Tito were about to move on Trieste, thus threatening a fight with the Anglo-American armies in Italy, Stalin forcefully told Tito to back down. Stalin was unwilling to risk a confrontation with the West on behalf of national Communist parties in Europe, which were at a distance from his own armies and thus beyond his direct control.

The Western Communist parties were loyal to Stalin but he did not respond in kind. In France he undercut the heavily armed partisans, Communists who had ideas of seizing power, by recognizing De Gaulle's regime; in China he urged Mao to negotiate a settlement with Chiang; and in Greece, where the Communist partisans, with the aid of the Yugoslavs, were fighting a reactionary monarch buttressed by British armor and men, Stalin refused to lend any assistance for fear of drawing a Western military response. "What do you think, that Great Britain and the United States—the United States, the most powerful nation in the world —will permit you to break their line of communication in the Mediterranean?" asked Stalin of Yugoslav Milovan Djilas in 1948. "Nonsense," he went on, answering his own question. "And we have no navy. The uprising in Greece must be stopped, and as quickly as possible." Stalin in 1946, like Bismarck in 1871, did not want to overextend himself. But Truman had come to share with the Western Communist parties the illusion of a unified Communist movement with Russia as its heart. Stalin, it appears, suffered from no such illusion. Despite the widespread belief to the contrary, in Greece and elsewhere the interests of the national Communist parties were strictly subordinate to Stalin's primary concern for Russian national power.

The distinction between Soviet imperial behavior in Europe and in the Near East was lost on Truman and his advisers, who had been thrown off balance by Stalin's refusal to dance to the American music. From an American perspective, it made little sense to have fought a war for the balance of power and U.S. markets in Europe only to have it fall to the native Communist parties, presumably under the control of Moscow. Having committed itself to the defense of Western Europe, the United States now found itself forced to deal with the economic problems of its military wards.

Truman's inclination was to nurse the ailing Europeans with economic aid, but he faced a formidable obstacle in the 80th Congress. The 1946 congressional elections had been a disaster for the Democrats. Split between the warring Wallaceites and middle-of-the-roaders and riddled by Catholic defections, the Democrats had been easy pickings for the Republicans, who, scoring massive gains, took control of both houses of the congress for their first taste of power since 1932. It had been a bitter campaign, in which Truman's supposed "appeasement" of the Russians and the alleged Communist control of the CIO were the major Republican issues. Playing on the widespread public distrust of big-labor leaders like the miners' John L. Lewis—himself a Republican—and public criticism of the postwar wave of strikes, the Republicans hammered away at the alleged role of "Communist agitators" in fomenting labor "strife." The *Republican News* openly accused labor leaders and New Dealers of trying to Sovietize the United States. The Republicans were aided by J. Edgar Hoover. Hoover, director of the FBI, who had gotten his start in Red-hunting twenty years earlier during the post-World War I anti-Red hysteria, called for eternal vigilance against not only the 100,000 Communists he said were on the loose in America but their unseen millions of sympathizers as well. The emotional currents were running with the Red-baiters. FDR's picture was ripped off the walls of Democratic clubhouses in ethnic neighborhoods and burned as the betrayer of Eastern Europe.

Truman, an unelected and increasingly unpopular President, was in a position neither to resist the rightward drift nor to gain the aid he wanted to fight Communism in Western Europe. In 1946 Truman's leadership was so little regarded and the Republican tide so strong that a prominent leader in his own party, Senator Fulbright of Arkansas, suggested he step down and hand the presidency over to the Republican leader of the House. The new Congress that floated in on the conservative and neo-isolationist tide of 1946 was deeply traditionalist and hostile to socialism. Powerful governments emerge either from fighting foreign enemies or from restructuring traditional domestic practices, and the neo-isolationists wanted nothing to do with either. They wanted to roll back government and return to the supposedly halcyon days of Herbert Hoover. Their passion was to unscramble all the omelets cooked by the New Deal. They wanted tax cuts, anti-labor legislation, and a crusade to purge "the Reds" from what they always described as the "bloated" bureaucracy. In foreign policy they wanted nothing so much as to have the outside world go away. Their leader, Robert Taft, was reported to have said that "I have been charged with moving in on foreign policy; the truth is that foreign policy has moved in on me." In foreign affairs their deep-seated hatred for Communism was at odds with their over-riding concern for cutting taxes and government. Foreign aid, or welfare for the Europeans as they called it, seemed part of a socialist plot to weaken America from within by justifying a strong government and draining the Treasury. Their view was aptly summed up by one spokesman who was convinced that New Deal "Communism" was even more of a threat than the Soviet variety.

Truman's immediate problem was a warning from the British that they could no longer afford to prop up the anti-Communist rebels in Greece. Greece had been devastated by the German occupation; roads, bridges, and whole cities had been destroyed, leaving a population in which as many as 85 percent of the children were tubercular. During the war the British and the Americans had supported a motley group of partisans, many of whom were Communist, to fight the Germans. The Communists' role in the resistance, said American Ambassador Lincoln MacVeagh, had enabled them to become the natural leaders of the country. They were, in his words, "the best," "the most vital fellows" in Greece. But at war's end the British insisted on reinstalling the anti-Communist King George, who was neither Greek nor popular. The result, according to MacVeagh, was "not one of the nice old revolutions we used to have in the old days." Faced with the prospect of fighting Communism by supporting a right-wing monarchy, Truman could have backed away and looked for another opportunity to draw the line with the Russians. But Truman was unwilling to back off. He was convinced that the deteriorating situation across Europe meant that the United States had to act and to act fast if Communists aligned with the Soviets weren't to seize power along a broad front. He could have begun prudently by calling on Congress to provide limited aid to support the Greek anti-Communists, but there was little chance that such a request would pass in a Congress which contained so many budget-conscious isolationists already warning Truman not to try to fill Britain's vacated imperial role.

Stymied, Truman sent World War II hero General George Marshall, who had replaced Byrnes as Secretary of State, before a group of congressional leaders to plead the Administration's case for aid to Greece. Marshall, sticking to the facts, gave a low-key presentation which failed to move the skeptics. It was then that Undersecretary Acheson seized the day with hell-and-brimstone rhetoric. "We are met at Armageddon," he told the congressmen. Acheson, who had an extremely low opinion of the intelligence of the members of Congress, went on, in a 1940s version of the domino theory, to warn that "like apples in a barrel infected by one rotten one, the corruption of Greece would infect Iran and all to the east." Asia Minor, Europe, and Egypt would surely be next. Then, rising to fevered heights, he wooed the rubes with an enticing pitch. "The Soviet Union," he said, "was playing one of the greatest gambles in history at minimal cost . . . We and we alone [are] in a position to break up that play." After listening to Acheson, a stunned Vandenberg told Truman "there's only one way to get" what you want. "That is to make a personal appearance before Congress and scare the hell out of the American people." And scare them he did. Truman, with the aid of Acheson, who emerges as "Iago or Paul Revere depending on your point of view," launched, verbally at least, a crusade in the name of the American creed and all that was holy.

Truman's March 12, 1947, speech before Congress announcing the Truman Doctrine was the United States' public declaration of Cold War. In 1940, Roosevelt, referring to the Nazis, said that World War II was "not an ordinary war" but instead was "a revolution imposed by force of arms which threatens all men everywhere." Truman was now making the same claim about the Communist-led war against the Greek monarchy. Playing every note of the anti-Communist keyboard, Truman echoed Lincoln's famous "House Divided" speech, in which the Great Emancipator had warned that the country could not long stand half free and half slave. Truman carried this warning to a world which he divided between the forces of light and democracy based on "free elections, . . . individual liberty, freedom of speech and religion, and freedom from political oppression" and the forces of darkness and totalitarianism based on "terror and oppression." The time had come, he proclaimed in the apocalyptic terms of a final confrontation, when "nearly every nation must choose between alternative ways of life." The United States, he vowed, would always "support free peoples [meaning non-Communist] who are resisting attempted subjugation by armed minorities or outside pressures."

A revealing letter written to his daughter the day after the speech makes it clear just how deeply Truman had repudiated wartime policies. "The attempt of Lenin, Trotsky, Stalin et al. to fool the world and the American Crackpot Association, represented by Jos. Davies, Henry Wallace, Claude Pepper and the actors and artists in immoral Greenwich Village, is just like Hitler and Mussolini's so-called socialist states." The high-hat phonies might have been fooled by the Reds, but not Harry Truman, the small-town boy.

The Truman Doctrine may have been justified for Western Europe, where the slogan "freedom of speech" was something more than a phrase learned in a foreign textbook, but what of the rest of the world? Were the traditional oligarchies of, say, Latin America any more liberal, any more freedom-loving than the totalitarian bureaucrats? Truman never once directly mentioned the Russians in his speech. Instead he talked of totalitarian regimes, implying both Hitler's Germany and Stalin's Russia, whose ability to totally mobilize their populations for the ends of the state put them on a permanent war footing.

Totalitarian regimes, provided they were also major industrial powers, might very well become a threat to the United States. But were armed rebellions against non-Communist regimes around the world, most of which were traditional or military dictatorships, also a threat to the United States?

The isolationists and the generally pro-Soviet liberals saw from their very different vantage points that Truman's vow threatened to put the United States in the impossible position of foolishly trying to hold back the ceaseless waves of rebellion and revolution unleashed by the growth of the world capitalist economy, which had everywhere shattered traditional societies and left little in its place. "The Communists were successful," explained Henry Wallace sanguinely, because "the world was being swept by revolution as ordinary people fought for a better life and the Communists had made themselves the natural leaders of that revolution." Wallace was joined in a strange counterpoint by Charles and Anne Morrow Lindbergh, the country's leading isolationists, who, viewing the world with disdain, believed that war and fascism in Europe were merely the most malign form—"the scum on the wave of the future"—of what in reality was a worldwide revolution.

The Lindberghs were prophetic, for Hitler was truly one of the most important revolutionaries of the twentieth century. The Führer's virulent brand of nationalism led through a European civil war to the loss of Europe's worldwide domination. While the great powers were destroying each other, the colonial world began to free itself. Hitler himself was aware of this. He made a point of attacking British and French imperialism. Like Lenin, he foresaw the swift emergence of Asian and Third World nationalisms, and he was particularly taken by the Moslem world, describing the Islamic peoples as Germany's best friend. Startling as it may seem today, Egypt's Anwar Sadat, operating on the principle that the enemy of my enemy is my friend, was both an admirer and a collaborator of the Nazis. In much the same manner, other Third World leaders around the globe were attracted to the Soviet Union, for, whatever the horrors of Stalin's crimes at home, Russia was a stalwart foe of the Western powers who had for so long exploited the colonial nations.

It was the popular appeal of the anticolonialist mass movements that particularly irked Americans. "The revolutions which formerly took place in the world had nothing in them that interested the bulk of mankind," said Tom Paine, referring to America as the beacon of the downtrodden. But now, unlike the traditional autocracies, America had set itself against the new revolutions of fascism and Communism and also claimed to represent the democratic and popular will.

Hitler had offered the Arabs a politics of vengeance which "breached the pale of traditional diplomatic practice" and provided a stylistic model for dictators to follow, but Stalin and the U.S.S.R. offered a far more appealing model for most emerging nations. Russia, a backward nation which had modernized itself, was an inspiration for Third World leaders. After its revolution, Russia had not only taken its place as a great power; as a latecomer to the game of great nations, it also offered aid to other newcomers in the struggle against the status quo powers Hitler had railed against.

If, as he promised, Truman aided every country whose rebels were attracted to the Soviets, "Russia would," in the words of one

isolationist, " 'play firebug,' while America would play 'fireman.' "
Washington, said the internationalist Walter Lippmann, would
have to race pell-mell around the globe "recruiting, subsidizing
and supporting a heterogeneous array of satellites, clients, de-
pendents, and puppets." Describing the Truman Doctrine as a
"big hot generalization," Lippmann foresaw a situation in which
the United States would find itself called upon to defend unstable
dictatorial regimes in the name of anti-Communism. Faced with
such demands, the United States would have to "disown our
puppets, which would be tantamount to appeasement and defeat
and the loss of face," or else support them "at an incalculable cost
on an unintended, unforeseen and perhaps undesirable issue." Lippmann's eloquence was paralleled by the raspy tones of outraged
isolationists who felt their pocketbooks bleeding. Once "Uncle
Sucker tried to deter Communism with cash," they fretted, "all the
spigoty 'republics' will develop active and very threatening Communist parties even if they have to import them." "The cry of
'wolf, wolf' will be raised by every royal punk the world over."

The isolationist romantic attachment to Asia aside, America's
primary interests, said Lippmann, were in Europe and it was there,
he insisted, that the United States should focus its anti-Communist
attentions. He would have been surprised to discover a considerable measure of agreement from the White House. Truman and
his advisers had not, despite their rhetoric, yet lost sight of the
limits of even American power. "The line must be drawn somewhere," wrote Undersecretary of State Robert Lovett, "or the
United States would find itself in the position of underwriting the
security of the whole world." Truman recognized that he had to
pick and choose among objectives, and he made money for
Europe's economic recovery his chief priority, even at the cost of
military expenditures, which still remained quite limited.

Directly contradicting the implications of the Truman speech,
Acheson, speaking for the Administration, specifically rejected the
idea that the Truman Doctrine provided a precedent for giving
military aid for countries other than Greece. There was no
thought, for instance, to giving military aid to South Korea, a
matter that would later lead to conspiratorial recriminations. And
pointing in particular to China, where the Administration was
looking for ways to scale down American commitment to Chiang,

a likely loser in the Chinese civil war, Acheson emphasized that aid to foreign nations would be taken on a case-by-case basis.

One nation Truman was prepared to help was Communist Yugoslavia. The Yugoslavs were perhaps the most ideological and militant of the Eastern European Communist parties. Strongly committed to Marxist-Leninist ideology, Tito had no hesitation in persecuting the Catholic Church or his political enemies. When in 1946 two unarmed U.S. transport planes strayed over Yugoslavian airspace, he shot them down, producing more than a few tense moments, since Tito's very close ties with Stalin led the Americans mistakenly to assume that the Russians were behind the incident. Loyal Communist that he was, Tito was also a devout nationalist; he and his supporters took great pride in the fact that they had largely liberated themselves from Nazi rule. Tito had plans for a Yugoslavian sphere of influence which was to include Greece —whose Communists he was aiding in the civil war—as well as Bulgaria and Albania. This was vetoed by Stalin, who had no desire to see a non-Russian center of power on his flank. When in a clash of rival Communist imperialisms Stalin tried to depose Tito in a coup, the Yugoslav leader drew upon his countrymen's nationalism and defied the Russians. To the amazement of the West, "the communist chieftain of a primitive Balkan country with a population of only 16 million said 'no' to Stalin, chased out Soviet minions, imprisoned Soviet partisans, and dared the Russians to do their worst." Tito's breakaway ended his support for the Greek rebels, helping to end the civil war there, and demonstrated the overwhelming importance of nationalism, a lesson the United States would later forget. For a while, however, there was hope in the State Department that Mao might become an Asian Tito.

Truman's difficulties, to return to Congress, were that the sizable isolationist contingent in Congress was opposed, on principle, to foreign aid. But now Truman had them mousetrapped. After all their warnings about the Red menace, it would be very hard to vote against proposals to fight it. As one observer saw it, "Truman had issued a challenge to the Soviet Union in one of the bluntest statements ever made in peacetime by a head of state. Congress could not repudiate him, or even amend his proposal substantially without giving encouragement to Communists everywhere." To guard his flank, Truman also proposed to take the lead in fighting

"Communism" within the government. Administering his own homeopathic cure, he announced a loyalty program for federal employees. This cynical ploy drew the fire of anti-Communist liberals like James Wechsler, who denounced "the artificial uproar" and danger to civil liberties posed by Truman's plan. The program, it turned out, uprooted such dangerous subversives as James Kutcher, a legless veteran working as a Veterans Administration clerk, on the basis of his membership in a Trotskyist sect which had little love for "Uncle Joe." In the bizarre logic of the Cold War, a search for that largely imaginary creature, the Communist mole buried deep in the New Deal bureaucracy, opened the back door for money to flow to European socialists by way of aid to Greek monarchists.

It was victory but at a price. To win, Truman had mortgaged his European policy, however well advised, to his crusading rhetoric. And whatever his administration's true goals, by announcing the need to fight Communism everywhere he had entered a hall of mirrors where perception would be more important than reality. For having announced such a policy, if he failed to respond to a Communist victory it would appear to the world that America lacked the will to fight its sworn enemies.

In June 1947, after angling for half a year, the White House finally proposed what it wanted all along, massive aid for the economic reconstruction of Western Europe. Called the Marshall Plan, after the Secretary of State, it was actually designed by George Kennan, who had regretted the military tone of the Truman Doctrine, to allow the Europeans jointly to reorganize their economies with U.S. support. The precondition for the American subvention was coordinated and often socialist transnational planning aimed at modernizing Europe's economic structures. The U.S. government, Republicans correctly pointed out, was underwriting policies that would never be tolerated in America. For Republicans the socialism of the anti-Nazi resistance fighters leading the New Europe was simply a continuation of the planned economies of Hitler, Mussolini, and Pétain.

The Soviets were invited to take part in the Marshall Plan, formally known as the European Recovery Program (ERP), but recognizing that the Plan was in part directed against them, they declined both for themselves and for their Eastern European satellites, many of whom were eager to participate. In America, Henry Wallace denounced the "Martial Plan" and scoffed that the initials ERP really stood for "Erase the Russian Peril." But most liberals, including Helen Gahagan Douglas, later to be smeared as a "pinko" by Richard Nixon, and even Truman critics like I. F. Stone, praised it as a constructive alternative to Truman Doctrine militarism.

Molotov denounced Marshall aid as an attempt by American capitalists to capture new markets and prevent a new depression at home; he was largely correct. The money for Marshall aid strained an already inflation-prone economy. But Truman, like many Americans, spent the 1940s looking over his shoulder at the 1930s and a depression which had been brought on, in part, by the contraction of international trade after World War I. He was willing to go to considerable lengths to prevent a repetition. The Marshall Plan, then, was both a hedge against depression and a means of securing Western Europe.

As might be expected, the brunt of the opposition to the Plan came from Republicans who unleashed a torrent of criticism about "sob sister proposals," "European TVAs," and the "rat holes of Europe." They asked why Truman was willing to send money to Britain's socialist government but unwilling to clean "the vermin out of our own house." But the Republican isolationists were not the only ones reluctant to funnel millions of dollars into Europe. The crisis conditions which seemed to have justified Truman Doctrine money for Greece were fading in Europe after De Gaulle had roundly beaten the French Communists at the polls. Surveying the scene, Lippmann concluded that "the Russians had lost the Cold War and they know it." And no less a figure than the sober General Marshall publicly admitted that "the advance of Communism had been stemmed." What, then, was the point of the Marshall aid? "The only way to win the support of the Congress for the Marshall monies," said Lippmann, "was to frighten it." But Truman had already played that card. In desperation he organized a massive pressure campaign on behalf of the Plan. Picking up support from that oft-sought-after breed "the enlightened businessman," liberals, and labor leaders, he had the tax-cutting Congress deluged with mail and petitions, but to little avail. The

President seemed destined for a major defeat, and then came Czechoslovakia!

In February 1948 the Czech government, Eastern Europe's only democracy, was toppled in a Soviet-backed coup. Nine months earlier a Communist coup in Hungary, removing the last remaining independent elements there, created little alarm in the West. Czechoslovakia was different; it had been the model nation—democratic, yet pro-Soviet—for those Western liberals who hoped for a reconciliation with the U.S.S.R. But perhaps even more important, Czechoslovakia, because it had been given up to Hitler at the infamous Munich conference a decade earlier, was a symbol of Western appeasement in the face of totalitarian aggression. This time it was Russian troops marching into Czechoslovakia, and Truman spoke for millions in Europe and America when he said that the coup had "sent a shock through the civilized world." We were, he believed, "faced with exactly the same situation with which Britain and France [were] faced in 1938–39 with Hitler."

A war panic seized the nation. "A cold fear," said a Chicago reporter, "is gripping the people." The Washington *Post*, responding also to Soviet pressure on Finland, captured the nation's fears with a front-page map of Europe, the areas controlled by Russia shaded. The caption stated: "Russia moves westward—where next?" General Clay sent an urgent message from Berlin warning that war might break out "with dramatic suddenness," while administration hard-liner James Forrestal talked of the possibility of a preemptive strike against the Russians. There was nothing, it seemed, to prevent the Russian Army from marching to the Channel. Even the usually cool Lippmann was caught up in the frenzy. He urged "immediate mobilization, the draft, . . . war powers over industry, and the declaration of national emergency."

Hot on the heels of the Czech coup came a crisis over Allied West Berlin, isolated deep in the heart of Soviet-controlled East Germany. The Soviets, angered by Allied moves toward the creation of a separate and anti-Soviet West German state, responded in June 1948 by shutting off Allied access to the city. A new war panic developed. Again there was talk in Washington of a preemptive strike. Britain's Labor government, by now also thoroughly disillusioned with the U.S.S.R., called for a direct show of force to challenge the blockade. Berlin had become a symbol worth protecting, though, as Truman made clear, not worth dying for. Truman, acting out of an exaggerated appreciation of Russian military strength, decided not to call Stalin's bluff; instead he ordered an airlift to supply the city with food and fuel. Not to be ended until May 1949, the airlift, which kept the Berliners alive while avoiding a confrontation, became a symbol of Western resolve to resist Russian imperialism. In the eyes of the American public the moral map of Europe was being redrawn, so that it was now common to talk openly with the West Germans of "our common enemy Russia."

When the smoke had cleared, however, it became apparent that, rather than being prelude to an invasion of Western Europe, the coup and the blockade were Russian responses to the Marshall Plan and the dangers of a rearmed West Germany. A revived Western economy was sure to act as a powerful magnet on countries like Poland and Czechoslovakia, which were eager to participate in the Marshall Plan and Western financial arrangements. Unable to bind her satellites by trade or culture, Mother Russia reacted in her traditionally crude and military fashion. The Marshall Plan had aided the free societies of Western Europe at the cost of further confining Eastern Europe. H. Stuart Hughes, a historian who had served in the State Department during these crises, aptly described them as part of "an elaborate counterpoint in which our government and that of the Soviet Union seemed to be working almost hand in hand to simplify the ideological map."

The Czech and Berlin crises played into Truman's hand on the domestic scene. Reviled from all sides, Truman was likely to be beaten in the 1948 presidential election, if he was nominated. Truman's star had fallen so fast that desperate anti-Communist liberals, organized into the Americans for Democratic Action (ADA), pleaded with General Dwight D. Eisenhower to come forth and save the party and the nation, even though Eisenhower was neither a Democrat nor a liberal. The General declined to mount the liberals' white steed, later to be ridden by John F. Kennedy, while Southern white conservatives, disgruntled over Truman's support for civil rights, decided that if they couldn't mount the Democratic donkey they would whip it with a breakaway Dixiecrat candidate for the presidency. Meanwhile the Wallace Democrats, still worshipping at the shrine of FDR, determined to punish Truman for his hard line with the Soviets by creating a Progressive Party with the former Vice-President as its standard bearer.

The GOP, it seemed, couldn't lose. The Republican sap had been rising since 1940, and 1948 was to be the year to tap that flow. True, their candidate, Thomas E. Dewey, was a stuffed shirt and his vacuous prose—"You know that your future is ahead of you" —was numbing, and yes, Dewey was reported to be able to strut like a peacock while sitting down, but even this was not enough to slow, let alone stem, the Republican tide.

Here was the making of an irresistibly appealing story, to be told over and over again by journalists and historians: the tale of how a beleaguered Truman, beset by traitors to his left and right, given up for dead, fought back against the man with the heart of a bank teller, and rose from the political grave to win the presidency. Only clichés could describe it, and few Hollywood script-writers have produced better plots. The problem is that the focus on the colorful campaign, in which a plurality voted for plucky Harry, obscured the deeper emotions behind the election; a sizable minority of Americans had come to hate Truman as the symbol of all they thought had gone wrong in America. What was thought of as a triumph was instead the first act of a tragedy.

The country, wrote Walter Lippmann, "has been wanting to have a conservative administration since 1944" and would have "something like a nervous breakdown if it is frustrated much longer." Lippmann exaggerated in talking of the country at large; rather, he had described the feeling of conservative and isolationist Republicans, those for whom General Douglas MacArthur was speaking when he said that "our American way of life is forever doomed . . . unless the New Deal can be stopped." The isolationists are perhaps better described as Asialationists,* since most of them, while noninterventionists regarding Europe, were strong interventionists in the Far East, where America could act unilaterally in the theater of her supposed destiny. Both MacArthur, who sought the presidential nomination in 1944, and Taft, who had the

---

* "Asialationist" is a term coined by historian Arthur M. Schlesinger, Jr., to describe the contradictory attitudes of postwar isolationists.

lion's share of isolationist support and had tried in 1940, were dismayed at Dewey's nomination. For the third time in eight years the nomination had gone to the Europhile, cosmopolitan, Eastern wing of the party, which had made its peace with the New Deal. That was easy enough for them to do, but what of the small Midwestern manufacturer battling trade unions to maintain his profit margin? Neither he nor the small-town politicos with a burning hatred for Washington's intrusions in their affairs had made peace with the Roosevelt "revolution."

In the late 1930s the Republican heirs of Grant and Sherman found themselves making common cause with the children of Lee and Jackson against Roosevelt's centralizing tendencies. Southern Democrats, though interventionist and far more supportive of the New Deal, were frightened by the growth of a federal government powerful enough to affect race relations.

The new expectations which came out of the war left Southern employers flabbergasted. As one returning black corporal explained it: "I spent four years in the Army to free a bunch of Frenchmen and Dutchmen, and I'm hanged if I'm going to let the Alabama version of the Germans kick me around when I'm back home. No sirree-bob! I went into the Army a nigger; I'm coming out a *man!*" Returning black veterans were reluctant to return to their old menial jobs. "Cotton Pickers, Where Are You?" asked the Memphis *Press-Scimitar*, while the Raleigh *News and Observer* was so angered by veterans collecting government benefits rather than returning to low-wage work that it suggested that the unemployed "ought to be forced to watch themselves starve." Southern employers were so resistant to higher wages and so concerned with bludgeoning workers back into prewar conditions that they appealed to the War Department to retain German POWs to work in the pulp and paper factories and citrus fields.

Midwestern businessmen had received some relief from labor pressures in the form of the 1947 Taft-Hartley Act, denounced as a slave-labor bill by the AFL-CIO, which outlawed the closed shop and thus made it more difficult to organize. But no relief was forthcoming for Southern employers; instead, with the Truman Fair Employment Practices Commission, the federal government was threatening unprecedented involvement in Southern labor "relations." Coming at a time when such bulwarks of Southern power as the poll tax, the all-white primary, and the two-thirds rule, which gave Southerners a veto over the Democratic nominee, were being eliminated, the FEPC brought on a panic among the region's gentry.

The county courthouse politicos of the South responded by playing on old fears, referring to Truman's civil rights program as a "Democratic version of Reconstruction." Some offered a "principled" defense of states' rights, but most simply shouted "nigger" or "Communism" at the top of their lungs. Joe Ervin, younger brother of Watergate's "Senator Sam," saw the FEPC as leading the country down the road to British socialism. Others weren't so subtle, suggesting the FEPC was nothing less than a plot to Sovietize America. Eugene Cox, a representative from Georgia, claimed to see "the hand of Stalin" behind CIO attempts to organize the black vote. With racketeers in patriotism sprouting everywhere, states' rights, racism, and anti-labor sentiment were fused in a countercampaign to hold back the changes unleashed by the war. It was one of those "patriots," Senator Theodore Bilbo of Mississippi, who had taken bribes from a half dozen military contractors during the war, who told his followers, "The time to see the nigger is the night before the election" and "If you don't know what I mean you are just plain dumb."

Whatever doubts credulous Southerns might have had about the Communist plot to destabilize the South were probably erased when Henry Wallace and his vice-presidential candidate, Glenn Taylor, defied precedent and concern for their personal safety by campaigning to racially mixed audiences across the South. When Taylor tried to speak to a black group in Birmingham, he was arrested by Sheriff Eugene "Bull" Connor, who explained: "There's not enough room in town for Bull and the Commies." Taylor emerged unscathed but others weren't so lucky; Wallace was repeatedly pelted by eggs as his supporters were jeered, threatened, and even knifed and beaten as they tried to attend his rallies.

Wallace's personal courage in confronting racism was overshadowed in his campaign by a streak of mysticism which affected his personal and his political judgment. At the Progressive Party convention, he first meditated and then spoke of his followers as Gideon's army, a brave band of biblical warriors who "by God's grace" would usher in "the people's peace" leading to the century of the common man. It was thanks to Wallace's interest in the occult that the Great Pyramid, with an eye at the apex peering out, appears on the back of the dollar bill. Wallace was particularly drawn to the pyramid's motto, *Novus Ordo Seclorum*, the New Order of the Ages, a phrase that California's Governor Jerry Brown was later to repopularize. Right-wing journalists, picking up on this strand in Wallace's personality, questioned the candidate roughly during the campaign as to whether he was in fact the author of the so-called guru letters, an alleged correspondence between Wallace and a Russian theosophist which was filled with bizarre incantations and referred to FDR as "The Flaming One." When Wallace refused to deny authorship he became something of a laughingstock, further diminishing the impact of his sometimes prescient words on American race relations and foreign policy.

Wallace had from the start denounced the Truman Doctrine as "a curious mixture of power politics and international carpetbagging," warning that in enforcing it "America will become the most hated nation in the world." Wallace, however, had little to offer in the way of an alternative. His appeal to the memory of FDR and the wartime policy of cooperation probably did more to defame Roosevelt's reputation than boost the Progressive Party's presidential chances. Wallace's insistence that we could "do business with Stalin" led him to overlook or apologize for the massively murderous repression in the U.S.S.R., which, while passed over in wartime, could no longer so easily be swept under the rug. Similarly, his sympathies led him to see that the Czech coup was a response to the Marshall Plan, yet they also led him to manufacture out of whole cloth a right-wing coup, planned in the American Embassy, which had precipitated the Russian takeover. Out of touch with a tax-cutting Congress and a public jealous of American national sovereignty, he proposed as an alternative to the Marshall Plan a far more expensive program financed solely by American money but administered by the UN. When the Berlin crisis startled the American consciousness, Wallace responded with dated vitriol charging that the real danger was fascism here at home set off by industrialists who had formented recurrent war scares in order to militarize the country. American industrialists were in fact supporting reduced military expenditures to lower taxes.

Wallace's credibility was further damaged by the obvious role played in his campaign by the American Communist Party. An independent leftist, the journalist I. F. Stone, decided that "a vote for Wallace would be a vote for peace." Even so, he was disturbed by the extent of Communist influence in the Progressive Party, and complained of "the stultifications and idiocies, the splits and heresy hunts which make the Communists so ludicrous a spectacle half the time." Wallace consoled himself by telling critics that since he was an outspoken Christian and advocate of progressive capitalism, it was he who was using the Communists and not the other way around. Truman, sensing both an opportunity and the deep-seated desire for peace, responded by outflanking Wallace. He increasingly spoke of his desire for peace and launched several largely diversionary diplomatic efforts to show that he meant what he said. At the same time, Truman, following the advice of Clark Clifford, began to turn Wallace into a lightning rod to fend off Republican charges that he was soft on the Reds. Echoing Wallace's earlier rhetoric about the Republicans and Hitler, Truman charged that "a vote for Wallace . . . is a vote for all the things for which Stalin, Molotov and Vishinsky stand."

In the spring of 1948 the Gallup poll found that 65 percent of the people it polled thought that foreign policy problems were the most important issue in the campaign and 73 percent felt Truman was being too easy on the Russians. For most politicians this would have been raw meat, but not for Thomas Dewey, the man with the soul of a bank teller. Dewey, calculating he was ahead, decided to sit on his lead. Dewey pressed his opinions on neither domestic nor foreign policy. "No presidential candidate in the future," said the Louisville *Courier-Journal* wryly, "will be so inept that four of his major speeches can be boiled down to these four historic sentences: Agriculture is important. Our rivers are full of fish. You cannot have freedom without liberty. The future lies ahead. [We might add a fifth: The TVA is a fine thing, and we must make certain that nothing like it happens again.]" Freed from his foreign policy vulnerabilities, Truman attacked the do-nothing Republican-controlled Congress and cleverly appealed to every domestic interest group aided by the New Deal. Truman turned the election into a referendum on the New Deal and won handily despite the Dixiecrats and Progressives. For Republicans the lesson was clear: if they wanted to regain power they would have to go back to the Red-baiting assault on the Democrats' foreign policy which had been so successful in 1946. It was hard to sympathize with Dewey for his embarrassing defeat. He was, said one reporter, a man who had "completely missed . . . the very emotion of the past 30 years." In the face of the tidal pull of irrational impulses about to sweep the nation into McCarthyism, there could have been no better time for such a bloodless President.

In November 1948, three days before the presidential election, the headlines in the New York *Times* read: "Manchuria Is Lost by Chiang Regime." It was the beginning of the end both for Truman's unwanted ally, Chiang's Chinese Nationalists, and for Truman's second administration. Within a year the Chinese Communists rolled across China, forcing Chiang to flee to Taiwan. Shortly after Mao's victory the Russians exploded their first atomic bomb, long before they were supposed to have such a capability, frightening an already anxious public. To intensify matters, the Soviet A-bomb and the "fall" of China were played out against the backdrop of the Hiss case. Hiss, a prominent New Dealer and participant at Yalta, was accused of being a Russian agent and his two trials for perjury opened all the festering wounds left by the New Deal and the fight over American intervention. "The shocks of 1949," wrote historian Eric Goldman, "loosed within American life a vast impatience, a turbulent bitterness, a rancor akin to revolt. . . . It brought into rococo coalition bankers and charwomen, urban priests and the Protestant farmlands of the Midwest, longtime New Deal voters and Senator Robert A. Taft."

Chiang was a strange ally. In the 1920s, before his conversion to Christianity, he had been, like so many Third World nationalists, close to the Kremlin. Stalin, who always had an affinity for Chiang, supported him against the advice of Trotsky, who was a supporter of Mao. In World War II, FDR tried to use Chiang's manpower to fight the Japanese as he had used Stalin's to halt the Germans. But Chiang was far less interested in fighting the Japanese invaders than in holding power against Mao's challenge. American advisers despised the Generalissimo. The chief American military adviser, "Vinegar Joe" Stilwell, was revulsed by the corruption and decadence surrounding Chiang's court. He derided Chiang as "the peanut," whereas he so came to admire the Communist general Chu Teh that he said he would be proud to "shoulder a rifle" with such a man. Stilwell's feelings were not shared by an army intelligence captain, John Birch, who would be killed in an encounter with the "Chi-coms," but they were shared by most American foreign service officers in China. These young officials realized that America's interests in Asia could be best served by weaning Mao away from Stalin to create Titoism *avant la lettre*. FDR, also appalled by Chiang, even considered assassinating the Generalissimo to further the war effort, but nothing came of the plan and Chiang became a permanent burden for American policy makers. With the war's end and the shift in national mood, the wartime criticism of Chiang was seen in a new light as part of an elaborate Communist plot directed from the Kremlin.

By early 1948 nearly half of Chiang's Nationalist troops had defected and as much as 80 percent of the American equipment given Chiang had either fallen into Communist hands or been sold on the black market. Chiang, said the American Ambassador, was "the best asset the Communists have"; compared to the Generalissimo, Czar Nicholas "was foresighted and daring." Truman had had enough of the "Chiangs, Kungs, and Soongs," the prominent Chinese clans behind the Nationalists; saying "they were all thieves, every last one of them," he moved to terminate U.S. aid. He was met with frenzied outcries from Asialationists and the powerful China lobby, which wasn't above financing its work on Capitol Hill by trading in illegal drugs.

The GOP was split between the followers of Vandenberg and Taft on European matters, but it was united in its anguish over what was described as the "loss" of China, as if it were ours to lose. Maps in *Time* and *Life* showed dramatically how with Mao's victory over 40 percent of the world's population and almost the entire land mass of Eurasia came under Communist control. For Republicans the fall of China was a foreign policy trauma equal to the victory of the New Deal at home. Just as the New Deal had betrayed Republican principles of government and allowed alien social elements to gain power in Washington, Chiang's fall meant an end to the belief that America's future lay in Asia.

The more measured Republicans like Henry Luce responded by trying to hold Truman's feet to the fire. Luce's *Life*, referring to the universal premises of the Truman Doctrine, pointed up the contradiction between the President's policies in Western Europe and Asia. Hoisting the President by his own petard, he asked how it could be that "at the very moment the government recognized the global nature of the conflict, the Chinese front is given up for lost"? If there was only one world Communism there could be only one containment and in Asia Chiang was its flag bearer.

Others wouldn't be as kind; where Luce saw inconsistency some Asialationists, shouting "treason," were ready to storm the barricades. How was it possible, Asialationists asked, that the United States, the most powerful nation in the world, had been able to ally itself with Russia, which then proceeded to vastly expand its empire, but was unable to halt the spread of Communism in Asia? Their answer was a mixture of devil theory and popular theology. They denied that Truman's failures could be attributed to miscalculation, stupidity, or circumstance; instead they charged disloyalty and treason "mixed with the sin of pride which made policy makers forsake the will of the people for their own superior vision." Roosevelt and Truman, arrogant men drawn to un-American ideologies, had, they claimed, worked diligently to undermine the traditional values upon which America was based. In the U.S.S.R. such sinners would have been branded Trotskyites and shot. In America very few died but many were swept up in a carnival of hate.

The devil dealers were joined by Catholic Democrats like young Congressman John F. Kennedy. Every bit his isolationist father's son, Kennedy "recounted" to a Boston audience the whole "incredible" history of how China had been betrayed by our policy-making "pinks," concluding with an emotional note: "This," he said, "is the tragic story of China, whose freedom we once fought to preserve. What our young men had saved, our diplomats and our President have frittered away." MacArthur was so pleased with the speech that he praised it effusively and quoted extensively from it in his own talks.

Catholic Democrats and Republicans were joined, as well, in their common hatred of Dean Acheson, the man who came to symbolize all that the conspiracy hunters were against. "Acheson," wrote literary critic Leslie Fiedler, seemed "the projection of all the hostilities of the Midwestern mind at bay; his waxed mustache, his mincing accent, his personal loyalty to a traitor [Hiss] who also belonged to the Harvard Club; one is never quite sure that he was not invented by a . . . cartoonist." The hatred for Acheson was as much a matter of culture as of policy. The Asialationists, in fact, had no alternative proposals for Asia; they, like Truman, were unwilling to send troops to China. But if they didn't know what they wanted they knew what they hated. "I look at that fellow" Acheson, said a seething Senator Hugh Butler of Nebraska. "I watch his smart aleck manner and his British clothes and that New Dealism, everlasting New Dealism in everything he says and does, and I want to shout, Get Out! Get Out! You stand for everything that has been wrong in the United States for years."

Republicans, inconsolable over the loss of China and bereft of alternatives short of nuclear war, poured vitriol over Acheson, the man they loved to hate. Acheson, who had far less of a constituency in Congress than did Chiang, responded by describing his tormentors as "primitives." With the fevered attacks on Acheson the ordinary props and costumes of the national political stage were stripped away to reveal the white-hot anger and unleashed frustrations of nearly twenty years of Republican exile. Acting as much to punish their enemies as to revive true Americanism, the Congress was turned into a living theater, a psychodrama in which senators and representatives felt free to spin out their wildest fantasies of homosexuality, intrigue, and treason, all of which were said to lay behind the New Deal.

In the midst of these outbursts of expressive as opposed to instrumental politics, the Russians exploded their first atomic bomb. The timing couldn't have been worse. While politicians talked of how our security had been stripped from us, a vulnerable public was subjected to a stream of lurid war scare stories from the popular magazines. Our scientists had estimated that the Russians probably wouldn't be able to make a bomb till 1955. How could those barbarians have gotten a bomb so quickly? They never could have done it on their own, so it must have been the work of spies, likes the ones already caught as part of the Soviet spy network in Canada. And who were the spies among us? Were they ordinary men and women loyal to their families and country? No, they were intellectuals fanatically loyal to ideas, but without an elementary sense of obligation to their fellow Americans. In short, they were people like Dean Acheson's friend Alger Hiss.

On the face of it, it seems strange that the Hiss case would generate emotions so powerful that they have yet to fully subside. Hiss was accused of having stolen some minimally important documents while working in the federal bureaucracy in the 1930s. The New York *Times* sometimes prints information of far more value, and other spy cases, which involved the compromising of atomic secrets, had only a fraction of the impact of the Hiss case. What transfigured the case is that the affair became a national Passion play in which all the political hostilities set off by the New Deal, the Spanish Civil War, American intervention in World War II, and the Cold War were personalized and played out in the conflict between Hiss and his former friend and accuser, Whittaker Chambers.

Hiss of Harvard was every bit as dapper and "superior" as Acheson. He had been with FDR at Yalta, and he was the president of the prestigious Carnegie Endowment for Peace. Hiss, the symbol of the liberal establishment, made little effort to hide his disdain for his questioners when he was brought up before the notorious "yahoos" of the House Un-American Activities Committee. A young congressman from California, Richard M. Nixon, led the pursuit of Hiss, and it was in that chase that liberal America conceived its everlasting hatred for "Tricky Dick." But Hiss's chief accuser was Whittaker Chambers, a man whose tortured life was of truly Dostoevskian proportions. As rumpled and anguished as Hiss was calm and aloof, Chambers, by the 1940s an editor for Luce's *Time* magazine, had once been in the Communist underground. In the 1930s, when support for the "Soviet experiment" ran wide and deep among American reformers, Hiss and Chambers had been friends. But then Chambers lost his faith in Communism and after a period of labored soul-searching found a new faith, Christianity, to anchor him. Repentant, the reformed Communist threw himself into the task of saving the Christian West from the Red peril. Chambers, whose Christianity was, like Chiang's, seen to be all the more genuine because of his former life, succeeded in presenting himself as a suffering Christlike victim of Communism who had broken with that heresy at the risk of his own life only in order to bring forth the message of salvation which was scoffed at by worldly-wise reformers.

Hiss's legal guilt or innocence was far less important than the symbolism of his two dramatic trials, which lasted from May 1948 to January 1950. It was the New Deal and its sympathy for the Soviet Union, and not just Alger Hiss, that had been put in the defendant's chair, accused of a mixture of treason and elitist arrogance.

Chambers, who felt himself under divine mandate to lie if necessary to halt the Communist Antichrist, nonetheless astutely described the trial's social meaning. "No feature of the Hiss case is more obvious or troubling as history," he wrote, "than the jagged fissure, which it did not so much open as reveal, between the plain men and women of the nation, and those who affected to act, think and speak for them. It was, not invariably, but in general, the 'best people' who were for Alger Hiss . . ." Though aided by the Republican Party and financed with Texas oil money, anti-Communism had an enormous popular appeal among working-class Catholics and Midwestern farmers, people who had long borne the brunt of the Eastern establishment's snobbishness. The establishment had been wrong about the Soviet Union and now it was going to pay for it. It was going to be taught that, in a democratic society, no one can pretend to being socially superior for long without being called to order. The trial then laid bare what Leslie Fiedler called the black socialism of American life, the egalitarian hatred of social pretension and sometimes intellect and quality which was the bedrock upon which Wisconsin Senator Joseph McCarthy was to build his career as the last and "greatest" of the isolationists.

The howls set off by the fall of China, the conviction of Alger Hiss, and the Russian A-bomb became a "roaring bitterness" with the political arrival of Joe McCarthy. McCarthy seemed to be able to make sense of all these calamities. He claimed to have evidence of a gigantic Communist plot, a "conspiracy so immense and an infamy so black as to dwarf any previous such venture in the history of man." And all this was centered in the very heart of the American government. McCarthy, a genius at creating publicity, would dominate American political life during the period of the

Korean War, from early 1950 through 1954. Even the election of Eisenhower as President in 1952 took place under the shadow of what became known as McCarthyism.

The senator first came to national attention with his sensational speech in Wheeling, West Virginia, in February 1950. The exact words of his talk remain in dispute. What is clear is that, in the course of his rambling speech, he waved a piece of paper and shouted something like the following: "I have here in my hand a list of 205—a list of names that were made known to the Secretary of State [Acheson] as being members of the Communist Party and who nevertheless are still working and shaping State Department policy." Reporters recognized McCarthy's accusations as a big story. They followed him from his talk to the airport and asked for a copy of his list. But he refused to provide one. The next night he gave a speech in Reno, Nevada, and there he mentioned a list of 57 Communists. In Salt Lake City, a week later, the number was 81.

Joe McCarthy was the tribune of revenge. Part Irish, part German, a Catholic Midwesterner, McCarthy combined within himself all the streams of resentment that had welled up into the politics of getting even. German-Americans, wrote Samuel Lubell, felt a "burning desire to vindicate their opposition to the last war ... the way the peace turned out was cited as proof that 'Germany and Russia should have been allowed to fight it out among themselves.' " McCarthy gave public voice to those feelings. Lubell found that he could "go into any German-American community in the country and that a talk with a typical resident becomes a virtual playback of McCarthy speeches." Joe McCarthy first gained national attention when he severely criticized American soldiers for their role in the Malmédy incident, in which GIs were accused of severely mistreating German POWs after the war. Isolationists cited the incident as proof that Americans were no better than Nazis and thus had no right to pass judgment as they had done at Nuremberg.

When the Malmédy affair died down, McCarthy, a brass-knuckles politician, looked for another way to hammer away on behalf of his own and his many constituents' passions. He found it in a conversation with Father Edmund Walsh of Georgetown University. Walsh, as I noted earlier, was a prominent Catholic critic of the Russo-American alliance. The author of numerous books on the threat of world Communism, he urged McCarthy to pick up the cleansing cudgels of the anti-Communist crusade. McCarthy obliged.

He was not only a master of the "big lie"—the accusation so astounding that it might just be true—but also expert at what Richard Rovere has called "the multiple untruth," in which a press conference called in the morning to announce a press conference for the afternoon would lead to a third appearance in which he contradicted the previous morning's statements. But reporters who were personally critical of him never pinned him down or forced him to produce his documentation.

There was nothing in McCarthy's accusations that hadn't been repeated ad nauseam by Asialationists. But McCarthy's personal style and ability to express and embody their anger was unique. Unlike Nixon, who was a certified stuffed shirt, McCarthy was bold and brazen, a standing rebuke to established authority. He came on like a real-life version of the 1940s movie tough guys Humphrey Bogart and John Garfield. Billing himself "Tail Gunner Joe," the fighting hero from World War II, he made a point of showing the public how different he was from the "homos" and "Commiecrats" who supposedly ran Washington. This avenging "angel" made "little pretense to religiosity or any species of moral rectitude"; he was "closer to the hipster than the organization man." He attacked all the symbols of national authority—the Army, the Protestant clergy, the civil service, the Eastern establishment—all of whom he held responsible for the "disasters" of American foreign policy, from fighting Germany to the fall of Chiang. In his Wheeling speech he declared that it was "not the less fortunate" Americans "who have been selling this nation out but rather those who have had all the benefits," like the "bright young men" in the State Department who were "born with silver spoons in their mouths." Determined to rough up the "pretty boys" who supposedly made their living sucking the blood of ordinary guys, McCarthy didn't want the world to think him respectable. And that was his appeal. He was the gut fighter, the politician who liked to be photographed "sleeping, disheveled, on the office couch like a bum on a park bench," or coming out of the shower with a towel wrapped around his torso like Rocky Marciano.

Forget for a moment that this political street fighter was financed by oil companies looking to gut the New Deal; it was a great script and fascinating show. But the results were frightening and tragic. Traditional American virtues like concern for questions of guilt and innocence were lost as Republican politicians around the country saw in McCarthy the chance to seize the initiative.

The highly respected Senator Taft urged McCarthy on, telling the "Tail Gunner": "If one case doesn't work, try another." Some people, particularly intellectuals and liberals, were guilty, not because of anything they had done, but simply because of who they were. Some of the consequences were laughable. Local schools tried to remove *Robin Hood* from their shelves because its theme was "Red" and the Cincinnati Reds solemnly changed their name to "Red Legs." But as the cancer of McCarthyism, the tactic of hounding those whose ideas were deemed un-American, spread, thousands upon thousands of lives were ruined across the country as local inquisitions drove schoolteachers, trade unionists, and civil servants from their jobs. McCarthy and his minions had no program, no goal; their effort was fueled by the sweet taste of revenge. They wanted to humble their victims with what Victor Navasky has called the ritual of degradation. They wanted intellectuals, scientists, writers, and people in the media who were supporters of the New Deal to be humbled and humiliated, so that all those who betrayed the canons of true Americanism, all those who had been "wrong" about Franklin Roosevelt, would be driven from the stage of American life.

The McCarthyites vilified Acheson for being insufficiently anti-Communist while the left accused him of being a war-minded militarist. Both were partly right. Liberal and leftist critics were angered by the way Acheson consistently downplayed diplomacy in dealing with the Soviets. Ironically for a man widely caricatured as a smooth-talking fancy pants, Acheson seemed to have an obsessive fear of bargaining with the Russians. His insistence on " 'negotiating from strength' meant in effect that there could be no negotiations, because U.S. power could never be sufficient to allay his fears." To foster American military strength, Acheson, maneuvering outside the normal State Department channels, prepared what came to be known as National Security Council (NSC) 68. Completed in the spring of 1949, the document called for a vast military buildup of American forces accompanied by psychological warfare to engage the Russians in a vast global struggle. Truman's Secretary of Defense, Louis Johnson, opposed the plan as dangerous and inflationary. Truman concurred and NSC 68 was temporarily shelved.

Chiang and Taiwan were to have no part in this contest for the world. Acheson wanted nothing so much as to have Mao quickly conquer Taiwan, definitively ending the Chinese civil war and opening the way for an American-Chinese rapprochement. In an important speech before the National Press Club given in January 1950, Acheson defined America's military interests in Asia as running on a line from the Aleutian Islands through American-occupied Japan and on to the Philippines. This offshore or perimeter strategy significantly excluded South Korea, Taiwan, and Indochina.

In June 1950, Communist North Korea, under the leadership of the "Glorious" Kim Il Sung, as he sometimes described himself, launched a surprise invasion of American-supported South Korea. The Cold War had suddenly turned hot, and Acheson's numerous enemies were sure that his Press Club speech had been little more than an invitation for the attack. For his part, Acheson, like many others, feared that the attack was a diversionary feint, a prelude to the invasion of Western Europe.

Korea had long been an arena for big power conflict. It was the United States which had opened Korea to the modern world by sending Civil War hero General Sherman there on a mission in 1866. Russia and Japan fought over Korea in 1905. Japan won that war, but in the wake of World War II Russia reasserted its claims by backing Kim's Communist regime, which occupied Korea north of the 38th parallel. The United States supported the conservative nationalist Syngman Rhee in the South. Kim Il Sung and Syngman Rhee were each determined to unify the country under his sole leadership. The Americans, fearing a military move by Rhee, gave him only limited arms. The Russians were less scrupulous in this matter. As Khrushchev gently explains in his memoirs, "the North Koreans," after being heavily armed by Stalin, tried "to prod South Korea with the point of a bayonet." Kim had evidently convinced the Russians that military pressure would, in Khrushchev's words, touch off an "internal explosion in

South Korea." The Russians, however, were probably surprised when an overaggressive Kim tried for a direct conquest. In either case, the Russians stood to benefit from the victory of their client. Besides embarrassing the Americans, Kim's triumph would serve as a warning to both Japan and Mao, should the Chinese leader entertain any thoughts of assuming the mantle of revolutionary leadership in Asia.

Truman responded cautiously; he refrained initially from linking the Russians to the attack, and while gradually ordering limited American support for the South Koreans, he made it clear to Moscow that U.S. aims were limited. While a surprised Truman assessed the situation, Washington held its breath. Would Truman again abandon Asia? But Truman, without consulting Congress, which alone is vested with the power to declare war under the Constitution, sent substantial military aid to South Korea under the guise of UN support. After a half decade of bitter attacks on the Democrats' foreign policy, the Republicans relented. "Never before," said Joseph Harsh of the *Christian Science Monitor*, "have I felt such a sense of relief and unity pass through the city." Korea, commented *U.S. News & World Report*, has let "Secretary Acheson off the hook on the Communist issue." The lesson wasn't lost on future Presidents, who remembered how a beleaguered Truman bought relief from critics by striking out boldly against the Communists.

There were many at the time who thought that it was McCarthyism which had forced Truman to respond. But Acheson had made it clear that the American response was dictated not so much by domestic politics as by the memory of Munich and the perceptions of the rest of the world. "To back away from this challenge," wrote Acheson, "in view of our capacity for meeting it, would be highly destructive of the power and prestige of the United States. By prestige I mean the shadow cast by power." America, by the Secretary's own admission, had no overwhelming geopolitical or economic interest in South Korea. America was fighting for the perception of power. This was to be a symbolic war, a war to demonstrate American will.

The American response to the North Korean assault "must have been one of the greatest surprises of Stalin's life. Having acquiesced in the loss of China, these unpredictable people now balked at the loss of a territory they themselves had characterized as unimportant."

The United States was totally unprepared for war. The few American troops and the small South Korean Army were routed by the well-prepared and well-equipped North Korean attack. Trapped in a defensive perimeter around Pusan in southeastern Korea, the UN forces, which were almost entirely American, were on the verge of being driven into the sea. Goaded by the American defeats, the Asialationists, who had been holding their fire, again opened up their guns on Truman.

McCarthy served notice on "Communists, fellow travelers and dupes that they are not going to be able to hide and protect themselves behind a war which"—referring to the way Acheson had excluded Korea and Taiwan from the U.S. defensive perimeter—"would not have been necessary except for their acts." But behind this immediate maneuvering lay the still simmering issue of America's involvement in World War II. This led to an extraordinary exchange of "pin the tail on Stalin," played by Senator William Jenner of Indiana, one of the "primitives," and the Trumanite Senator Joseph Tydings of Maryland, a sharp critic of "Tail Gunner Joe." Tydings, whose reelection bid may have been brought down by McCarthy, played on the parallel positions of the isolationists and the Soviets much as interventionists had played on a similar congruence between the Nazis and the isolationists. Tydings attacked Jenner's vote against the Marshall Plan, noting that "Joe Stalin and the *Daily Worker* and the Senator [Jenner] all vote the same way." Jenner, attaching himself to the same tattered banner that Tydings had wrapped himself in, said he was not "obligated to squander our substance in suicidal attempts to underwrite everybody else's interests and security except our own." Then, responding to Tydings' boast of the medals the senator from Maryland had received from General Pershing in World War I, Jenner commented tartly: ". . . there is another medal which will probably come to him. It will be very large, and emblazoned with a single name: 'Thanks, from good old Joe, for a job well done.' " Politics had been reduced to competitive Red-baiting.

The Asialationist critique was inconsistent. On the one hand, McCarthy insisted that if Truman wanted to demonstrate his patriotism he could do so by getting rid of "alien-minded radicals and moral perverts" in Washington. This suggested that the real enemy was in America, not abroad. Yet this was combined with a romantic attachment to Chiang and a deep desire to halt the spread of Communism. In this vein McCarthy attacked one of Acheson's weak points. "Either Acheson was wrong when he referred" to Taft's suggestion "that we aid the anti-Communist forces on Taiwan as a 'silly venture' or, if Acheson was right, the President is now engaged in a 'silly venture' in Korea." Acheson's reply that Russia was a permanent enemy, while Mao was a potential friend, was by then beside the point. Any meaningful political distinctions had long been dissolved in the acids of anti-Communism.

Truman's political fate was now closely tied to the war in Korea. His fortunes took a sharp turn upward in September 1950, when General Douglas MacArthur pulled off one of the most daring and successful moves in military history. Trapped in the Pusan perimeter, the General launched an amphibious invasion against North Korea, landing at Inchon. In one strike MacArthur had both broken free of North Korean entrapment and turned the tables on the enemy. The North Korean military collapsed, leaving little between MacArthur and the Chinese border to the north.

The victory brought a new set of problems. It now seemed possible not only to demonstrate American will by preserving South Korea but to roll back Communism and bring a united Korea into the American camp. In their different ways both MacArthur and Acheson were intoxicated with such possibilities, though such a move north risked inviting Chinese intervention, as Mao was sure to be unhappy about having the army of Chiang's allies on his border. British Prime Minister Clement Attlee urged restraint, warning that a move north would push Mao ever more solidly into Russia's arms. But in the euphoria of victory the temptation proved too much and Washington agreed to MacArthur's quest for a total victory even as it tried to assure the Chinese that it had no aggressive intentions toward them.

Ignoring diplomatic warnings from the Chinese, MacArthur drove north toward the Yalu River against only limited resistance. But then a trickle of Chinese troops turned into a torrent. In early November, MacArthur's men were routed by wave after wave of Chinese "volunteers." What followed was a costly seesaw struggle across the 38th parallel with growing American casualties and little to show for them.

Truman was reluctant to commit additional American energies to Korea. He was afraid the war was leaving Europe unprotected, so he was willing to cut his losses and make a settlement based on a division between North and South Korea. MacArthur, on the other hand, still hoped for liberation and complete victory. Convinced that he was a master of the Oriental mind—MacArthur had not set foot in the United States since 1936, living all that time in Asia—the champion of the Asia Firsters in World War II reacted like a "gambler attempting to recover his losses by raising the stakes." Acting on his own authority, he threatened to extend the war to China itself if the Chinese did not withdraw their forces from Korea. Faced with a direct challenge to his authority, Truman relieved MacArthur of his command and the General returned to the United States and a hero's welcome.

MacArthur, though away from America for many years, retained a sense of the American temperament. Literally millions of admiring people greeted him to cheer on his defiance of the increasingly unpopular Truman. MacArthur and the public believed that "there was no substitute for victory." Either we should fight to win, he thought, or get out. The policy of limited war that Truman was pursuing was intolerable. Either America was fighting in the name of high moral principles, in which case we should be going all out, or we shouldn't be fighting at all. Limited war, said MacArthur, was simply another name for appeasing Communism. Nor, said MacArthur, could the nation "ignore the insidious forces working from within America." Taking a direct shot at the man who fired him, he denounced Truman's use of the terms "red herring and witch-hunt" to brush off the dangers of subversion at home.

When Senator Brien McMahon of Connecticut asked MacArthur who the enemy was, the General replied: "Communism." Did this mean Communism as evidenced in Russia or China? McMahon asked. MacArthur replied: "I mean all over the world, including the interior of many of the fine democratic countries." MacArthur's answer pointed up the weakness of his position. How did one go about fighting Reds everywhere without creating the bureaucracy at home which Republicans equated with Communism? The answer, said MacArthur and his supporters, was nuclear weapons and air power. These appealed to them not because Taft and MacArthur were particularly bloodthirsty; on the contrary, MacArthur decried the meat-grinder tactics of limited war which brought "killing Chinese to the fore." Rather, nuclear weapons delivered by air offered the promise of allowing the United States to influence the world without fully being part of it. It would allow the United States to project its power without an inflationary and freedom-curtailing buildup of conventional forces and it would keep the United States free of entangling alliances. These were appealing possibilities, but they suggested that the United States would have to be willing to use atomic weapons against China, thus risking war with Russia to gain the limited objective of victory in Korea. The risk wasn't proportional to what was to be gained. In the absence of a viable alternative, the hostility to Truman's limited war grew even as MacArthur and his alternative slowly faded.

Truman and Acheson fared no better than MacArthur in giving a satisfactory answer as to who the enemy was. If North Korea was the real enemy, why all the fuss? They could easily be taken care of. But if it wasn't really North Korea, if it was really China behind the war, then why not go after China, why consign American boys to fight and die in a proxy war? And besides, if it was true that it was Russia who stood behind China, why should the Russians be allowed off the hook? If the Russians really were responsible, then maybe MacArthur made sense and we should settle the score with Russia sooner rather than later when the Soviets had rebuilt their military establishment. Neither Truman nor his Secretary of State could give satisfactory public answers to these questions because in effect they had committed the United States to a symbolic action designed to win nothing so much as American military credibility.

After the first decisive year of fighting the war settled into a long stalemate which wasn't broken until Stalin died and Eisenhower replaced a beleaguered Truman in the presidency. The United States had saved South Korea from the undoubted depredations of the ruthless Kim, but at enormous cost. The war provided a justification for an enormous U.S. military buildup along the lines proposed in NSC 68 at a time when the Russians were by no means a military threat; China was forced into an unnatural alliance with North Vietnam and the U.S.S.R., while America covertly supported a secret war on China from Taiwan, enraging the Chinese and eventually leading to involvement in another limited war in Asia.

The tragedy of America's militarized and increasingly imperial world view was that the Cold War had in fact already been won, in the one place where it was winnable, Europe. A stable Europe was on its way to economic recovery while the supposed Soviet "victories" in China and Poland proved illusory. Starting with Korea, the United States would prove to be its own worst enemy in foreign affairs.

4

Truman, Eisenhower, and the Politics of Prosperity

Everything is going to be prettier, you're not going to have any more bad dreams, you're going to have all the things people have, your life is going to be living, laughing, fighting and loving.
—SPENCER TRACY in *A Guy Named Joe*

IN APRIL 1945, *Newsweek*, discussing the New Deal's departure from the American ideal of limited government, declared that "the era of experimentation was over." Truman concurred. "I don't want any experiments, the American people," he said, "have been through a lot of experiments, and they want a rest."

Truman's call for a respite was paralleled in Europe, where French resistance hero and philosopher Albert Camus pronounced "the end of ideologies." After twenty years of war and revolution, Camus argued, there was both a yearning for tranquillity and an unwillingness to vest hopes for the future in the hero of the 1930s, the common man. The future was to be based, not on the profound conflicts of class and conscience which "sprang from hopes of transcendence," but on the careful management of the economy in pursuit of material well-being." The domination of man by man [was] to be replaced by the administration of things." The old struggles of class, religion, and race were to be dissolved by economic growth. "Politics," said John Kennedy in 1962, near the end of this period of postwar tranquillity, was to be kept away from "basic clashes of philosophy and ideology" and directed to "ways and means of achieving common goals."

Growth and prosperity did provide a period of relative harmony, but it proved to be short-lived. The dynamic of rapid growth would in the long run prove as disruptive of traditional ways as the New Deal itself. The disruption was built in to what *Fortune* proudly trumpeted as "Capitalism: The Permanent Revolution."

At war's end the nation was still dug in behind the mental trenches of the 1930s. Military victory, it was feared, might herald an end to temporary wartime prosperity and a return to depression. Henry Wallace spoke for many economists and policy makers when he warned that without proper planning and expanded markets America could still be engulfed by the violent revolutions that had swept across Europe. Journalists, recalling the experience of post-World War I Germany, suggested that jobless veterans might turn to freebooting or fascism. Would there be enough jobs? Experts were predicting postwar unemployment of between 8 and 20 million. As late as 1946, a *Fortune* survey of 1,500 leading businessmen found that a large majority believed a major depression with large-scale unemployment would recur within ten years.

These fears were muted, however, as much by the government's effective handling of reconversion as by the glow of wartime prosperity. Between 1939 and 1945 the country's economic output had soared from $91 to $167 billion. During the war, when Roosevelt began planning for a postwar economy based on the speedy reconversion to private ownership and the lifting of wartime price controls, half the nation's economic output was for the military. When peace came, Truman, following in FDR's train, moved quickly to reduce the government's role in the economy, thus forgoing what Wallace hoped for and so many businessmen feared, a genuinely mixed economy. The government moved rapidly to divest itself of the assets it had acquired to produce military hardware. By the end of 1945 more than 90 percent of the wartime industries were back to civilian production. Surplus government property was sold at giveaway prices to private owners and the high wartime taxes were reduced.

In contrast to the experience after World War I, reconversion after World War II was a great success. The economy returned to peacetime production more smoothly and efficiently than anyone expected. "The result was a boom that began as soon as the war had ended," as the nation's production jumped from $167 billion in 1945 to $241 billion by 1950.

Inflation, not unemployment, became the big postwar problem. During the war, military production and strict rationing limited consumer demand. With few consumer goods available on which to spend their bountiful wartime earnings, Americans saved $140 billion between 1941 and 1945. When the war ended, those dollars were available to buy consumer goods yet to be produced. The prices of the limited supply of goods soared.

Truman tried to halt the rapid rise in prices by at first maintaining and then only gradually lifting the wartime wage and price controls administered by social scientists like the young John Kenneth Galbraith at the Office of Price Administration (OPA). But the public responded to proposals for the gradual end of controls in much the same way they responded to plans to bring the GIs home slowly. After fifteen years of depression and war, people had money in their pockets and they wanted to spend it. For a time the nation had the worst of both worlds—the tangles of bureaucratic controls and a growing black market. *Fortune* reported that stockings which were officially priced at under a dollar were selling for $7.50 on the black market.

Republicans and businessmen, sensing a chance to put themselves on the popular side of an economic issue, launched a fierce attack on the OPA as the opening wedge of a broader assault on the New Deal itself. For neither the first nor the last time, spokesmen for business denounced the "paternal busybodies" in Washington while insisting that only a return to the laws of supply and demand would allow production to catch up with demand. Flaying bureaucrats was once again a popular sport.

By this time Republicans had gotten the hang of using antifascist rhetoric for their own purposes. Borrowing from the Austrian theoretician of laissez-faire, Friedrich von Hayek, whose still popular 1945 best seller *The Road to Serfdom* argued that New Deal economic interventionism was a second cousin to Nazism, Republicans began to call the OPA administrators "the single most important collection of American fascists we've got." For his part, the right-wing radio commentator Fulton Lewis, Jr., hinted that the OPA really had links to Moscow. No matter, the message put out by the Chamber of Commerce and the National Association of Manufacturers was clear and effective: price controls had to go.

After a series of bitter fights, Truman relented and lifted controls completely. The results were disastrous for the consumer. Prices jumped 25 percent in one month while earnings declined 12 percent. A headline in the New York *Daily News* on beef prices read: "Prices Soar, Buyers Sore. Steers Jumped over the Moon." Faced with the difficult choice of living with rapid inflation or reimposing the unpopular controls, Truman equivocated. His critics began to joke: "To err is Truman." The enormous growth of productive power in the economy, however, came to Truman's rescue. With more and more goods available, prices began to level off even without controls.

The fight over controls was one of numerous battles fought in the immediate postwar years between the heirs and enemies of the New Deal. The Depression greatly weakened the public standing of American business. But the success of industry in arming the Allies revived public confidence. Business and its spokesmen began to take the offensive against labor and its allies.

There were still relics, representatives of small business, like Robert Taft, who remained indifferent to their public images. In the midst of the controversy over the OPA, Taft was asked what his solution was. He answered tersely: "Eat less." Big business looked on Taft as an anachronism, but they were willing to join him in attacking big government and bureaucracy (as if large corporations weren't themselves bureaucratic). Increasingly, however, business tried to counter the appeal of the welfare state with the image of welfare capitalism resting upon a new social contract between business and society, if not between business and labor.

The "new" businessman, the public was told, was not the predator of yesteryear who brought on the Great Depression; rather, he was a responsible citizen who took the interests of society and not just his shareholders into account. This new version of the lion lying down with the lamb was accompanied by a publicity offensive against unions which both ridiculed union jurisdictional disputes and blamed labor for rising prices.

Labor had also gained in strength during the war. The ranks of the country's unions swelled from about 9 million members in

1940 to about 14.5 million in 1945. At this high point, from which labor membership has since steadily declined, unions represented more than a third of the labor force. The war, however, was only a mixed blessing. It produced enormous wage gains, but it also heightened public criticism of restrictive craft practices and produced a fierce hatred for the nation's most prominent labor leader, the miners' fiery John L. Lewis. When Lewis, a prime mover in the creation of the CIO, twice called his men out on strike, *Stars and Stripes*, the service paper, "damn[ed]" his "coal black soul."

Even before the war ended in Asia, the gradual loss of overtime pay, rapidly rising prices, and the growing surplus of labor as soldiers returned home led to fears that labor would be hard-pressed to hold on to its wartime gains. Beginning in the months before V-J Day, a trickle of illegal walkouts swelled until by the fall of 1945 the trickle had become a flood. By January 1946 workers had "hit the bricks" in the auto, oil refining, electrical, and steel industries. In 1946 more than 4.5 million workers went out on strike.

The immediate conflict between business and labor was basically over how to divide the profits from increased productivity. Between 1939 and 1945 productivity in American industry had doubled without wages keeping pace. Profits similarly outpaced wages. Pointing to the enormous profits from wartime contracts, union leaders argued that wages could be raised substantially without decreasing profits. When the management of General Motors argued that wage increases meant price increases, United Auto Workers leader Walter Reuther called for GM to open its books to the public. General Motors refused, and like most large companies, agreed to sizable wage increases, which it then passed on to its customers in the form of higher prices, helping to set off the first of the many postwar rounds of inflationary agreements. Despite Reuther's efforts, labor bore the brunt of political criticism, as when Nebraska's Senator Kenneth Wherry, casting himself in the mold of the common man, asked "How long will Americans tolerate big labor's use of the strike bludgeon to get . . . inflated unrealistic pay scales that hamper productivity, slow conversion and deny goods to the average American?" Further coal strikes and a rail strike in which a dyspeptic Truman threatened to draft the strikers gave credence to the wave of big business propaganda suggesting that labor, not big business, was a threat to American democracy.

Anti-union sentiment culminated with the passage in 1947 of the Taft-Hartley Act, which, said Senator Taft, was designed to "roll back" the power granted unions by the New Deal. Taft-Hartley outlawed a number of labor practices, including the closed (all-union) shop and the secondary boycott. It also penalized unions that engaged in jurisdictional disputes and required all union leaders to swear under oath that they were not part of the "Red Menace," though owners were given no such test. Labor denounced the bill as a slave-labor act, but, despite Truman's veto, it passed.

The palpably conservative mood signaled by the fight over the OPA and Taft-Hartley doomed most of Truman's proposals for a Fair Deal to extend the Roosevelt "revolution." New TVAs, proposals for European-style national health insurance, federal aid to education, a Fair Employment Practices Commission to protect blacks against job discrimination, and the attempt to maintain federal control over the valuable tideland oil reserves, were all beaten back. Truman was, however, able to secure an increase in the minimum wage and legislation extending Social Security to nearly 10 million people in addition to the 35 million already covered.

In effect there was a standoff: the New Deal was neither advanced nor dismantled. The character of the deadlock can perhaps best be seen in the Employment Act of 1946. First proposed in 1945, the original version of the bill called for broad presidential powers and national economic planning to keep people employed. In the face of a storm of opposition, the word "Full" was stricken from the title and instead of specifying the powers available to the President, the act established a Council of Economic Advisers while suggesting that government in some unspecified way was responsible for the nation's overall economic performance. Although the bill as passed was a defeat for the liberals, it nonetheless marked the first legislative acceptance of modified Keynesianism for the national economy.

Ideological currents aside, big government was here to stay, and this was nowhere better illustrated than in veterans affairs. The GI Bill of Rights passed in 1944 was to have an extraordinary impact on American life. Two and a quarter million returning veterans used their benefits to attend college, democratizing the universities in the process. Home ownership was similarly democratized. In 1940, 44 percent of American families owned their own homes. By 1960, the figure was over 60 percent, in large measure because of government-backed Veterans Administration (VA) mortgages. VA mortgages allowed a returning GI to purchase a house with little or no down payment. Finally, veterans were given preferential hiring in federal and state jobs, so that by 1959 more than half the federal work force consisted of veterans.

The programs for veterans were, in effect, the first of the massive entitlement programs like Medicaid and Medicare that would transform the national budget in the 1970s. The idea behind the programs was not just to reward the veterans for their bravery and courage—after all, many had not been in combat—but also to compensate them for the time taken out of their careers. The principle of compensatory aid both provided the model for other groups later deemed to be disadvantaged and set the precedent for conflicts engendered by compensatory action. Unions, for instance, criticized the "superseniority" created for veterans which undermined traditional seniority practices, while employers turned the new policy to their own advantage by replacing union workers with grateful veterans. Women and blacks struggling to hold on to wartime jobs were displaced by the returning GIs and then were accused of being unpatriotic when they complained. These conflicts might have grown more severe but for the rising tide of economic prosperity.

Whether reviled as the age of conformity or revered as "Those Happy Days," the 1950s are remembered as a time when individuals tended their own careers or family gardens to the exclusion of the commonweal. This mood, sometimes attributed to the intimidations of Senator McCarthy or the grandfatherly blandness of Eisenhower, preceded the senator and the President. Rather than being imposed, the mood flowed naturally from the desire of a depression- and war-scarred nation to taste the fruits of peace and prosperity.

The young were matured by the war experience, so that the returning GIs, who set the cultural tone of the late 1940s, were serious and purposeful before their time. Some worked at two and three jobs; others opened small businesses with VA loans. But most shunned small business for the security of a union or corporate job.

The veterans on campus created their own, no-nonsense mood. They disdained panty raids and the like; instead they dashed through the curriculum on their way to a shot at the corporate brass ring. Surveying the graduating class of 1949, *Fortune* found that, above all, these young men in a hurry wanted to avoid risk. Only one in fifty wanted to go into business for himself. "Security," said *Fortune*, "has become the big goal. . . . [They] want to work for somebody else . . . preferably somebody big." As one graduating veteran put it: "I know AT&T might not be very exciting, but there will always be an AT&T."

The drive and determination of these young men on the make was underwritten by a belief in not only an American Age but an age in which science and technology held out hope for an ever-brighter future. A good deal of what had once seemed science fiction became facts of everyday life. Between 1945 and 1950 American technology perfected the automatic car transmission, the electric clothes dryer, the automatic garbage disposal unit, and the long-playing record. These new products came at a time when growing numbers of Americans were able to buy vacuum cleaners, electric ranges, refrigerators, and freezers stocked with food grown more cheaply because of DDT and the mechanization of agriculture, and then in a new process quick-frozen. Plastics, which had seen limited use for ornamental objects, were developed during the war, in new and more durable forms, as replacements for rubber, wood, and metal. In the postwar years plastic provided new "wonder" fibers, long-lasting nylon for clothing, inexpensive food wraps, light but strong and easy-to-clean Styrofoam containers, inexpensive but attractive vinyl floor coverings, light plastic cabinets to replace heavy metal ones, and an array of low-priced plastic toys.

The fastest-selling new product of the period, television, was used to market all the other new items. One million television sets were sold in 1948, seven and a half million in 1949, and by 1953 half of all homes had a set. Television, advertisers quickly discovered, was an extraordinary marketing device. Unlike radio or newspapers, it was national in scope, uniting the diverse regions into one gigantic market. TV, by coming directly into the home with close-up pictures of new products, could cultivate the consumers' desires in an intimate, relaxed setting. The allure of many new products, plastic floor covering for instance, came from both their functional and symbolic value as emblems of modernity. What better way to hawk "newness" than on television, itself the prime symbol of instant access to once-remote events, places, and products.

The federal government had played a major role in the wartime development of plastics, but when peace came the industry was turned over gratis to corporate giants like Du Pont, who basked in the reflected glory of what had been a joint achievement. The Du Pont slogan, "Better living through chemistry," later parodied by the promoters of LSD, captured the spirit of the hour. The corporations reviled in the 1930s as bastions of corporate greed became model institutions, the "public service enterprises" of the postwar era.

The dramatic innovations of the period captured the public imagination, but they were not as important for driving the economy forward as the less publicized substitution of low-cost oil and natural gas for muscle and coal. One of the reasons John L. Lewis' miners clashed so sharply with Truman, a generally pro-labor President, was that coal-mining jobs were imperiled by the increased availability of cheaper, cleaner, and more efficient energy sources. Lewis responded with a form of arbitrage; rather than holding on to as many jobs as possible, he pioneered extensive welfare benefits and job security provisions for those miners who would continue to work. The miners were the first but by no means the last of the postwar workers who would be displaced by an increasingly mechanized and automated economy.

Cheap oil allowed manufacturers to adopt new, highly efficient machine technologies that substituted mechanical power for man-power. Productivity was based in part on the ability of manufacturers to use three or four times as much energy per unit of production as in other industrial countries. Men and women working with high-energy power-driven tools were able to produce far more than their prewar counterparts.

Dramatic advances in medicine ensured that people would be able to live longer, healthier lives while they strained less. Despite the fierce opposition of the American Medical Association, the government played a major role in protecting public health. Federal money underwrote the research which mass-produced antibiotics like penicillin and the "mycin" drugs that attacked dread communicable diseases like tuberculosis and syphilis.

One sign of optimism was the postwar baby boom. In 1946 there was a dramatic rise in the divorce rate as marriages, strained by the separation of war, broke apart. This was accompanied and followed, though, by a rapid rise in the marriage rate until the percentage of the married population reached unprecedented and since unequaled proportions. These new marriages produced an equally extraordinary rise in the birth rate. The nation's population had grown by only about 9 million in the 1930s; it grew 19 million in the 1940s and 28 million in the 1950s. The population boom led in turn to a demand for housing, furniture, and a variety of other consumer durables, thus further fueling the prosperity which underlay the birth boom.

The wonders of this new world were such that, according to Norman Vincent Peale, the best-selling author and leading spokesman for liberal Protestantism, hard work and self-sacrifice were no longer necessary to enter the kingdom of the elect. In the age of scientific wonders, the Bible itself, he said, should be seen as a simple yet scientific system of successful living that works. It could make you over into a wealthy and powerful businessman if you were faithful to easy-to-follow rules which would activate and actualize your energies. For Dr. Peale, a spokesman for his age, religion was to be the handmaiden of personal success.

While the political world was mired in seemingly endless wrangles over the New Deal, private life was aglow with possibilities. The glossy, full-color Sunday newspaper supplements were filled with stories of the wondrous future science had in store for us. After finishing their twenty-five hours of rewarding work in beautiful functional buildings of glass and plastic, Mr. and Mrs. U.S.A. were to be whisked away by personal helicopter to one of many weekend mountain retreats. After a walk in the insect-free wooded glades, Mr. Average Worker would return to a solar-heated glass house filled with Bauhaus furniture. There, after reaching for a cold beer in the refrigerator, he would settle down to watch the finest performers in the world brought directly into his living room through the wonders of television. What more could anyone ask? The country was on the road to Elysium.

Throwing away their pen-and-ink past, Americans picked up one of the small new wonders of the age, the ball-point pen (advertised as "the fantastic atomic age miraculous pen"), and signed a new social contract. In return for the cornucopia present and promised, they agreed to renounce political meddling for rule by the enlightened businessmen who administered the engines of progress. Those businessmen in turn "chose" General Dwight D. Eisenhower as the honorary chief engineer for the voyage.

If the Republicans had not been so sharply divided between their Main Street (Taft) and Wall Street (Dewey) factions, the Democrats would have seemed like "easy pickin's" in the 1952 presidential race. Truman had been unable to generate popular support since American troops were bogged down in Korea. The President, whose reputation would later undergo a revival, had slumped to a positive rating of just 26 percent in the polls. Bombarded with accusations of being soft on Communism and burdened with an unpopular "limited war," Truman also saw a number of his Missouri cronies indicted for taking kickbacks on government contracts. His staunchest defender, the New York *Post*, was reduced to pointing out that, despite his failings, he was after all "a member of the human race." Truman, who had thoughts of running again, withdrew. Republicans, gleefully summarizing Truman's troubles as KC^2, "Korea, Communism, and Corruption," saw the President's unpopularity as a chance to roll back the New Deal.

The two leading Republican presidential aspirants, Taft and Eisenhower, were united in their belief that the 1952 elections were "the last chance to stop the drift to socialism." But they were deeply divided by constituency, style, and attitudes toward Europe. Taft was the undisputed leader of both the "corn belt conservatives" and the senatorial Republicans, but his unsmiling, uncompromising, and erratic style and his anti-European animus made him a frightening figure to the party's cosmopolitan Eastern establishment. Taft's principled and unstinting criticism of the New Deal struck Dewey Republicans as suicidal for a party which had to reach out beyond the Midwestern Protestant faithful and appeal to Democrats and independents. Republican businessmen found Taft's homilies on free enterprise naïve. They wanted to use government for their own ends, not eliminate it.

Eisenhower was far more appealing to Deweyite businessmen than the traditionalist Taft. Eisenhower was every bit as conservative on domestic issues as Taft. His postwar diaries are filled with apocalyptic warnings about how "the preservation of freedom" was threatened by the "internal Munichs" of union victories in the coal fields and the "paternalism" and "dictatorship" of the New Deal. His candidacy was motivated, as his diaries make clear, by a belief that perhaps he alone could save the nation from the peril of "creeping socialism." While campaigning, Eisenhower, as sociologist Dennis Wrong has described it, would hold up an egg "and indignantly enumerating the taxes on it, suggest that even chickens were financially oppressed by the welfare state."

Both Ike and Taft were heavily influenced by Herbert Hoover, a man Eisenhower "admired extravagantly." Ike was capable of being every bit as callous as Hoover; he dismissed the fears of working America with the taunt: "If all they want is security, they can go to prison." But unlike Taft, Eisenhower was fully at home in the world of large organizations and public relations. And while in the view of many Wall Street bankers Taft threatened to start World War III, Eisenhower the Atlanticist, the hero of World War II, was a man fully sympathetic with the close business ties between the United States and Western Europe.

Eisenhower had made his reputation, not as a line commander, but as a military diplomat and organizer of vast military enterprises like the invasion of Normandy. In the words of one historian, Ike was "the product of the organizational revolution which had transformed American life in the 20th century." He was "a member of the new managerial class which led the great public and private bureaucracies that dominated the nation." He was a skillful manager of men, a tactful compromiser who emphasized teamwork.

Eisenhower felt most at home in the company of wealthy and powerful men. He had a contempt for the disorder of electoral politics and he loathed what he saw as the petty selfishness of the masses. Politicians catering to that selfishness, he argued, produced the "handout state" that threatened the freedom of the enterprising. But the public had little intimation of these hard-line views, which he kept to himself and his corporate golfing partners. Unlike Taft, who had a reputation for partisanship, Eisenhower, a careful shepherd of his own public image, had cultivated a reputation for being above the political fray. Also unlike Taft, he was aware of the liabilities of the Republican Party, commenting acidly, "Don't the darn fools [the Taftites] realize that the public thinks the dollar sign is the only respected symbol in the Republican Party?" Blessed with a winning smile and a common manner, Eisenhower had none of Taft's drawbacks. He was, said Walter Lippmann, "a kind of dream boy," a chaste vessel "into which the public could pour all its hopes."

Eisenhower seemed the ideal candidate to bring the Republicans out of the political wilderness. But his fight against Taft for the nomination was a bitter one. The small-town Republicans, pushed aside first by the amateur Willkie and then by the two-time loser Dewey, were in no mood to see their hero, Robert Taft, displaced by another representative of the Eastern establishment, no matter how popular. It was a measure of the hostility wrought by twenty years of defeat that after Eisenhower had secured the nomination, a woman leaving the convention hotel was heard to say, "This means eight more years of socialism." For the Republican right, which would later regroup as the Goldwaterites, the Eisenhower nomination was a cruel blow, yet another confirmation that the country which had once been theirs by birthright had slipped, perhaps irretrievably, from their grasp.

For its part, the Democratic Party was not only badly divided between Northerners and Southerners on civil rights and between anti-Communist liberals and conservatives on foreign policy and civil liberties; it was also exhausted, done in by its own success in managing capitalism. After twenty years of winning as the business-baiting party of the common man, prosperity had returned, while, as H. Stuart Hughes put it, the "common man had lost his aura of sainthood" and the corporations were once again widely admired. The majority of Democratic voters, who only a few short years before had been battling the malefactors of wealth, were now fairly well off. Before the war only the top 10 percent of wage earners, generally Republicans, paid significant income taxes, but by 1944 the boom had brought even lower-middle-income workers into the government's net and they were increasingly receptive to Republican criticisms about high taxes. Besides, even the liberal intellectuals who had supported the New Deal were having second thoughts about big business, which, it turned out, might not be so bad after all. The OPA's John Kenneth Galbraith explained with his theory of "countervailing power" how business was no longer a danger to the Republic because its power was checked by big government and big labor, and Daniel Bell gained a wide audience for his argument that the society had become increasingly plural- istic—that is, broken up into many competing groups—and was no longer in danger of being dominated by the scions of the Liberty Lobby.

Battered and divided, the Democrats turned away from the plebeian Truman to embrace aristocratic Adlai E. Stevenson, governor of Illinois, as their standard bearer. The Princeton- educated Stevenson, whose grandmother had been a founder of the DAR and whose grandfather had served as Grover Cleveland's Vice-President, was a candidate Henry Adams could have approved of. Stevenson didn't pretend to be "one of the people," like Eisenhower; he presented himself as being above petty politics. Imitation is the sincerest form of flattery, and in choosing Steven- son, after earlier being unable to secure Eisenhower, the Democrats were paying tribute to the General in an election whose outcome was never in doubt.

The two men were so much alike they formed a mutual admiration society. Eisenhower had said that his regard for Stevenson was so high that if he had known the Governor was going to be the Democratic nominee he never would have gone into politics, while Stevenson told Walter Lippmann: "There's no man around who can beat Eisenhower and what's more, I don't see any good reason why anyone should want to." Stevenson never deigned to speak in the name of "the poor or the workers or the 'one-third' of a nation" submerged in poverty. Stevenson's break with the New Deal spirit brought plaudits from the con- servative press, which praised him for avoiding Truman's anti- plutocratic rhetoric. A Europe Firster in foreign policy, opposed to public housing (something even Taft approved of), federal aid for education, and federal health insurance, Stevenson was a thoroughgoing conservative who was in favor of Taft-Hartley and the states' rights that precluded civil rights for black America.

The two men were separated largely by style and their attitude toward McCarthy. For his party, Eisenhower shamelessly truckled before the senator because, as his diaries make clear, he agreed with McCarthy about the dangers of creeping socialism and a Democratic sellout at Yalta. When McCarthy viciously attacked General George Marshall, the Army Chief of Staff during World War II and Eisenhower's mentor, Ike refused to come to Marshall's aid. Eisenhower quibbled with McCarthy about the senator's crude methods but went out of his way to avoid criticizing the witch-hunts. When asked if he could support McCarthy, Eisenhower replied that he was second to none in his determination that "any kind of communistic, subversive or pinkish influence be uprooted from responsible places in our government," adding only that the job could best be done through existing mechanisms.

It was Stevenson's criticism of McCarthy and above all his detached, ironic style that made him a hero, not to the traditional working-class base of the Democratic Party, but to its intellectuals. Stevenson's portrayal of himself as "a tragically lonely figure" out of place in an increasingly vulgar and materialistic America, "who had paid for his devotion to public service with his own loss of public happiness," made him enormously appealing to liberal intellectuals. They saw Stevenson's "sense of separation from his audience as an emblem of the intellectual condition." Intellectuals, said critic Irving Howe, were gratified to see Stevenson winding his witty way through American politics, "acting out from on high their political impulses." The emphasis on Stevenson's style, his detached, sardonic (if sometimes snobbish) humor—the Republicans, he cracked, were trying "to replace the New Dealers with the Car Dealers"—marked a change in the internal life of the Democratic Party. The support Stevenson received from professionals and academics was a portent of the "New Politics" that was to emerge in the 1960s.

Eisenhower's problems in the election came less from the Democrats than from his own running mate, Richard M. Nixon. California's Senator Nixon was a rough-and-tumble anti-Communist who had made his reputation with the Hiss case. Placed on the ticket as a bridge between the Eastern establishment and the far right, Nixon played his role to the hilt, attacking Stevenson as "Adlai the appeaser with a Ph.D. from Dean Acheson's College of Cowardly Communist Containment." But Nixon's career and the Republican ticket were put in jeopardy when the New York *Post* revealed that a millionaires' club in California had illegally provided Nixon with an $18,000 slush fund.

Up until the scandal the Republican crusade against "Korea, Communism, and Corruption" had kept the Democrats on the defensive. At first Nixon tried to pass off the charges as left-wing smears, but when that didn't work he tried a bold strike to cut the ground out from an attempt by Eisenhower to drop him. He went on the relatively young medium of television to stage, in what came to be called the Checkers Speech, a remarkably successful version of prime-time political soap opera. Coming before the nation as a supplicant, Nixon made a point of his family's financial difficulties and his long struggle to make something of himself. Casting himself in the unusual role, for a Republican, of the average Joe, he explained how the gifts he received, such as a cocker spaniel named Checkers, were accepted for the sake of his family. The speech was a stunning success. Film tycoon Darryl Zanuck phoned Nixon to tell him it was "the most tremendous performance I've ever seen." The pathos of his appeal won over the audience accustomed to thinking of Republicans as fat cats. In an anticipation of his later strategies as President, Nixon had succeeded in identifying himself with what came to be called middle America.

The scandal had little effect on the election. Eisenhower carried 39 states and 442 electoral votes to only 9 states and 89 electoral votes for Stevenson. A shocked Democrat announced that "the natural order had come to an end."

The themes of the new administration, a mixture of God and business, were set at the inauguration, which featured the homburg hats and formal dress absent from Washington during the New Deal years. Eisenhower's supporters marched down Pennsylvania Avenue in tuxedos, trailing what was called "God's Float," emblazoned with the slogans "In God We Trust" (which Eisenhower was to add to the dollar bill) and "Freedom of Worship." The float was topped by a strange object which was supposed to represent a nondenominational church but which one stunned clergyman described as "an oversized model of a deformed molar left over from a dental exhibit."

The new administration was built on a bedrock of nineteenth-century certainty. Eisenhower and his two most important domestic cabinet officials, Charles Wilson, president of General Motors, and

George Humphrey, of Cleveland's National Steel Company, were all born in 1890, products of the Midwestern heartland and a time of peace and relatively fixed beliefs that preceded what was to be a century of war and revolution. It was a time Herbert Hoover described as "the happiest period in man's history." Satisfied with themselves and convinced that their success was a reflection of timeless and nearly immutable principles, Humphrey and Wilson were the leaders of a Cabinet of Protestant businessmen jokingly described as "the eight millionaires and a plumber." The plumber, Secretary of Labor Martin Durkin, was the only Catholic in the group and he resigned after eight months.

Previously insulated from the rough-and-tumble of politics, Secretary Wilson got the Administration into temporary hot water when he publicly expressed what the entire Cabinet believed, that "what was good for our country was good for General Motors and vice versa." The slogan, simplified and distorted, made the newspapers as "What's good for General Motors is good for the country." This set off a public relations furor, and Stevenson had a little fun mocking Wilson. "I for one," he said "do not believe that the general welfare has become a subsidiary of General Motors." For his part, Wilson was puzzled by the furor. He thought he was simply giving voice to what "everyone" already believed. And in a sense he was right. The acceptance of big business had become a fact of life. "In the 1950s huge corporations dominated almost every area of business. There were 325,000 manufacturing companies in the United States in 1955, but the fifty largest counted for 27 percent of all manufacturers' sales. The fifty biggest corporations in all fields that year" accounted for one-fourth of the total Gross National Product (GNP). General Motors alone had sales equal to 3 percent of the GNP. In a sense then, the economy had been socialized into private hands. A fairly small group of businessmen now made private decisions that determined a good deal of the economic and public life of the country.

Big businessmen, like their socialist critics, recognized that the distinctions between private choices and public policy, business and politics, no longer made any sense. In a world of giant corporations it was planning rather than the market that ordered the economy. And, warned Paul Hoffman of Studebaker, a leading Eisenhower supporter, "if business failed to plan" for the society at large, then "the government would and collectivism would come to America by default rather than design." The New Deal had failed, in this view, not because it had planned, but because its brain trusters and ward heelers didn't know how to plan according to sound business principles. The government, said the corporate leader, was simply the nation's largest business, and to be successful it had to be run like any other giant corporation.

Eisenhower was sure he wanted to run the government on sound business principles. This meant reducing the size of the federal government, balancing the budget, and dismantling elements of the New Deal. But he was unsure of how to package his program. Aware that, despite the new prosperity, big business was still held responsible for the Depression, he tried at various times to label his approach "dynamic conservatism," "progressive moderation," or "moderate progressivism." But oxymoronic labels aside, what Eisenhower wanted above all was to balance the budget and return the economy to private control. He was particularly interested in dismantling the TVA, the giant public power company created by the New Deal. Speaking of the TVA, he is reputed to have said, "By God, I'd like to sell the whole thing but I suppose we can't go that far." Instead of selling the TVA, he tried to undercut it by awarding a new contract for a major Tennessee Valley power plant to the firm of Dixon-Yates. But a congressional investigation uncovered shady dealings in the way the contract was let. A scandal erupted and an embarrassed Administration had to sue to block the very contract it had negotiated.

Eisenhower's efforts to curb government spending met with two other embarrassments. The Administration was faced with a public outcry when Secretary of Commerce Sinclair Weeks fired the chief of the Bureau of Standards for reporting that AD-2X, a commercial battery additive, was useless. Weeks didn't deny it was useless. But he thought that AD-2X should be allowed the "test of the marketplace." A similar furor erupted over the actions of the Republicans' first woman cabinet member, Oveta Culp Hobby, the Secretary of the newly created Department of Health, Education, and Welfare (HEW). Hobby opposed the free distribution of Dr. Jonas Salk's newly developed polio vaccine for children, objecting that this would amount to socialized medicine.

Complaining about the way bureaucrats "nag, irritate and hound every businessman in the United States," Eisenhower moved to take the federal government out of the offshore oil business. Truman had argued that the rich deposits of oil which lay just off the coast should be held by the federal government in trust for the entire nation. But Eisenhower, smelling a plot to foil private enterprise, pushed through legislation turning the development of these rich deposits over to the states, which in turn leased them at very low rates to private oil companies. The wealth generated from these deposits off Texas, California, and Louisiana was instrumental in creating the climate of economic growth of what came to be called the Sun Belt.

When it served the interests of the Administration's major business supporters, such as General Motors, Eisenhower was willing to bend principle. While General Motors was doing its best to eliminate public transportation as a competitor to the automobile, the General in the White House was promoting the costliest peacetime program in our history, the Federal Highway Act of 1956. Supported by auto and tire manufacturers and construction companies, the bill provided for more than $25 billion over twenty-five years to create a system of interstate highways. Along with the accelerated depreciation allowances for new plant construction which encouraged business to move out of the older cities, the Highway Act played a major role in undermining the viability of the nation's older cities.

Eisenhower was initially successful in reducing government spending and the federal payroll. In his first year of office, he eliminated 200,000 federal workers and cut federal spending by 10 percent. But he was forced to halt these cutbacks when the economy went into a tailspin in late 1953. His first reaction to the downturn was to issue statements suggesting that the problems would pass, so that there was no need to alter his course. For many Americans, however, this sounded like a rerun of Hoover's discredited policies, and Eisenhower was forced to respond. Where the Democrats would have reacted largely with Keynesian fiscal policy, expanding government spending to stimulate demand, Eisenhower turned to monetary weapons to fight the inflation, easing consumer credit requirements to nurture spending.

The issue was no longer whether we would have a free or managed economy, but how the economy would be managed.

5

From Utopia to Dystopia

Americans are "a happy people" doing exactly what they choose.
—"IKE"

IN THE 1950s the pivot of American life shifted from production to consumption, from blue- to white-collar work, from adulthood to childhood, from old city neighborhoods to new suburban communities.

White America was both pushed and pulled out of the old cities. During the 1950s about 1.8 million black Americans were driven off the farms of the rural South by the mechanization of cotton production. Economically redundant, they faced a choice between a marginal existence in subsistence agriculture or a trek North to follow those blacks lured to the cities by defense jobs during World War II. Most moved North to the once-thriving cities. Their arrival hastened the departure of people at the other end of the technological axis; some two million men and women who had become part of the technical-managerial complex organizing the modern economy were leaving the city for the suburbs.

Many of the new suburbanites were state and local government employees whose ranks increased by more than half during the Eisenhower years. Others were scientists, engineers, and technicians, the people everyone else increasingly depended on to fill the American cornucopia. But whether they were in the private or the public sector, they were the most rapidly growing element in the work force, the new men, the organization men who staffed the nation's giant bureaucracies.

"What must be grasped," said C. Wright Mills, summing up the situation, "is the picture of society as a great salesroom, an enormous file, an incorporated brain, a new universe of management and manipulation." The family farmer and the independent entrepreneur, the people who traditionally formed the backbone of American society, were receding on the horizon. At the start of World War II one American in thirteen lived on a farm. Between 1940 and 1960 the farm population declined by nine million people; by 1969 only one American in twenty lived on a farm. As for independent entrepreneurs, by the mid-1950s they were outnumbered four to one by people who earned their living from wages. And the economy was continually "inventing new professions to build out the roster—new kinds of hired bureaucrats, captive technicians, 'social engineers,' or gal Fridays."

It was hard to define what these "paper pushers" did or why their companies paid them so much. They were, said political scientist Andrew Hacker, paid to "manage and plan and coordinate; they travel and confer and investigate possibilities; they sit at meetings and talk on the telephone; they write letters and draft memoranda; they check up to see how things are coming along; they provide opinions and they relate to suppliers and retailers, stockholders and unions, government agencies and the public." In short, they did not engage in productive labor as Americans had once understood it.

Initially uprooted by the war, trained in the new industries and technologies that had developed in the 1920s, 1930s, and 1940s, the people of the suburbs were, it appeared, thoroughly modern types. They were unhappy with the dirt, congestion, and crime of the cities. But they were also drawn to the suburbs by the arcadian appeal of rural life. This was nothing new. "The pursuit of country happiness" had always been "a recognized part of a city dweller's dream life." In the years between World War I and World War II, 75 percent of the nation's new housing had been built in the suburbs. But even so, until after World War II they were confined to the well-to-do upper middle class. What postwar prosperity and government subsidies achieved was the democratization of the suburbs.

The flight from the cities was encouraged by government policies. The federal government's massive expenditures on highways, its subsidized mortgages for veterans, tax advantages for home ownership, and the development of mass-production techniques to produce cheaper houses put the suburbs within reach of all but the poorest white city dwellers. But there was also an anti-urban, anti-technological, anti-modern undertone to suburban aspirations. This was part of what sociologist Bennett Berger calls "complex pastoralism: the use of modern techniques to re-create the Jeffersonian idyll of homeowning freeholders."

The promoters of suburban developments understood this pastoral lure. Their promotions mocked polluted and problem-ridden cities and spoke of the "respite and refuge" offered by a countryside community "where life is healthier and less pressurized." With no irony intended, suburban communities were often named after the nature they displaced—thus the Pine and Cedar Grove Estates, the Fresh Meadows and Stone Hill developments.

It is easy to mock suburban optimism; its utopian sense of hope and possibility now seems part of a distant and naïve past. But there was a great deal that was attractive and even fulfilling. By 1960, for the first time, more Americans owned their own homes than rented. Suburban tracts recalled the lost splendor and simplicity of the nineteenth century, but they also anticipated elements of the commune and ecology movements of the 1960s and 1970s.

The growth of home ownership was but one part of what, at least for the middle classes, was the growing democratization of life's pleasures. Between 1945 and 1970 the real weekly earnings of factory workers grew by 50 percent, and this did not include the increasingly attractive fringe-benefit packages that allowed many unionized workers to receive prepaid medical and dental benefits as well as prorated pensions. The enormous growth in real wealth gave the American social structure the shape more of a diamond than a pyramid, with a vastly expanded middle class. The proportion of families and unattached individuals with an annual income of $10,000 or more (in standard 1968 dollars) rose from 9 percent in 1947 to 33 percent in 1968, while that below $3,000 fell from 47 percent in 1947 to 19 percent in 1968. This is not to suggest, however, that the upper class had disappeared, for, as economist Paul Samuelson has pointed out, "if we made an income pyramid out of children's blocks, with each portraying $1,000 of income, the peak would be far higher than the Eiffel Tower, but almost all of us would be within a yard of the ground." The very wealthy still held a vastly disproportionate percentage of the nation's wealth. What was new was the disposable income available to middle-income families.

Before the war the class boundaries between the upper middle class and those below them were unmistakably marked by the presence of servants in the wealthier homes. The wartime demand for labor and the ideology of the New Deal served dramatically to reduce the number of full-time servants, so that in the 1950s a broad band of families used their disposable income to purchase a wide range of household labor-saving appliances. In 1925 the number of refrigerators was minuscule; by 1956, 96 percent of American homes had them. Two-thirds had vacuum cleaners and nearly 89 percent had washing machines. Families which had earlier rented deep-freeze lockers for a dollar or two a month were now buying them, as they either redesigned once-cramped kitchens or moved into new modern ones which had the kind of appliances and workspaces once associated with homes in which servants did the work.

If a family lacked the ready cash to remodel and create its dream kitchen, it could do the job on credit. As quickly as disposable income had grown, credit had grown even faster. "Some 60 percent of all automobile purchases, usually cited as the single most important element in the consumer economy, took place on credit, the terms of which were often as generous as $100 down and three years to pay." This was less like buying a car than renting it at a low monthly charge. The broad availability of credit allowed a large percentage of the population to enjoy (although not always pay for) approximately the same package of consumer durables. At the turn of the century Thorstein Veblen had warned that American workers might mistake the abolition of scarcity for the abolition of capitalism. In the 1950s numerous commentators mistook the growth of mass consumption for the end of class divisions.

At a time when the nation seemed assured of an ever-brighter future, its children were looked upon as a national asset. "When I see my grandchildren, these lovely clods of human clay given us by God," said Wisconsin's Senator Alexander Wiley in 1948, "I reflect that each of us is a sculptor of that soft, receptive clay. . . . We can make of it a masterpiece of human art." Previous generations, the very wealthy excepted, had been raised in an environment of scarcity, where strength of character was essential for survival, in the literal sense of that much-abused term. The term "character" comes from the Greek "to be deeply marked." Parents traditionally hoped to deeply mark their children with the classic virtues of self-discipline in order to prepare them for life as adults. But the children of affluence were to be spared the harsh task of acquiring self-control.

In a world of scarcity, family life almost always centered on the breadwinning father. With father working ten- or twelve-hour days in field or factory and mother tied to the arduous task of maintaining a home without modern conveniences, children were shaped by the sometimes harsh but often effective patriarchal authority which fired the clay of unformed souls. Children of the 1950s, however, belonged to a far more democratic and child-centered family. Abundance meant that father's authority was no longer buttressed by economic necessity. Living in the new world of suburban affluence, cut off literally and figuratively from the world of the grandparents, the suburban mother and father turned to a new indoor recreation, the scientific rearing of children. They read Dr. Arnold Gesell's *The Child from Five to Ten* and Dr. Benjamin Spock's *The Pocket Book of Baby and Child Care*, the most popular book of the postwar era, with more than 20 million copies sold. These experts emphasized the importance of fun, play, love, and understanding. Children were no longer animal spirits to be restrained or vessels to be filled with adultness. Rather, said the experts, they were marvelous beings who needed tender loving care far more than order and self-discipline. "The child who cried in 1914 was a petty tyrant seeking slavish attention. The child who cried in 1947 was a lovely little creature that was worth all the attention you could give it." "For the children's sake" became an unanswerable riposte in household disputes.

Expert advice attacked the old distinction between what was

pleasant and what was good for the child. In the new "fun morality" baby's wants and needs were said to be one and the same. The job of parents was not so much to mold the children into obedience as to allow them to express themselves. Children raised by such methods, it was said, would be free of the neurotic and violent behavior which, as all had been made aware by the popularization of Freud, stemmed from repression. They were to grow up to be happy and spontaneous individuals, free of the burdens that had tormented all who had come before them.

By the mid-1950s the "average Joe" had a job and technical training that placed him several notches above the station his father had achieved. He took great pride in owning his own home in which his wife prepared nutritious meals with modern appliances and raised children who were "given all the advantages the parents had never had." He enjoyed opportunities for travel and recreation undreamed of by previous generations, and there seemed little doubt that things could only get better. Few suspected that prosperity could produce its own undoing.

A decade later this idyll was in ruins. The children, whether fighting in strange wars against an unseen enemy or rebelling at home, seemed desperately unhappy. The nutritious meals prepared by the most modern methods were revealed to have contained carcinognic substances, and the wife who had cooked that meal was no longer able to stay at home to organize family life. Feminist or not, she had been pushed by inflation into the job market. The middle-class values which provided the bedrock of certainty in the 1950s were eroding under attack from all directions; in short, the utopian promise of the 1950s lay in ruins. What had happened?

The very forces which had created the 1950s idyll were undermining it. The extraordinary growth of American capitalism had given individuals far more options than they had ever enjoyed before but only at an enormous price. What was from one angle the freedom to leave the city behind to pioneer in the suburbs was from another the breaking of traditional ties and the loss of older identities. "Nobody truly occupies a station in life any more," moaned novelist Saul Bellow. "There are displaced persons everywhere." The man who moved from blue- to white-collar work also moved into a new social world where his old ways of living were no longer acceptable. Where he once bowled and played canasta, now he had to play bridge and golf. His wife had to raise the kids without the support of the parents and sisters and aunts who had usually done so much to make the task of caring for young children bearable. And while the family's first automobile allowed it to escape city squalor, its second car often allowed the children to escape family togetherness. In 1956 Charles Wilson's General Motors launched an ad campaign to promote the idea of a second car by depicting "a family happily grilling hamburgers in front of their two cars." The caption read: "Going Our Separate Ways We've Never Been So Close." And then addressing the centripetal consequences of a second car, the text read: "The family with two cars gets twice as many chores completed, so there is more leisure to enjoy *together!*" Together? Unlikely, since the older children in particular were likely to be drawn by television and the movies and the emerging youth culture centering on such figures as James Dean and Elvis Presley. For them the second car would be a chance to cruise with their friends rather than spend another dull evening with the folks.

In a nation which had glorified hard work, prosperity and leisure produced discontents. The traditional virtues of thrift, persistence, and craftsmanship that had helped produce prosperity were being undercut by it. What need was there for craftsmanship in a world of automated machines, and why be concerned with thrift and savings when credit was so easily available in the "enjoy now–pay later society"? If work had given our lives meaning earlier, where was meaning in a world in which the old motto "Waste not, want not" was replaced by "It's only money"? And if prosperity was no longer related to hard work in the automated society, what were children to be told about work? Were children, in the words of David Riesman, merely "consumer trainees"?

"Prosperity," wrote Russell Lynes in a *Surfeit of Honey*, "produces not only plenty but curiously empty values and a national uneasiness. . . . Cars get gaudier, hi-fi sets get hi-er; beer can openers become mink-bearing; open fields get swallowed up to make future slums; slums are town down to make parking lots; pasture becomes drive-in movies; drive-in movie operators provide heaters so one does not have to desert one's status symbol even in winter."

For a growing minority of suburbanites, particularly among the better-educated, the excesses of consumption produced, to borrow Tocqueville's phrase, a "strange melancholy." Something "which . . . haunts the inhabitants of democratic countries in the midst of their abundance." It was a "strange disgust at life which sometimes seizes upon them in the midst of calm and easy circumstances." This disgust led some to abstain from consumer purchases as a way of making a social statement. Without the grid of struggle to define existence, life came to seem meaningless. Threatened by what they felt was a purposeless existence, they looked for a new sense of direction. This quest for purpose and meaning led some to quietism, withdrawal, and the inner contemplation of Zen Buddhism.

The new "beat" (as in beatitude) scene had an appeal closely parallel to Zen. The beats represented another version of "complex pastoralism." They were poets and writers, products of the city culture, and their leaders, such as Allen Ginsberg and Jack Kerouac, preached the virtues of instinct and authenticity. In love with an idealized version of adolescence, Ginsberg insisted that masturbation was a transcendent experience, one of many open to all who gave up materialism and rationality in order, in the words of the poem "Howl," to see that:

> The world is holy!
> The Soul is holy!
> The skin is holy!
> Everything is holy!
> Everywhere is holy!
> Everyday is an eternity!
> Everyman's an angel!

Ginsberg's juvenilia was to have great appeal in the 1960s, but for the moment most of those who were discontented turned to the political arena, and they were disappointed by what they saw.

Raymond J. Saulnier, chairman of Eisenhower's Council of Economic Advisers, set off a furor with his remarks before Congress. "As I understand an economy, its ultimate purpose is to produce more consumer goods. This," he told the legislators, "is the goal. This is the object of everything we are working at: to produce things for consumers." The statement enraged traditionalists and liberals. Traditionalists saw the statement as just another example of moral decline and well-heeled self-indulgence, while liberals insisted that social and not individual ends should be given the highest priority. Saulnier's boss, "Ike," who said to the nation, "Everybody ought to be happy every day," remained unruffled by the reaction. The President was a decidedly uninspirational figure. He told Americans to "play hard, have fun doing it and despise wickedness."

For those who wanted more in the way of inspiration and meaning, the President suggested a turn to religion (Ike had the words "In God we trust" added to the currency). Religion enjoyed a renewed though superficial popularity. Church attendance burgeoned and the country was blanketed with TV spot commercials reminding Americans that "the family that prays together stays together." For her part, the buxom movie star Jane Russell discovered that she too loved God and "when you get to know him, you'll find he's a living doll." This new religious interest was disdained by cosmopolitan liberals, who saw it as just another example of how anything could be mass-marketed, and it was denounced by traditional conservatives. "The U.S.," wrote a leading conservative, Russell Kirk, "has embraced a religion-in-general that is 'progressively evacuated of content.' " This "Christianity amounts to little more than a vague spirit of friendliness, a willingness to support churches—providing these churches demand no real sacrifices and preach no exacting doctrines." This "ethos of sociability" was a far cry from the earlier agonizing and soul-searching Protestanism which demanded rigorous self-examination.

Both conservative traditionalists and 1950s liberals denounced Eisenhower's reign of immediate gratification. What is surprising is that they did so in strikingly similar terms. They complained about the shallow, vulgar, conformist, money-grubbing character of American life. As Anthony Harrigan, a conservative, put it: "Alleged progress has come in the form of billboards and leveled forests. Juke joints, hamburger stands, curio shops, motels and neon signs have spread across the highways, spilling concrete-block blights of ugliness and impermanence . . ." A leading liberal intellectual, John Kenneth Galbraith concurred: "The family which takes its mauve and cerise air-conditioned, power-steered, and power-braked automobile out for a tour passes through cities that are badly paved, made hideous by litter, blighted buildings, [and] billboards . . . They pass on into a countryside that has been rendered largely invisible by commercial art . . . they picnic on exquisitely packaged food from a portable icebox by a polluted stream and go on to spend the night at a park which is a menace to public health and morals. Just before dozing off on an air mattress, beneath a nylon tent, amid the stench of decaying refuse, they may reflect vaguely on the curious unevenness of their blessings." Both men were brimming over with contempt for America's middle-class parvenus. They demanded an end to the national binge.

The vulgar, newly arrived middle class, they agreed, was simply too weak to resist the blandishments of mass advertising and mass merchandising. They were horrified by the nihilism of consumer sovereignty which, in Bentham's famous expression, means that "pin push is as good as poetry" or, in modern terms, "bingo is as good as Bach." And they both appreciated the paradox whereby the proliferation of individual choices in pursuit of personal pleasure leads to public outcomes like pollution, which no one desires. In a democracy, said Santayana, "people do what they wish but do not get what they want." The credulous untutored masses, the argument went on, were victimized by advertising. They were trapped on a squirrel wheel of contrived consumption. Cultural democracy had gone far enough. These empty people had to be told how to live, they needed a tutelary state to teach them how to behave. The American conservatives hoped for a cleansing wave of spiritual reform that would wash away the decadence of the modern—that is, post-Herbert Hoover—world. Such a wave would remove the monstrous deposits of modernity like the giant corporation and the welfare state, thus allowing a return to the lost world of frugality, private conscience, and individual responsibility. The liberals hoped to ride modernity into a future where the state would be used to re-create the vital public life which had supposedly thrived before it was undercut by the growing possibilities for private pleasures.

The liberal critique was to prove far more important, and its chief spokesman, the witty Harvard economist John Kenneth Galbraith, was to become the high priest of middle-class reform. According to Galbraith, a former adviser to Adlai Stevenson, "what ails the affluent society is a glut of the wrong goods, private consumption as opposed to government services. The corporations" said Galbraith in 1957, laying out what would be the liberal agenda for the next ten years, "had solved the problem of production. What remained was for the government to put its surpluses to proper, sound uses." The market mechanism, he said, served frivolous appetites, not real needs. What the nation really needed, Galbraith wrote in his best-selling *The Affluent Society*, was more money for the roads, schools, and public parks with which a truly cultured society could be created. To get the money for these public goods, Galbraith proposed a sales tax, which, though highly regressive, would serve the double purpose of cutting down on "unnecessary consumer expenditures" while providing funds for public projects organized by bright and thoughtful fellows like himself.

Galbraith's technocratic vision of socialism without spirit, a counterreformation from above, made but passing mention of the poverty and despair of millions of black as well as white Americans. Nonetheless, this new liberalism which emphasized questions of quality rather than quantity was enormously appealing to the nation's fast-growing population of academics and professionals. Galbraith's latent message offered them an inverted form of status snobbery. They could show their superiority to run-of-the-mill Americans, not by more and better purchases, which was becoming increasingly difficult as "the great game of consumption became free for all," but by rejecting consumption in the name of higher goals. And at the same time they could support worthy social goals such as aid to education and more beautiful parks.

Galbraith's admirers, one wag pointed out, were people driving Porsches complaining about the bad taste of people driving cars with tail fins. Though Galbraith was a self-proclaimed "voice in the wilderness" during the 1950s, his ideas came into common currency in the 1960s.

6

The Sputnik Years

If you ask me whether a country with no highly developed
sense of national purpose, with an overwhelming accent of life
on personal comfort, with a dearth of public services and a surfeit
of privately sold gadgetry, with insufficient social discipline
even to keep its major industries running without grievous
interruption—if you ask me whether such a country has over
the long run good chances of competing with a purposeful,
serious and disciplined society such as that of the Soviet Union,
I must say that answer is no.

—GEORGE F. KENNAN, 1959

JOHN KENNETH GALBRAITH'S CALL, in *The Affluent Society* (1957),
for an activist government to meet the challenge of reform couldn't
have been better timed. The book appeared just a few weeks before
the Soviets launched Sputnik, the world's first earth-orbiting satellite. This great technological feat on the part of the supposedly
backward, though clearly purposeful Russians shook the foundations of America's postwar self-confidence. The response to Sputnik was the hinge on which the nation's politics would swing into
the 1960s.

In 1955 and 1956 the Democrats, out of power and hungry for
an issue to use against the popular Eisenhower, took their turn at
foreign policy demagoguery. They charged that the Republicans
had allowed a "bomber gap" to develop between the United States
and the U.S.S.R. The charge was made despite the Soviets' relative lack of interest in bombers. Unlike the Americans, who en-
circled the Soviet Union with air bases, the Russians lacked military
facilities near the American homeland, so Stalin had pushed the
Soviet military to develop long-range missiles. Their efforts paid

off in August 1957, when the Russians became the first to successfully test an ICBM. Forty-four days later they pressed their advantage by putting Sputnik (Russian for "traveler") into orbit. Taken together, the two achievements implied that the Soviet Union would soon be in a position to launch a missile with a nuclear warhead capable of traveling 5,000 miles in twenty minutes with sufficient accuracy to destroy a target as limited as the Capitol in Washington. "We should," said Senate Majority Leader Lyndon Johnson, admit "frankly and without evasion that the Russians have beaten us at our own game—daring scientific advances in the atomic age." It was not only pride in American technical superiority which was shattered but the axioms of Eisenhower's foreign and military policy as well.

From the moment he entered office Eisenhower made every effort, at least verbally, to distance himself and his Secretary of State, John Foster Dulles, from the policies of the outgoing Secretary of State, Dean Acheson, who had been hounded and humiliated by the ideologues of the Republican right. Eisenhower and Dulles had, in fact, help formulate the Truman-Acheson policies, but faced with fierce opposition to limited war in Korea and strong criticism of budget-busting military expenditures, the new administration formulated a "New Look" foreign policy. Both Eisenhower and Truman firmly believed in containment, but where Truman saw nuclear weapons as a last resort, Eisenhower's "New Look" brought them to the fore of American policy at a time when the United States still had an effective nuclear monopoly.

Nuclear weapons had a twofold appeal. First, they were far cheaper to produce and deploy than conventional arms, an important consideration for the budget-conscious Republicans, who feared that big deficits created by military expenditures would undermine the very society they were designed to protect. Secondly, nuclear weapons promised to restore the initiative to the United States. Rather than simply responding to Third World revolutions set off by the Communists—Eisenhower and Dulles believed that all radical nationalist movements were in fact Communist—the United States could use the threat of nuclear weapons to foreclose Russian opportunism. This reliance on atomic weaponry shaped foreign policy. Since the H-bomb was to be the weapon of first resort, the United States had to be willing "to flash a nuclear bomb every time [it] wanted to threaten the use of force." It had to act as if no distinction existed between nuclear and non-nuclear weapons. Or as Eisenhower put it during the confrontation between the United States and Red China over the tiny islands of Quemoy and Matsu: "I see no reason why [atomic weapons] shouldn't be used just exactly as you would use a bullet or anything else." This was not bluster. The Administration was seriously prepared to use nuclear weapons for limited objectives. To make this threat credible, Dulles developed what came to be called "brinkmanship." It was an international game of chicken. To show the enemy that you weren't afraid, you had to be willing to run right up to the edge of the abyss without jumping off, in the expectation that your daring and courage would frighten off the Soviets, who were being threatened with "massive retaliation"— that is, total destruction. Containment, it seemed, required either limited wars or nuclear chicken.

American unwillingness to rethink containment in the light of Sputnik led first to proposals for "limited nuclear war" and then to an ongoing crisis with the European allies. Until Sputnik, Europe lay under the protection of the American nuclear umbrella. Should the Soviets use their overwhelming conventional superiority—the Warsaw Pact had three times as many tanks as NATO— the United States, it was assumed, would forestall the Russians with the counterthreat of nuclear attack. What made the American threat credible was that the Russians would be unable to respond in kind. But Sputnik dramatically raised the price of European defense. If the United States were to threaten the Soviets with H-bombs, it would now do so at the risk of its own destruction. This meant, said France's Charles de Gaulle, that the United States could no longer be counted on to defend Europe, because no nation would risk suicide in the defense of another. Insisting that France now had to have its own nuclear arsenal, De Gaulle began to withdraw France from NATO, splitting the Western camp.

In order to allay the European fears of American abandonment, Americans like Henry Kissinger, then a little-known professor working for Nelson Rockefeller, and the Rand Corporation's Herman Kahn tried to show how it was possible to fight a limited nuclear war to hold back the Russians. But, protested the Europeans, a limited nuclear war in Europe would destroy what the United States was pledged to defend. The United States was caught in a dilemma: on the one hand, its commitment to defend Europe even at the risk of self-annihilation was no longer fully credible; on the other, its alternative strategy frightened the people it was supposed to protect. Unresolvable without an expensive buildup of conventional arms, which the Europeans were unwilling to pay for, this dilemma would continue to fester well into the early 1980s, when it again came to the forefront of American diplomatic concerns.

The split between De Gaulle and the United States was paralleled by the growing tensions between Khrushchev and China's Chairman Mao Zedong. Khrushchev used the launching of Sputnik to wage a ferocious propaganda offensive. Labeling the ICBM the "ultimate weapon," he was free with his threats of destruction, implying that a turning point had been reached in the power relationship between the U.S.S.R. and the United States. "Over and over," reported *Newsweek*, Khrushchev said "in one way or another: 'We will bury you.' . . . Watching his face freeze with purpose, his little eyes flash, no one could doubt that he meant it." But no such turning point had been achieved. The Russians had severely strained their resources to produce their first ICBMs, and rather than move ahead rapidly to produce more, they were slowing the pace of their weapons development. Khrushchev's warnings, then, were largely bombast unmatched by actions, something neither the Americans nor the Chinese realized. When, in the wake of Sputnik, Mao trumpeted the triumph of "the East Wind" (Russia and China) over "the West Wind" (the Western powers), he talked as if he believed his own words about the United States being a "paper tiger" and he expected the Russians to press their advantage by more actively supporting wars of "national liberation" around the globe, whatever the risk. For his part, Mao, lauded by some Western liberals as a great humanitarian, announced that China was willing to sustain 200 to 300 million casualties if that's what it took to defeat the United States in a nuclear exchange. Khrushchev, who understood full well that the United States was not a paper tiger, was unwilling to allow the Chinese to put him into a conflict with the United States. Caught in the web spun by his own bellicose rhetoric, Khrushchev criticized the Chinese, who responded in kind, deepening the chasm between the erstwhile comrades.

Sputnik coincided with an economic downturn in America and Russian boasts that they would soon surpass us economically. All the "outs" of the 1950s—Democrats, intellectuals, scientists, and reformers—seized upon Sputnik as the lightning rod for their accumulated grievances. Instead of being extolled as a wise grand-fatherly leader, Eisenhower was castigated as "a symbol of an America grown complacent, fat and unconcerned: an America about to be overtaken by a smart hungry rival." "With super-markets as our temple and the singing commercial as our litany," asked Adlai Stevenson, referring to the Russian challenge, "are we likely to fire the world with an irresistible vision of America's exalted purposes and inspiring way of life?"

Stevenson's questions were echoed from coast to coast by a host of university presidents smarting from the gibes (not to mention minimal funds) directed their way by Republicans who had boasted of their "progress in rooting out eggheads" from the lairs of government. America, said the presidents of Harvard, Yale, and Princeton, suffered from "a general slackening of will," a glorification of "the cheap and tawdry" in pursuit of more "di-version, personal comfort and safety." What was needed, they insisted, was a government led by modern men of science who could provide the faith and meaning once supplied by religion. Your wish is our command, replied politicians of various moderate stripes, and for the next several years the country witnessed a frenzied sweepstakes to define "the national purpose."

The fear and anxiety of Eisenhower's most vocal critics were not shared by the nation at large. A 1960 Gallup poll found that despite Sputnik and all the sermons it produced, Americans were "relaxed, unadventurous, comfortably satisfied with their way of life and blandly optimistic about the future." On foreign affairs they seemed a "pond of calm and contentment." This "serene and buoyant" mood, as a visiting journalist described it, served only to inflate further the fears of America's leaders, who saw such an attitude as confirmation of their worries about American compla-cency in the face of the Communist threat.

These fears of complacency gave a new group of politicians their chance to perform on a national stage. These new men—"patricians with a common touch"—looked on Taft Republicans and New Deal Democrats as relics. Devotees of what came to be called the "Smooth Deal," they were suave, well-tailored men of breeding and intelligence who came of age during World War II when the nation was filled with a sense of destiny and purpose. Republicans Nelson Rockefeller (whose 1958 slogan of a "New Frontier" was later appropriated by John F. Kennedy), Charles Percy, and John Lindsay, Democrats Joseph Clark, John F. Kennedy, and Robert Meyner, presented themselves as the tribunes of a new, more stylish, more sophisticated America that was about to take its place not only as a great power but as a great civilization. They were rich men bidding to free the nation from the slough of crass commercialism and democratic materialism to meet the Communist challenge. If advertising, to use Huey Long's famous slogan, had made "every man a king," then the patrician warriors—most notably Kennedy and Rockefeller—planned to make those kings foot soldiers again in pursuit of an ennobling national cause.

It was Rockefeller who set the mold, but John F. Kennedy who perfected it. Heir to a huge fortune, brother of the chairman of the vast Chase Manhattan Bank, Nelson Rockefeller won the governorship of the Empire State in 1958 by defeating rival patrician Averell Harriman, heir to another banking fortune and an architect of Truman's foreign policy. Aided by the public relations machine which won him office, "Rocky," as his press releases described him, proceeded to create a parallel national government-in-waiting while governor. A liberal insofar as he was free with the taxpayers' money and interested in clearing away troublesome social issues so that the "real" challenge of the times, Soviet power, could be met, Rocky and his brothers created a number of commissions staffed by house intellectuals like Henry Kissinger. The commission reports, not surprisingly, warned that the country faced "a critical situation." "The nation," it was argued, was "in grave danger, threatened by the rulers of one-third of mankind" (Russia and China). The apocalyptic conclusions of the Rockefeller brothers echoed the Gaither Report, written under the leadership of H. Rowan Gaither, Jr., chairman of the Ford Foundation. Gaither argued that the Russians would soon have the capacity to hit America with a knockout nuclear blow. The social scientists at the prestigious Rand Corporation, the most important of a growing number of think tanks, went even further. Their studies indicated that the nation was in such grave danger it ought to consider plans for surrender.

In New York, Rockefeller tried to meet that imagined challenge by pursuing his own foreign policy. To prepare the state for an attack by Russian ICBMs, he waged a vigorous campaign to provide every home with a fallout shelter so that the United States could fight and win a nuclear exchange. Using his vast network of hired press agents and friendly journalists to present himself as a "doer"—Max Lerner described him as "a man of action whom intellectuals want"—Rockefeller was preparing to remake the country in the name of a national crisis that would demand sacrifices from the public and the leadership of a "great" man like himself.

Rockefeller was never to have that opportunity. His journey to the Republican presidential nomination was waylaid time and again by the heirs of Taft, who hated the New York governor with a burning passion. Many modern Republicans would learn from Rockefeller's defeats and make tracks for the Democratic Party. It was the "Smooth Deal" Democrat Jack Kennedy who would carry "Rocky's" foreign policy ideas into the White House.

The story of John F. Kennedy is inseparable from that of his father, Joseph P. Kennedy. It is a tale of unlimited ambition, for Joe Kennedy was a man of gargantuan drives. The grandson of Irish immigrants, he inherited a small trust company from his father, a politician and saloonkeeper, and built it into a multimillion-dollar empire. He made quick profits in banking, Hollywood, liquor, and land and moved on because power, not wealth, was his goal. "In a nation without royalty of birth his was a royalty of success." But he was proudest of the four sons produced by his marriage to Rose Fitzgerald. Thwarted in his ambition to become a national political figure, he raised his sons for a life in politics. "My work is my boys," he was fond of exclaiming. The boys, Joe, Jack, Robert, and Edward, were filled with a love of the active life and the cult of courage as preached by the Englishmen T. E. Lawrence (of Arabia) and John Buchan, author of *The Thirty-nine Steps*.

Jack's senior thesis at Harvard, "While England Slept," was a study of British democracy's failure to prepare for Germany's challenge. The thesis was laced with doubt about the ability of a free society to defend itself against a totalitarian threat. "The efforts of democracies are disjointed," he wrote. "They don't have the intensity or long-range view that dictators do . . ." Impressed by the efficiency and order of fascism in Italy, he speculated that "democracy might be an unaffordable luxury." In times of crisis democracies might have to submit to what he called "voluntary totalitarianism," including the internal suppression of dissent, if they were to survive. Joe Kennedy saw an opportunity to use the thesis in promoting Jack's career. He had a close friend, New York *Times* columnist Arthur Krock, rewrite what Jack's Harvard advisers thought was a mediocre study, and he promoted the book like one of his Hollywood movies. He later told Krock: "We're going to sell Jack like soap flakes." It was the beginning of a JFK legend built on money and Joe Kennedy's influence.

When war came, Jack was drawn into his father's isolationist and pro-German circle, with nearly disastrous results. Young Jack, an ensign, became infatuated with a Danish journalist working on the isolationist Washington *Times-Herald*. Inga Arvid was a former Miss Denmark who had accompanied Hitler to the 1936 Berlin Olympics, where the Führer described her as "a perfect example of Nordic beauty." There was evidence that Ms. Arvid was engaged in espionage for the Germans, and the FBI was well aware of the torrid affair between Arvid and Kennedy. Jack had no desire to give her up to go to war, but when his father got wind of the situation he used his influence to pull the reluctant warrior from the field of love to that of battle. If the story of the affair had surfaced before 1960, Kennedy might never have been elected President. As it was, he was forced out to sea and his historic misadventure as commander of PT-109. A mistake on Kennedy's part (incredibly, he allowed his small quick ship to be rammed by a Japanese destroyer) led to two deaths, some standard wartime heroism in the rescue of overboard sailors, and a Silver Star for the inept commander. Joe Kennedy brought in writer John Hersey to describe the "adventure" for *The New Yorker*. The story made it seem as though young Jack was preparing his boat for attack rather than being accidentally rammed, but of such are modern American legends made. Not since Teddy Roosevelt's charge up San Juan Hill in a Brooks Brothers suit had a minor military adventure been so successfully marketed. The Founding Father, looking to touch downscale readers, thoughtfully arranged to have *The Reader's Digest* run a condensed version of the article.

Back home, yet another legend was created, that of Jack Kennedy the Boston Irish pol, though he was none of the above. Although Boston was the family's ancestral home, Jack grew up in posh Scarsdale and Hyannisport and knew little of the city. His successful campaign for Congress, directed by his father's organization, was the privileged young man's first contact with the Irish or any other working class.

In Congress, Kennedy voted the economic interests of his working-class constituency, but he made it clear he had more in common with Theodore than Franklin Roosevelt. Described by friends as an "ultraconservative," Jack fully adopted his father's free-market beliefs and raging anti-Communism. "Jack," said one friend, "could no more insulate himself from his father's thinking than escape his genes." Criticized for not being a true New Deal liberal, Jack responded: "I'd be happy to tell them, I'm not a liberal at all."

Kennedy was bored by Congress and most of his fellow representatives. One of his few friends on the Hill was another first-termer, Joe McCarthy from Wisconsin. Kennedy served on the Education and Labor committees, on which he shared a hostility toward big labor and Communism with another young congressman, Richard M. Nixon. The two were divided by party, not belief. Before Nixon made his mark in the Hiss case, Kennedy had made a small reputation for using the Labor Committee for his own smoother and more aristocratic brand of heresy-hunting.

After he was elected to the Senate in 1952, his upper-chamber career was notable for general inactivity except in those matters which might garner publicity. He distinguished himself by "writing" a book about great senators called *Profiles in Courage* and by being the only Democrat who didn't censure McCarthy, leading some to quip that Kennedy needed "more courage and less profile." The book, which won a Pulitzer Prize, was written by Ted Sorensen, a member of his staff, but this too would come out only after his death. At the time, the image of young Jack as not only Washington's most eligible bachelor but a highly literate scholar as well won him plaudits from the national press, his real constituency.

Kennedy began running for the 1960 presidential nomination the day he lost his bid for the second spot on the 1956 ticket. After Sputnik, the "missile gap" became the ideal vehicle for his presidential aspirations. It allowed him to attack Eisenhower's bookkeeper mentality, his unwillingness to fund larger military expenditures with larger deficits, and his "soft sentimentalism"— a term he used to describe Eisenhower's interest in diplomatic negotiations. The Cold War chickens Eisenhower had nurtured were coming home to roost. Now it was the Democrats who demagogically hurled accusations of being "soft on Communism."

The "tide of events," warned Kennedy, was running against America. Unless a heroic leader acted soon to rally the nation on every level—economic, ideological, and military—we would be swept aside by a younger, tougher, more determined Soviet Union. Their missile power, he said, "will be the shield from behind which they will slowly but surely advance—through Sputnik diplomacy, limited brush-fire wars, . . . internal revolution . . . and blackmail. The periphery of the Free World will slowly be nibbled away." Turning his youth to his advantage, Kennedy called for a new American resolve, a mobilization of will and resources led by a new generation able enough to face up to the impending contest. All in all, it was a vision and a call to action that could have come straight from the pages of John Buchan's heroic novels of aristocratic adventure which he had always loved.

Eisenhower refused to rise to the bait. It was not that he was unwilling to take strong anti-Communist measures. In Iran and Guatemala, he had used the CIA to overthrow reformist governments because of their supposedly pro-Communist taints, and he was planning a similar measure against the revolutionary Cuban government of Fidel Castro. But these actions had involved covert activities and limited resources. The kind of massive public campaign and enormous military expenditures Kennedy was calling for seemed imprudent and unnecessary to Eisenhower. Imprudent because vast and costly measures threatened to distort and undermine the free society they were designed to protect. And unnecessary because Eisenhower knew there was no missile gap. Secret U-2 planes flying high above the Soviet Union made it clear that Khrushchev's blustery rhetoric was by no means matched by Soviet military might. The Russians were unable to afford many ICBMs. The United States continued to maintain a wide margin of superiority.

Eisenhower and Secretary of Defense Thomas Gates made every effort to reassure the nation and the press that the country was in no danger. But there was little they could do to stem the tide of liberal hysteria coming from newspapers like the Washington *Post* and intellectuals like the respected historian Arthur Schlesinger, Jr. Ignoring the evidence presented by Gates, Schlesinger, a supporter of Kennedy, typified intellectuals who insistently repeated that "the reason we are falling behind lies in the lack of national purpose in our life." "No one," said Walter Lippmann, meaning no one who counted, "would listen to President Eisenhower's denials and assurances." The 1960s were about to open on a note of elite hysteria that was to grow in intensity throughout the coming decades.

It is usually said that Kennedy faced three major obstacles on his road to the Democratic nomination: prejudice against Catholics, liberal suspicion, and resentment from the party regulars. The first has been overestimated and the second was cleverly used to cancel out the third. By 1960 a candidate's Catholicism was no longer a major issue. In the 1950s the nation abandoned "stuffy" old religious disputes for a syrupy religion of good feelings. Catholics were elected to Congress in record numbers, and young Catholics like William F. Buckley, Jr., scion of another Catholic dynasty, and Eugene McCarthy were making their mark on the nation's political life. In 1956, Eisenhower, recognizing the growing importance of the Roman Catholic vote, seriously considered dumping Richard Nixon and replacing him on the Republican ticket with Frank Lausche, a conservative Catholic Democrat from Ohio.

By 1960 Kennedy was able to play the religious issue both ways. He generated a great deal of enthusiasm among Catholics, who of course were called upon to vote for one of their own. Before Protestant and mixed audiences, Kennedy invoked the memory of Al Smith and the anti-Catholic nativism of the 1920s, implying that a vote against him was a vote for bigotry.

A far more serious obstacle was opposition from the solons of Capitol Hill. "Within his own party Kennedy was considered too young, too rich, too independent and in too much of a hurry" to be President. Senate Majority leader Lyndon Baines Johnson, also a candidate for President, looked down on Kennedy as the spoiled son of a rich man, while Johnson's mentor and fellow Texan, Speaker of the House Sam Rayburn, disdained Kennedy as someone who was closer to journalists than to his colleagues on the Hill. But these were to be Kennedy's strengths. The traditional politics of men who knew each other on a face-to-face basis and were bound by patronage and party loyalty was being replaced by a new style in which television images and "selfless volunteers" set the tone.

Kennedy used his father's money, organization, and connections to build a parallel political machine largely independent of the Democratic Party. In the crucial West Virginia primary, Kennedy used sophisticated polling techniques and stunning television commercials to swamp the underfinanced and bewildered Hubert Humphrey, the true heir of the New Deal, in an overwhelmingly Protestant state.

"Style is the deference reason pays to uncertainty." Kennedy overcame liberal uncertainties by playing on style. For those to whom the word "Catholic" conjured up images of Franco and rabid McCarthyites, Kennedy made it clear that he wore his religion lightly. For Stevensonians, he emphasized his Harvard background, his urbanity, wit, and detachment, all of which were real enough. For the die-hard social reformers, he presented himself for the first time as a loyal scion of FDR.

There were liberals who could never forget that Jack Kennedy's father had been an "umbrella man," but far more important were those like the historian of the New Deal Arthur M. Schlesinger, Jr., novelist Norman Mailer, and economist/pundit John Kenneth Galbraith, who saw in Kennedy the maximum leader they had been pining for ever since FDR had passed away. Schlesinger seemed particularly overwrought with the promise of a Kennedy presidency. He referred to Kennedy as a Moses of sorts who would lead the nation from its Egyptian bondage (the Eisenhower presidency), a prince who would awaken the country from its "trance," an alchemist who could change the lunch-pail liberalism of the New Deal into the lifestyle liberalism of the future. For his part, Mailer was excited by the Kennedy who in a *Sports Illustrated* article called on Americans to toughen themselves mentally and physically, while Galbraith saw in Kennedy the possibility of a government by the best and the brightest from academia. All hoped that Kennedy could create a politics which would be something more than the sum of pleasures consumed by its individual citizens.

Their feelings toward Kennedy were echoed across the country by the new upper middle class, the junior officers of World War II who had gone on to fashion success for themselves in corporations and academia and now longed to see someone who reflected their success in high office. Kennedy channeled their enthusiasm into a powerful and effective volunteer vote-getting operation that functioned entirely outside the channels of the Democratic Party. These new enthusiasts, plus the old Stevensonian reformers won over to Kennedy, were as important for converting old-line party leaders as for bringing out the vote.

Finally, for those who were not attracted by Kennedy's style or promise, there was always the trump card, Richard Nixon. Support Kennedy because the alternative was the devil who had persecuted/prosecuted Alger Hiss. Nixon was still detested for his role in the witch-hunts, not only by liberals but by moderates like Sam Rayburn, who never forgave Ike's handpicked Vice-President for having accused so many colleagues of outright disloyalty.

Historians and commentators have emphasized the similarities in the positions and tactics of the two candidates. "The managerial revolution has come to politics," according to CBS's Eric Sevareid, "and Nixon and Kennedy are its first completely packaged products. The processed politician has finally arrived." The campaign was summed up by the debate in which neither man distinguished himself but which Kennedy won because of his good looks and Nixon's unflattering makeup. There is no doubt that when they served together in Congress there was little in the way of beliefs separating these two men. As Nixon himself put it during the debate: "Our disagreement is not about the goals for America, but only about the means to reach those goals." True enough, but Schlesinger had seen something. The goals of the two men might be the same, but Kennedy's call for an unconventional politics to meet those conventional goals helped pave the way for the tradition-shattering shocks of the 1960s.

7

The New Frontier in Power

Eisenhower embodied half the needs of the nation, the needs of the timid, the petrified, the sanctimonious and the sluggish. What was even worse, he did not divide the nation as a hero might (with dramatic dialogue as the result); he merely excluded one part of the nation from the other. The result was an alienation of the best minds and the bravest impulses from the faltering history that was made. America's need in those years was to take an existential turn, to walk into the nightmare, to face into that terrible logic of history which demanded that the country and its people must become more extraordinary and more adventurous or else perish.

—NORMAN MAILER

THE 1960 ELECTION WAS a very close race between two marginally popular politicians. Kennedy won the popular vote by two-tenths of 1 percent. A shift of a few thousand votes in Chicago or Texas could have swung the election to Nixon. There were indications of voter fraud in Texas, where Kennedy's vice-presidential candidate, Lyndon Johnson, was a man of commanding influence, and in Chicago, where the political machine of Mayor Richard Daley was strongly behind Kennedy. Nixon, however, declined to make an issue of the matter.

Kennedy narrowly captured the presidency, but the Democrats lost 20 seats in the House and 2 in the Senate. On paper, the new President's party had a comfortable majority in both houses, but a third of the Democrats were Southerners hostile to civil rights legislation and generally more conservative than Kennedy on domestic issues. Recognizing, as Arthur Schlesinger put it, that "great innovations should not be forced on slender majorities," Kennedy saw that the opportunity to make his mark was where his heart lay, foreign policy.

As World War II ended, the nation sensed that it was at the beginning of what *Time* magazine's Henry Luce called the "American Century." But that postwar promise of greatness remained unfulfilled. First Truman was unable to prevent China from slipping into the Communist camp and, even more ominously, under Eisenhower, China came to seem, not the exception, but the portent of peasant revolutions to come. This new "wave of the future" threatened to sweep across what Kennedy called "the great battleground for the defense of freedom . . . the whole southern half of the globe—Asia, Latin America, Africa and the Middle East." In the three years of Kennedy's presidency twenty-seven new nations were created, many by bloody anti-Western revolutions. The threat of these new dictatorial regimes was confirmed by the Cuban revolution of Fidel Castro. "Now," as one writer put it, "there are Communists right on top of us. The darkness has moved across the ocean."

Kennedy promised to break out of this "encirclement" with what he called a "New Frontier" for America. The "New Frontier" was to restore the lost promise of postwar greatness. Greatness required the kind of toughness Kennedy trumpeted in his inaugural address: "Let the word go forward from this time and place, to friend and foe alike, that the torch has been passed to a new generation of Americans—born in this century, tempered by war, disciplined by a hard and bitter peace, proud of our ancient heritage, and unwilling to permit the slow undoing of those human freedoms to which this nation has always been committed."

In his farewell address Eisenhower warned that the means the United States used to fight the Cold War might subvert the end of preserving freedom. Kennedy brushed these fears aside in the best-remembered lines from his inaugural: "Let every nation know . . . that we shall pay any price, bear any burden, meet any hardship, support any friend, oppose any foe, to assure the survival and success of liberty. This much we pledge—and more."

This Churchillian rhetoric led to a grand conclusion. America, asserted Kennedy, was in a great crisis. The ordinary rules of government had to be suspended so great leaders with extraordinary powers could come forth to save democracy from the new totalitarian challenge. "In the long history of the world," exclaimed Kennedy, "only a few generations have been granted the role of defending freedom in its maximum hour of danger. I do not shrink from this responsibility, I welcome it . . . And so, my fellow Americans, ask not what your country can do for you; ask what you can do for your country."

The men who were to help the President in his hour of self-proclaimed crisis were a mix of technocrats and militant liberals, the personal and political heirs to Teddy Roosevelt's activist presidency. They were men whose obvious talents and intellectual flair led to their being dubbed "the best and the brightest." The gray, deliberative businessmen of the Eisenhower era were replaced by a slew of *Harvard Law Review* editors and Phi Beta Kappa social scientists, part of a grand mobilization of expertise. Products of the great universities and science-based corporations of the 1950s, they belonged to a generation which was heady with its scientific successes with computers, rocketry, miracle wheat, super pesticides, and systems analysis, all of which were said to embody "the rosy dawn of a technotronic age." Young, hyperconfident, ambitious, and full of "viguh" like the President himself, they included Robert McNamara, Ford Motor Company whiz kid and systems analyst as Secretary of Defense, and brother Bobby Kennedy as Attorney General. The brightest of them all was McGeorge Bundy—summa cum laude at Groton, the first Yale student to get three perfect scores on his college entrance exams, and dean of Harvard College at thirty-four—as National Security Adviser. "Eloquent in discourse, and devastating in debate, [Bundy's] intellectual superiority was patently obvious." The effect, as Arthur Schlesinger saw it, was that "Washington seemed engaged in a collective effort to make itself brighter, gayer, more intellectual, more resolute. It was a golden interlude . . . One's life seemed almost to pass in review as one encountered Harvard classmates, wartime associates, faces seen after the war in ADA conventions, workers in Stevenson campaigns, academic colleagues, all united in a surge of hope and possibility."

The style and enthusiasm of these young men and the charm of Kennedy's blueblooded wife, Jacqueline, enthralled the nation. Finally, it seemed, America had a leadership worthy of the nation's greatness. No longer would we have to be ashamed of the frumpy bourgeois dinners at 1600 Pennsylvania Avenue. A new, modern, and even aristocratic spirit of glamour and adventure, which came to be called Camelot, was to fill our hitherto empty lives. Fueled by a contempt for the nation's sluggishly deliberative and bureaucratic political institutions and armed with the predictive methods and quantitative techniques of modern science, Kennedy's "happy band of brothers" looked on themselves as a guerrilla administration that would reshape both their own government and the world in the image of their own self-satisfied modernity.

The first test for these armchair adventurers came from Cuba, just ninety miles from Florida. Cuba had been virtually an American colony. By 1956 Americans owned 80 percent of Cuba's utilities, 40 percent of its sugar, 90 percent of its mining wealth, and enjoyed a ninety-nine-year lease on the island's strategic Guantánamo Bay naval base. Cuba had been ruled by Fulgencio Batista, a corrupt dictator who come to power as a reformer but then proceeded to make himself and his friends, including American gambling interests, wealthy while ruling over the rest of the country with the national army. But if Batista ruled, the United States reigned. Thrice in this century American marines landed in Cuba to restore order and ensure the protection of American economic interests. American power was so great in Cuba that, as a U.S. envoy to the island explained, "the American Ambassador was the second most important man in Cuba; sometimes even more important than the [Cuban] president."

The United States was so closely linked to Batista's corrupt reign that when the dictator was overthrown in 1959 by a diverse group of non-Communist revolutionaries led by Fidel Castro, the U.S. position was threatened as well. Castro, whose heroes were Robespierre and Napoleon, dreamed of a Cuba independent of American domination, and to achieve that goal he fatefully turned to the Russians, less out of ideology than out of a desire to consolidate his power and protect himself from the United States.

Khrushchev was jubilant. The Monroe Doctrine, he said, was dead, and he threatened, "figuratively speaking," to destroy the United States if it attacked the new Cuba. For Americans perpetually worried about the dangers of Communism, Cuba was the last straw. The Cuban-Soviet connection meant that foreign policy was no longer a remote matter. Faced with an obvious challenge to

American power, Kennedy responded by activating a plan for an invasion of Cuba devised by the outgoing Eisenhower administration. The plan for a landing at the Bay of Pigs in Cuba was modified by Kennedy to fit his idea of guerrilla government. "It was a bold plan," said journalist Henry Fairlie, "the kind that appealed to the Kennedy spirit. This kind of action, the Kennedy brothers felt, fitted the New Frontier. It was full of chance, certainly, but it was audacious, glamorous, new. It was irresistible." The attack would not be carried out by the regular American Army under the traditional chain of command; rather, a mixed group of Cuban refugees and CIA operatives (some of whom would later be involved in Watergate) would pull off a daring attack which in turn would set off a popular uprising. Kennedy, like so many Americans whose vision of Communism was formed by the Soviet-imposed regimes of Eastern Europe, simply could not believe that Castro's overthrow of Batista represented the true feelings of the Cuban people.

The invasion was a fiasco. The mixed CIA and Cuban exile force that landed at the Bay of Pigs on April 17, 1961, was routed by Castro's waiting army. Kennedy, recognizing that the invasion force's position was hopeless, decided not to escalate the conflict by sending in regular U.S. troops and thus openly admitting what was obvious to all, Washington's involvement. The anti-Castro Cubans felt betrayed by Kennedy. One of the exiles said it was "like learning that Superman is a fairy," a conclusion not so different from that of Khrushchev, who sensed in Kennedy's inaction a weakness to be exploited. The Russian leader, who had been a soldier in the Czar's army before Kennedy was born, already had a personal distaste for the callow American. He decided to test the young President. The Bay of Pigs set off a chain of events, a contest of wills that wound its way through yet another crisis over Berlin, a dangerous confrontation over Cuba, and the escalating American involvement in Vietnam.

Khrushchev served notice that he was about to play hardball by loudly reaffirming Russia's "sacred interest in wars of national liberation, including Vietnam," and then turned his attention to the central bone of contention between the United States and the U.S.S.R.—Germany and particularly Berlin. The linchpin of the

Western military position in Europe was the alliance between West Germany and the United States. It was Khrushchev's aim to break that tie either by neutralizing Germany, splitting the alliance, or forcing the United States to bargain away its military position in Western Europe. But his efforts were undermined by the hundreds of thousands of East Germans fleeing East Germany by way of the Allied sector of Berlin. To stem the flow, Khrushchev built what came to be known as the Berlin Wall, and he declared that the status of West Berlin would have to be resolved in a manner favorable to the U.S.S.R. within six months.

Kennedy was shaken by the Russian's bellicosity. The fight over Berlin was shaping up, in the words of Dean Acheson, as "a simple test of wills." Kennedy, worried that Khrushchev might think him weak, told New York *Post* reporter James Wechsler that "if Khrushchev wants to rub dirt in my nose, it's all over." Kennedy responded to Khrushchev's Berlin provocations by calling up the reserves and by further expanding the already unprecedented buildup of American military forces, a buildup which in itself had done a good deal to goad Khrushchev into his foolish bluster. Faced with Kennedy's willingness to go to the mat over Berlin, Khrushchev backed down and turned his attention to the new U.S. point of vulnerability, Cuba. For Khrushchev the road to a neutral Germany lay through Havana.

1962 was a year of bluster, bravado, and rising tensions. The Russians exploded a series of nuclear devices, one of them 3,000 times more powerful than the bomb at Hiroshima, to demonstrate their power, while Kennedy and McNamara began to suggest that the U.S. missiles were so powerful and accurate that they could be used in a successful first strike against Soviet military installations. In the midst of these threats and counterthreats, evidence of a Soviet military buildup in Cuba revived popular demands that Kennedy "do something about Castro." Then, in mid-October 1962, American U-2 spy planes discovered conclusive proof of what had been most feared. The Russians were installing in Cuba nuclear missiles capable of hitting most of the United States.

The danger from the missiles was not military. If the Russians had wanted to start a nuclear war, the missiles fired from their own territory would have been more than sufficient. The danger, as

Kennedy saw it, was political. If the Russians were allowed to get away with planting missiles ninety miles off U.S. shores, they would, he said, have gained the "appearance" of power. And since appearances contribute to reality, the missiles would, in his words, "have politically changed the balance of power."

Determined to respond, Kennedy rejected both Acheson's plan for an immediate strike and Stevenson's plan to react diplomatically. Instead he chose a naval blockade of Cuba, which gradually tightened around the island. The plan had the virtue of appearing to take a middle course, but in effect, by eschewing even quiet diplomacy before acting, it raised the stakes and forced an extraordinarily dangerous confrontation.

The blockade brought nearly unbearable tension as the country waited to see what would happen when the United States intercepted Soviet ships steaming toward Cuba. Then, to the great relief of everyone involved, the Soviet ships turned around. "We're eyeball to eyeball," said Secretary of State Dean Rusk, "and I think the other guy just blinked." But the test of wills wasn't over yet. Kennedy insisted that there might still have to be an invasion if the missiles weren't dismantled.

Shortly before the planned American attack that could have brought nuclear war, a deal was struck. Kennedy agreed not to invade Cuba in return for the withdrawal of the missiles. Kennedy had won; for the second time in two years he had successfully called Khrushchev's bluff. But in many ways it was a hollow victory. A humiliated Khrushchev came under great pressure from Kremlin hawks and the always hard-line Chinese Communists. Within a year, Khrushchev was deposed and replaced by men whose chief priority was the buildup of Soviet military might. Pledged never again to back down before American military strength, Khrushchev's successors began the largest peacetime military buildup the world has ever seen.

Kennedy's advisers were, as Robert Kennedy recalled them, "probably the brightest kind of group that you could ever get together," but, he went on, referring to the hard-line advice of Acheson and others, "if six of them had been President . . . I think that the world might have been blown up." The country had escaped the worst in Cuba, but those same advisers would realize their potential in what would truly become a disaster, Vietnam.

In order to understand Kennedy's escalation of the U.S. role in Vietnam, it is necessary to go back to the origins of American involvement in a land where America had neither investments nor markets. If one looks for the economic motivations for America's fateful encounter with the Third World in Vietnam, those motivations can be found, not in Asia, but in Europe and American plans for its economic recovery after World War II.

Cordell Hull, FDR's Secretary of State, blamed economic nationalism for both World War I and the Great Depression. In Hull's words: "Unhampered trade dovetails with peace; high tariffs, trade barriers and unfair economic exchange, with war." This was an Enlightenment view of the world in which the free exchange of economic resources was the one thing most likely to "bring the greatest possible prosperity to the greatest possible number." In a world of free trade men's aggressive instincts were to be channeled into peaceful economic competition rather than war.

America's opportunity to apply the principles of international free trade came in August 1941 with the signing of the Atlantic Charter between a United States still unwilling to enter the war and a besieged Britain. The Charter was strikingly reminiscent of Wilson's Fourteen Points. In the words of one British diplomat, it was a rehash of all the old Wilsonian "clichés" with its call for free trade, demilitarization, national self-determination, and de-colonization. Both Churchill and De Gaulle insisted that the right to decolonization should apply only to victims of Nazi aggression and only to people with white skin, and neither was eager to open his country's protected colonial markets to free trade and American competition.

Roosevelt made no secret of his disdain for De Gaulle and French colonialism. "France," he said, "has milked [Indochina] for a hundred years. The people of Indochina deserve something better than that." Roosevelt's rhetoric led prominent British and French figures of the left and right to accuse him of "encouraging rebellion among the subject races, thus creating a disorder from which the Soviet Union may profit." But Roosevelt's actions were a good deal more tempered than his rhetoric.

In the classic American manner, FDR hoped to "do well by doing good." That is, while he genuinely wanted to raise the standard of living of the "brown peoples" of the world, he wanted to do so through the classic American mechanism of free trade, and to be successful, a world economy based on free trade required a healthy Europe. So while the United States publicly supported decolonization, it hoped that Third World nationalist movements would proceed slowly so as not to destabilize the European powers who were still dependent on their empires. In other words, FDR wanted what Wilson had hoped for: an orderly transition from a world of colonies and closed imperial trading spheres to a globe bound together by unhindered commerce. But in the short run this transition had to be gradual enough to allow the European powers to use the colonies temporarily to fuel their postwar economic revival.

The Americans were forceful in pushing decolonization on the British and the Dutch, but the French were a different story. In 1947, while all of Europe seemed to be teetering on the brink of collapse, a wave of Communist-led strikes appeared to bring France to the verge of insurrection. At the same time, in Indochina the fighting between the French and the Viet Minh, led by Ho Chi Minh, was intensifying. American policy makers, increasingly preoccupied with fears of Communist expansion, began to view Ho, who had fought alongside the United States against the Japanese while the Vichy French collaborated with the Nipponese, as a tool of Moscow. The policy makers surmised that the Soviet purpose in Indochina was to involve French troops, retard French economic recovery through heavy military expenditures, and thus create the disorder necessary for a Communist takeover in France.

For their part, the French tried to wave the flag of anti-Communism in the Americans' face as often as possible. General Jean de Lattre de Tassigny, the World War II resistance leader, became the first to talk of falling dominoes if the West was defeated in Vietnam. He warned that in Vietnam "Southeast Asia, and even the whole of Asia, is at stake . . . Once Tonkin is lost, there is really no barrier before Suez." This inflated rhetoric had only a limited effect until June 1950, when the North Korean assault on South Korea gave credence to such warnings. After Korea, American officials saw Vietnam as yet another piece on the global chessboard threatened by international Communism.

The French found the Vietnamese Communist Party's blend of zeal and organization more than a match for their troops, and after a disastrous defeat in 1954 at Dien Bien Phu the French withdrew, leaving behind a regime led by the conservative nationalist Ngo Dinh Diem, who became the legatee of American support. For a half decade or so after 1954 there was relative quiet as the Diem regime seemed to prosper while the Communists in the North licked their wounds. But then in the early 1960s the Diem regime weakened. Diem had the support of his fellow Catholics concentrated in the cities and of the landlords, who made up about a fifth of the population. His repressive regime, however, had alienated the vast majority of Buddhist religious leaders and peasants, who were neither Communist nor anti-Communist in their inclinations. Diem's association with the Americans gave the popular and nationalist Ho a chance to finish what he had begun in the 1930s, the creation of a Vietnam free of foreign influences. More vigorous and aggressive than the interior peoples of Southeast Asia, Ho and his followers saw themselves as the natural rulers not only of the South but of Laos and Cambodia as well. While Buddhists burned themselves with gasoline to protest Diem's contempt for their traditions, Ho's soldiers infiltrated the South, where, aided by South Vietnamese supporters in the National Liberation Front and the general hostility to the regime, they effectively terrorized many of Diem's supporters. By 1962 it seemed likely that without American intervention the Diem regime would collapse.

The Kennedy administration viewed the developing crisis in Vietnam through the old prism of McCarthyism and the new lenses created by the American humiliation at the Bay of Pigs and Kennedy's subsequent confrontation with Khrushchev in Vienna. At the June 1961 Vienna Summit, held just two months after the Bay of Pigs, the Soviet leader alternated threats about Berlin with pledges of Soviet action on behalf of "sacred wars of liberation." Khrushchev taunted Kennedy with the specter of Communist and hence Soviet victory in Vietnam. When Kennedy returned he repeatedly told John Kenneth Galbraith: "There are just so many concessions that one can make to the Communists in one year and survive politically." And with one eye on the domestic political scene, he went on, saying, ". . . we just can't . . . have another defeat this year in Vietnam."

The United States had neither a long history of cultural ties nor major economic connections with Vietnam, but in the context of the United States-Soviet rivalry, "as a point of intersection between threat and commitment, it was everything." When asked to explain the American interest in Vietnam, the Administration's spokesmen emphasized perceptions. Or as a staff report put it, an American loss in Vietnam would "generate defeatism among governments and peoples in the non-Communist world, or give rise to frustrations at home." When asked why the loss of such an insignificant piece of real estate could produce such extraordinary consequences, the Administration's spokesmen talked of the indivisibility of U.S. commitments, as if all were of equal importance. In effect, a grandiose world view that refused to distinguish between vital and peripheral interests made U.S. policy hostage to any weak regime that came under Communist challenge.

Vietnam became a test of the Administration's inaugural commitment to "pay any price, bear any burden . . . to assure the survival . . . of liberty." For the gung-ho Kennedyites anxious to show how they could remold the world, Vietnam was a great opportunity to demonstrate their blend of heroic and technocratic leadership. Speaking in the clipped style of the social scientist, Secretary of Defense Robert McNamara said that America had "to prove in the Vietnamese test case that the free world can cope with Communist 'wars of liberation' as we have coped successfully with Communist aggression at other levels." Similarly, Kennedy's chief military adviser, Maxwell Taylor, reported that "the President repeatedly emphasized his desire to utilize the situation in Vietnam to study and test the techniques and equipment related to counter-insurgency." Vietnam, said Taylor, was a "laboratory" for the American military.

Europeans looking at the American scene were shocked that Kennedy had chosen Vietnam to be "a proving grounds for democracy." Americans, they pointed out, knew very little about Vietnam, but the information available suggested that there was little in the way of democratic tradition to build on in that over-whelmingly peasant and traditionalist society. But the lawyer/social engineers of the Administration saw this lack of specific knowledge about Vietnamese culture and history as an asset of sorts. Armed with abstract social science models about how economic and social development takes place, they were anxious to impose their hothouse ideas on an unwilling Vietnam. There was even an ironically idealist cast to this ignorance. Americans, free of the caste snobbery which had hindered European attempts to remake the lesser peoples of the world, were convinced that in their ideas about the inevitable stages of economic growth, stages modeled on the American experience, they had the keys to producing a prosperous commercial world free of Communist oppression. While the Kennedy administration, Bobby Kennedy in particular, was promoting the crack Green Berets as both the American answer to dedicated guerrilla fighters and a new model for American heroism, "Saigon was inundated with teams of American political and social scientists and every form of expert researching and analyzing from preconceived Western ideas every facet of Vietnamese life and motivation." While the courage and élan of the Green Berets were supposedly lifting the fighting spirit of the South Vietnamese Army, the American experts were form-ing a shadow government whose reforms were supposed to "win the hearts and minds of the Vietnamese people." Only belatedly would these experts come to realize that the bureaucrats and landlords of the Diem regime, who were supposedly America's partners in progress, were the chief obstacles to reform. The upshot was the worst of both worlds: Americans neither directed the South Vietnamese in a straightforward imperial manner nor worked with them as true partners. Instead, while the Americans and the Diem government worked at cross purposes, the country suffered from both the wrenching "reforms" of the social scientists, who often found it necessary to displace people from their ancestral villages, and the corruption of the Diem officials, who saw the American programs as an opportunity for increased graft.

Back home there was another, more successful grand mobiliza-tion of expertise, this one designed to redirect the emerging revolution of black Americans. The Second Reconstruction did not begin, as popular history would have it, with the Supreme Court's 1954 decision outlawing segregated schools. The modern civil rights movement began in the late 1930s when black and white radicals challenged FDR's calculated decision to downplay civil rights for fear of offending the Southern grandees of Capitol Hill. The radicals insisted that America live up to its creed of equality. In the words of Godfrey Hodgson: "It would no longer be possible to qualify the tenets of the American creed with a muttered sotto voce mental reservation: 'We hold these truths to be self-evident (except in Mississippi) that all men (except black men) are created equal.'"

It was World War II, as E. Franklin Frazier put it, which marked the point when large numbers of black people were "no longer willing to accept discrimination in housing and employment without protest." Struck by the discrepancy between a war against Nazi racism abroad while racial persecution was enshrined at home, blacks insisted that the time had come to redress their grievances. "A Jim Crow Army," the NAACP pointed out, "cannot fight for a free world." Putting it more sharply, a small but growing band of black nationalists called World War II "a white man's war." They reserved their sympathies for the Japanese, who showed that "colored people knew how to fight," and even the Germans, who, after all, were fighting the same British Empire that held millions of black Africans in its thrall. Less extreme than the nationalists, black journalist George Schuyler expressed an increasingly popular view when he argued that "our war is not against Hitler in Europe, but against the Hitlers in America."

The war, said the black Pittsburgh *Courier*, was an opportunity "to persuade, embarrass, compel and shame our government and nation . . . into a more enlightened attitude toward a tenth of its people." The man who seized that opportunity was the black socialist and trade union leader A. Philip Randolph. In 1941 Randolph channeled the rising black anger into a March on Washington Movement, which threatened to disrupt FDR's calls for wartime unity with a mass protest against segregation. To head off the threatened march of 50,000, Roosevelt agreed to create a Fair Employment Practices Commission, "the first national agency that explored discrimination in jobs and worked for equal employment."

The commission was denounced by Congressman Joe Ervin as socialistic, and Eugene "Bull" Connor, Birmingham's Commissioner of Public Safety, warned that the FEPC was creating "impudent, arrogant, law-breaking, violent and insolent" Negroes. The commission did nothing of the kind, but it did break through the regional logic which had governed race relations since the end of the First Reconstruction by creating an administrative bureaucracy which, along with the judiciary, slowly began to impose new racial rules on American society.

The first wave of the modern civil rights movement came to an end in the late 1940s, a casualty of the anti-Communist hysteria sweeping the country. Critics of American racism were deemed unpatriotic, if not simply subversive, for painting a picture of the United States that might give aid or comfort to its Soviet enemy. The end of this phase of the civil rights struggle was symbolized by the Peekskill riot of 1949, in which a jeering, chanting crowd of a thousand, led by American Legionnaires, attacked the black Communist Paul Robeson, who had come to that New York City suburb to give a political concert.

Even as the Peekskill mob was shouting: "Every nigger dies tonight," a new group of radicals, untainted by any association with Russia, were creating a new type of racial protest. Pacifists in World War II, A. J. Muste, James Farmer, and Bayard Rustin (a disciple of Randolph) pioneered nonviolent direct-action methods of confronting racism. Members of a new civil rights organization, the Congress of Racial Equality (CORE), they put themselves "on the line" in a series of dramatic freedom rides across the South. In the McCarthy era their rides bore no immediate gains, but CORE was a vital link to the development of the Student Non-violent Coordinating Committee (SNCC) a decade later. In the meantime the promise of direct action was overshadowed by a pathbreaking legal decision.

The 1954 decision of the Supreme Court in *Brown* v. *Board of Education of Topeka, Kansas,* to outlaw school segregation was the culmination of a series of court decisions beginning in the late 1930s that chipped away at the notion that racially separate education could be equal. The grounds on which the Court, led by Eisenhower appointee Chief Justice Earl Warren, reversed the 1896 decision of *Plessy* v. *Ferguson* have aroused a great deal of belated controversy. Rather than follow the line of dissent laid out by Justice John Marshall Harlan in the earlier case, arguing against segregation on straightforward moral grounds, the Warren Court based its judgment on a set of questionable sociological assumptions. The Court's reasoning aside, however, the historic decision stimulated the emergence of a massive civil rights movement.

The Supreme Court Justices were aware that the Brown decision was a mortal threat to three centuries of white supremacy. So while Chief Justice Warren insisted that "constitutional principles cannot be allowed to yield simply because of disagreement with them," the Court waited for more than a year to declare how its decision should be implemented. It pronounced cautiously that desegregation should move ahead "with all deliberate speed," a decision that angered blacks and did little to allay Southern white hostility. Throughout the South, White Citizens Council units were organized to sabotage the decision, with violence if necessary. "The Deep South Says Never" read the title of one of the Council's pamphlets. "If we submit to this unconstitutional, judge-made integration law," spouted one of the Council leaders, "the malignant powers, of atheism, Communism and mongrelization will surely follow." What did follow in the winter of 1955–56 was violence. A black voter registration worker was killed on the lawn of the Lincoln, Mississippi, county courthouse, and a fourteen-year-old black boy from Chicago was murdered in Money, Mississippi, for whistling at a white woman. Yet all this might have been tolerated if TV cameras hadn't begun to convey the meanness of Southern racism to Northern liberal audiences. "There was an unforgettable scene . . ." wrote Yale law professor Alexander Bickel, "in one CBS newscast from New Orleans, of a white mother fairly foaming at the mouth" trying to teach her little boy to hate by repeating "the ugly, spitting curse NIGGER! The effect," concluded Bickel, "was that an unprecedented number of Americans got a sense of what a slave auction must have been like."

While the gradual effect of the Court's decision was beginning to work its way through the South, a group of black women and men in Montgomery, Alabama ("the Cradle of the Confederacy"), emboldened by the Brown decision but disappointed by its lack of enforcement provisions, took matters into their own hands. On December 1, 1955, after returning from a training institute in nonviolent direct action, Mrs. Rosa Parks, a seamstress, refused to give up her seat in the front of a bus, as was the custom, to a white man. Her arrest sparked a momentous mass protest.

E. D. Nixon, a black trade unionist in the Randolph tradition and a leader of the local NAACP, seized on Mrs. Parks's arrest to rally the black community behind concerted action. Frustrated in his efforts, he turned to a young Montgomery minister, the Reverend Martin Luther King, Jr. King, who had a Ph.D. in theology, was the son of a well-to-do Atlanta preacher. He grew up in a home where "everybody preached against such things as adultery and stealing, but the one venial sin was ignorance." Pastor of the church for the city's black elite, "the big folks," he had the capacity to reach out and draw the entire black community into a disciplined organized boycott of the Montgomery bus system.

Montgomery's white leadership expected the boycott to fade quickly; after two grueling months they discovered that blacks were willing to walk for miles rather than give in. As an elderly black woman explained it, "My feets is tired but my soul is rested." Angered and under pressure from the city's merchants, who were losing millions of dollars' worth of business, the mayor announced a "get tough" policy. He joined the White Citizens Council and warned that "white people are firm in their convictions that they don't care whether the Negroes ever ride a city bus again if it means that the social fabric of our community is to be destroyed . . ."

When verbal threats failed, King was arrested and then released on bond; his home was bombed, bringing the city to the edge of a violent confrontation between heavily armed blacks and whites. King's response, writes Lerone Bennett, "changed the course of the protest and made King a living symbol." He asked his followers to get rid of their weapons. "We are not advocating violence. . . . We must love our white brothers no matter what they do to us." "Blood may flow in the streets of Montgomery before we receive our freedom," he told his congregation, "but it must be our blood that flows and not that of the white man."

Aided by Bayard Rustin and Glen Smiley, a minister trained in Gandhian passive resistance, King managed to keep the boycott going until a special three-judge U.S. District Court declared Alabama's laws requiring segregated bus seating unconstitutional.

However modest the goal seems in retrospect, the effect of the boycott victory was electrifying. Here at last was the victory black America had been waiting for. In the wake of the Montgomery triumph, King, with the financial aid of Northern white philanthropists and tactical advice from men who drew their experience from the Communist Party, forged a new organization, the Southern Christian Leadership Conference (SCLC). Together with older organizations, such as the NAACP, which had brought the suit in the Brown case, and the Urban League, SCLC forged a powerful mass movement for social justice. The movement's organizational muscle, however, was no match for the White Citizens Council's. Its real strength lay in the way it couched the struggle in terms of a contest between the black nonresisters' Christlike suffering and the bestiality of the white racists. It was a moral tableau that captured the conscience of Northern liberals. In the end, King believed, the blacks' discipline and self-sacrifice would lead to redemption and reconciliation.

The struggle for civil rights grew without the aid of President Eisenhower. Referring to the Brown decision, he called his appointment of Chief Justice Earl Warren "the biggest damn fool thing I ever did." He told Warren that Southerners "are not bad people. All they are concerned about is to see that their sweet little girls are not required to sit in school alongside some big overgrown Negroes." When Arkansas Governor Orville Faubus announced that the state's National Guard would block black students from entering Little Rock's Central High in defiance of a federal court order, Eisenhower hesitated until the mayor of Little Rock asked for federal troops to forestall mob violence. Only then did a reluctant Eisenhower send in federal troops to ensure compliance with the court order.

Nationally, the most effective arguments for civil rights traded on Cold War sentiments. The NAACP had some success arguing that segregation hurt the United States in its competition with Russia in the Third World. John Kennedy became sympathetic to that argument. But Kennedy, like Eisenhower before him, was careful, at least initially, not to offend the white South.

The newly elected Kennedy was acutely aware that black voters—he received 70 percent of the black vote—had been crucial in his narrow victory. Once elected, he tried to repay blacks with high-level appointments and an emphasis on supporting the black right to vote. But unwilling to offend the powerful Southern committee chairmen in Congress, he refused publicly to condemn segregation.

CORE, led by James Farmer, decided to force Kennedy's hand by re-creating the Freedom Rides of the 1940s. As Farmer explained it: "We planned the Freedom Ride with the specific intention of creating a crisis. We were counting on the bigots of the South to do our work for us. We figured that the government would have to respond if we created a situation that was headline news all over the world, and affected the nation's image abroad." Farmer figured correctly. Two busloads of Freedom Riders, a mixed group of older white pacifists and young blacks, were savagely beaten as they traveled through Alabama. Attorney General Robert Kennedy dispatched 500 federal marshals to protect the riders, but he was unwilling to endorse the ride's purposes or protest the riders' imprisonment by local authorities. Frightened by the explosive possibilities of recurring violence and upset by liberal criticism of the Administration's inaction, Robert Kennedy called for a cooling-off period. But soon a new wave of Freedom Rides were launched by a fledgling organization of white and black college students. The new organization, the Student Nonviolent Coordinating Committee (SNCC) had been created in 1960 when young college-educated blacks in Greensboro, North Carolina, decided to break the law and the taboo against interracial dining by sitting down at a segregated Woolworth's lunch counter and refusing to move until they were served. Robert Moses and Julian Bond, two future leaders of SNCC, said that watching the Greensboro sit-in on television changed their lives. Inspired by the courage and audacity of the sit-down demonstrators, a group of black and white students, many of whom were in divinity schools, came together, with money from the AFL-CIO and office space from the SCLC, to form what was frankly designed as an elite shock corps for the civil rights movement.

SNCC's multiracial militance reminded one observer of a "Popular Front Affair in the 1930s." But there was something strikingly new about them as well. In their courage and élan and their calls for a genuinely participatory democracy, the members of SNCC "were improvising a style and defining an ethic for [many in their] generation." The Kennedys, who aspired to run a guerrilla administration, couldn't help but admire SNCC's verve and courage, but acutely aware of how important the South was for any Democrat who hoped to be reelected, they refused to talk of the struggle in straightforward moral terms. Until Birmingham.

The Kennedys were wary of the unpredictability and potentially explosive character of the struggle over civil rights. Generally sympathetic to moderate black aspirations, they nonetheless doggedly tried to maintain control of the way the contest developed. On the one hand, they were unwilling to introduce voting rights or other civil rights legislation for fear of a humiliating defeat at the hands of Southern committee chairmen on the Hill. On the other hand, they feared that black direct action, nonviolent or not, would produce a bloodbath. Jack Kennedy said he was haunted by "this Southern problem." As late as 1962 not a single black attended white schools or colleges in Mississippi, Alabama, or South Carolina. The brothers' solution was to try to redirect civil rights energies "from buses to ballots." They argued that voter registration drives were the key to progress, in part, no doubt, because black ballots could offset retaliatory voting by Southern whites.

Civil rights leaders (aided by money from Northern liberals) were supportive of voter registration drives, but they were unwilling to wait for the day long in the future when it would pay dividends. Instead they again decided to force the issue, this time in Alabama, where in January 1963 George Wallace was elected governor vowing: "Segregation now! Segregation tomorrow! Segregation forever!" King planned a "socio-drama" for Birmingham. In April 1963 the Reverend King and his "nonviolent army," which included numerous grade-schoolers purposely recruited for the occasion, marched on Birmingham—specifically to desegregate the stores and upgrade black employment. There, in full view of the network TV cameras, the police, led by Commissioner of Safety Eugene "Bull" Connor, and the blue-helmeted troops of George Wallace's state police assaulted, beat, and pummeled helpless nonviolent demonstrators. The national newspapers featured a picture of a police dog, fangs bared, leaping at a black woman.

White violence, as Godfrey Hodgson has put it, "achieved more than black non-violence" that day in Birmingham. The response from outraged Northern liberals, the "constituency of conscience," who viewed the ugly scene on television, was all that King had hoped for. Jack Kennedy, who said the picture of the police dog made him sick, was forced to take strong action. First he used national and local business leaders to force a Birmingham desegregation agreement, and then he made the public pronouncement that blacks had long awaited. For the first time Kennedy spoke of civil rights in straightforward moral terms. Race, he declared, "is a moral issue . . . as old as the scriptures . . . as clear as the Constitution . . . A great change is at hand, and our task, our obligation, is to make that revolution, that change, peaceful and constructive for all." A moral crisis, he said, cannot be "quieted by token moves or talk. It is time to act in the Congress, in your state and local legislative body, and, above all, in all our daily lives." Hours later Medgar Evers, described as "the Negro most feared" by the segregationists of Mississippi, was murdered in Jackson, Mississippi. A week later Kennedy sent the Congress the strongest civil rights bill since Reconstruction. It called for a ban on segregation in all interstate public facilities, such as hotels, buses, and airline terminals, and asked for broad powers to protect black voting rights and initiate school desegregation suits.

Black leaders, seeking to capitalize on the momentum of Birmingham, planned the kind of massive march on Washington that A. Philip Randolph had threatened in 1941. The new march, organized by Bayard Rustin, with broad black and white liberal support, promised to be precisely the kind of unpredictable event the President feared. Again he intervened to channel developments his way. At first he tried to block the march, but "once Kennedy saw that we were determined to have it," Rustin recalls, "he decided to cooperate fully in order to ensure that it would be used to lobby Congress rather than denounce the President."

The march, held in August 1963, was an extraordinary success, as 250,000 demonstrators gathered peacefully around the Reflecting Pool on the Great Mall chanting: "Pass that bill! Pass that bill!" The highlight of the march was King's "I Have a Dream" speech: "I have a dream that one day this nation will rise up and live out the true meaning of its creed: We hold these truths to be self-evident that all men are created equal." This was the high point of the civil rights movement. Briefly it appeared that the walls of segregated Jericho would come tumbling down. They didn't, to everlasting bitterness. Already there were those at the march, such as SNCC leader John Lewis, who criticized Kennedy's bill proposal as too little too late. The bill, in fact, had little chance of Senate passage until that fateful day in Dallas (just a week after the murder of Diem in Vietnam) when the young President was assassinated.

It was Kennedy's luck to die—on November 22, 1963, in a bizarre shooting which has never been fully explained—with his aura of promise still intact. He was widely and deeply mourned by a nation who saw in his wit and charm a confirmation of its own success. Kennedy, as one taxi driver put it, was a "classy guy" and he meant it in both senses of the term. Mourned as a hero by a people who loved his public persona if not his limited accomplishments, he was deeply missed by blacks who remembered him for the reluctant though grandiloquent support he gave civil rights and by liberals who would soon turn against his foreign policy.

John Kennedy's goal, aside from his own self-aggrandizement, had been to re-create a sense of national purpose. The purported Russian threat was as much the opportunity as the reason for that re-creation. The drive for national purpose was more an exercise in therapeutic nationalism than a policy aimed at specific goals. "The United States," wrote one of Kennedy's aides, "needs a Grand Objective. . . . We behave as if . . . our real objective is to sit by our pools contemplating the spare tires around our middles. . . . The key consideration is not that the Grand Objective be exactly right, it is that we have one and that we start moving toward it."

What was to be so attractive about Kennedy's pursuit of the Grand Objective—as it turned out, a heightened conflict with the Russians—was that, the rhetoric and imagery of sacrifice aside, Kennedy demanded very little of the American people. There was, said Kennedy, no further need for "the great sort of 'passionate movements' which have stirred this country so often in the past." Instead Kennedy proposed to substitute himself and his band of brothers for the nation as a whole. It was their heroism, the heroism of their Green Berets, which was to justify the easy living of bourgeois society gone fat and stale.

Observers at the time noted the theatricality of Kennedy's call for heroism, activism, and sacrifice. Oscar Gass, for one, noted the discrepancy between the portentous "let the trumpets summon us again" language of Kennedy's speeches and the modest proposals for action. Kennedy called for heroic virtue but lived the life of café society; here was the core of what Tom Wolfe was to call "radical chic."

On the level of policy, Vietnam was Kennedy's legacy, but on the level of style, to which he owed so much, Kennedy bequeathed to the country a theatricality and activism that would soon overflow the channels of official Washington and flood onto the streets of the nation's cities. Instead of unifying the nation, Kennedy helped create the schism that would define a decade. He spawned both the "experts' war" in Vietnam and the upper-middle-class activism that would come to oppose it.

8

From the Great Society to

Black Power

This man is not a visionary or a radical: he is a middle of the road extremist.

—MAX ASCOLI on Lyndon Johnson

ON NOVEMBER 22, 1963, in the same plane that carried the slain chief executive's body back to Washington, Lyndon Baines Johnson was sworn in as the thirty-sixth President of the United States. Lyndon Johnson was a Rabelaisian, larger-than-life figure. A tall man from Texas, a state with a reputation for producing outsized characters, Johnson had the face of a riverboat gambler and the political skills of a master politician. He was only ten years older than Kennedy, but he came from a different generation and a different world. A product of Depression era poverty, Johnson's political views had been shaped in part by his political hero, Franklin Delano Roosevelt. Styling himself after FDR, Johnson liked to be called LBJ. If Kennedy had been born with a silver spoon in his mouth, Johnson grew up with the taste of dirt in his. He came from the desperately poor hill country of West Texas. "When I was young," Johnson told reporters, "poverty was so common that we didn't know it had a name."

° A self-made man, Johnson fought his way to the top of the Texas political heap. A man of wildly conflicting impulses, he was driven on the one hand by greed and an unquenchable thirst for success and on the other by a genuine concern for the plight of those who had shared his childhood poverty. Johnson's Texas was a one-party state. The Democratic Party in Texas was a circus tent organization that included everyone from right to left, from business big and little to labor, blacks, and Mexican-Americans. The key to success in that situation was to create a consensus everyone could live with. Johnson became a master of using his extraordinary persuasive skills to engineer agreement between diverse interests. Elected to Congress in 1937, he made his mark bringing together within the Democratic Party rapacious nouveau riche Texas oil millionaires and conscious-striken Northern liberals whose political divisions paralleled those of his own vast personality. He was elected to the Senate in 1948 by the narrowest of margins, leading his detractors to joke about "Landslide Lyndon." But once there, he rose, with the support of his fellow Texan and mentor, Speaker of the House Sam Rayburn, to become Majority Leader of the Senate in 1955 after serving only one term.

Johnson became one of the most powerful and effective Majority Leaders the Hill has ever known. He was an overpowering figure with the psychic energy of a natural phenomenon. When a congressman was asked why he had changed his mind on a key vote, he answered: "Well, it's this way. Lyndon got me by the lapels and put his face on top of mine and talked and talked and talked. I figured it was either getting drowned or joining." Extremely intelligent without being an intellectual, he was a reader of men, not books. Johnson, as an English reporter described it, "comes into a room slowly and warily, as if he means to smell out the allegiances of everyone in it." He combined a rare ability to look inside his fellow politicians with a near-photographic memory for details, so that, as one aide put it, "not a sparrow falls on Capitol Hill" without LBJ knowing.

The Kennedy loyalists and intellectuals were among the few who seemed totally immune to his political sway. They viewed the roughhewn Johnson as a boor and a usurper, much as FDR's retinue looked down on the man from Missouri, Harry S. Truman. For the Kennedyites, brother Bobby was the true heir to the throne, so that the Johnson presidency was simply an unfortunate interregnum. Kennedy's intellectual camp followers were exhilarated by a President who brought taste to the White House and recognition for them. Enthralled by the magic of Camelot, "they received his words and images," said literary critic Alfred Kazin, "as children 'read' the pictures in a storybook." Johnson, on the other hand, reminded intellectuals of what the rest of the country was like." He reminded us of who we were—and some, said Richard Whalen, conceived their dislike of him in that moment.

For his part, Johnson brushed aside the snubs and moved quickly to calm the nation by proclaiming his intent to carry on Kennedy's noble mission. As powerful as he was, Johnson was somewhat in awe of his Ivy League advisers, something that worried Rayburn. After an obviously impressed Johnson recited the extraordinary academic credentials of his Cabinet, the Speaker snorted, "I just wish one of them had been elected anything, even deputy sheriff." To prove he was worthy of the office and not just another parochial Southerner, Johnson moved quickly to push Kennedy's civil rights legislation, long blocked by his fellow Dixie politicians. As Johnson explained it: "If I didn't get out in front on this issue" the liberals "would get me . . . I had to produce a civil rights bill that was even stronger than the one they'd have gotten if Kennedy had lived." And produce he did. Defying all the writers, politicians, and analysts who spoke of the "deadlock of democracy," Johnson used his unparalleled skills to break the Southern filibuster. He pushed through Congress the most sweeping civil rights legislation since the end of the First Reconstruction. The 1964 Civil Rights Act, described by Supreme Court Justice Arthur Goldberg as "the vindication of human dignity," became the cornerstone of civil rights law. It provided legal and financial support for cities desegregating their schools, banned discrimination by businesses and unions, created an Equal Opportunities Commission to enforce that ban, and outlawed discrimination in places of public accommodation.

With the Civil Rights Act passed and his own legitimacy established, Johnson turned to putting his own stamp on the presidency. Declaring, "We are not helpless before the iron law of [traditional] economics," Johnson called for a "War on Poverty" as Kennedy had called for a war on Communism.

The "War," wrote *Time* magazine, reflected the "uniquely

American belief" that "evangelism, money and organization can lick just about anything." Americans generally believed that "a rising tide lifts all boats," but a spate of books on poverty, particularly Michael Harrington's powerful *The Other America*, showed that a substantial number of Americans, black and white, silently suffered from such serious deprivation that they would be unaided by the general prosperity. The very poor, argued anthropologist Oscar Lewis, were trapped in a culture of poverty, a culture which, in the words of Harrington, meant that "the poor are not like us. . . . They are a different kind of people."

Social science promised a way to reach the culturally distant world of severe poverty. On assuming the presidency Johnson inherited an economic growth rate that had more than doubled from 2.1 percent to 4.5 percent since 1960 and which, with mild inflation, was pouring extraordinary amounts of money into federal coffers. This "social surplus," the excess of revenues over expenditures, provided nearly four billion dollars a year for new public spending. The flow of money was so great that Governor Earl Long of Louisiana whimsically suggested massive spending for two highway systems, one reserved for drunks. Johnson's economic advisers assured him that the unprecedented surpluses would continue indefinitely. Pointing to the great success of the 1964 tax cut, which seemed to demonstrate their ability to put their theories into practice, the "new" economists claimed that, through Keynesian "demand management," they had discovered the secret of constant noninflationary growth. In short, the continuing surplus created by "demand management" meant that poverty could be abolished without undue sacrifice from the rest of the population. There would be a "maximum of reform with a minimum of social disruption."

While the economists were guiding the fiscal ship of state, their fellow experts, the sociologists, devised programs to provide the poor with nutritional aid, health and schooling benefits, job training, and even dignity and respect. The programs were institutionalized as part of Johnson's Economic Opportunity Act of 1964. The act appropriated nearly a billion dollars for projects such as the Head Start program to assist disadvantaged preschoolers, the Job Corps for high school dropouts, a domestic Peace Corps—

Volunteers in Service to America (VISTA)—a Neighborhood Youth Corps, and a Community Action Program designed for the "maximum feasible participation" by the poor it was meant to aid.

Flushed by his legislative successes, LBJ headed into the 1964 presidential campaign by asking for even broader social measures as part of what he called "The Great Society." Like Kennedy's New Frontier, the Great Society was a presidential answer to the quest for national and thus in many cases individual purpose in an increasingly secular age. It was to be the fulfillment of the American creed of equal opportunity—a grand mobilization of expertise, this time to fight poverty and disease, as depression, fascism, and Communism had been fought previously. In LBJ's own inspiring words: "This nation . . . has man's first chance to create a Great Society: a society of success without squalor, beauty without barrenness, of genius without the wretchedness of poverty. We can open the doors of learning. We can open the doors of opportunity and closed community—not just to the privileged few, but, thank God, we can open doors to everyone." Rhetoric (glorious though it was) aside, Johnson's proposals for a Great Society hinged on passing a twenty-five-year backlog of liberal Democratic legislation on health, education, racial discrimination, and conservation that had been sitting on the rear burner ever since the New Deal flame was snuffed out by the Republican/ Dixiecrat coalition in 1937.

The Great Society program, which vested vast new powers in the federal government, promised to rearrange the relationship between Washington and the rest of the nation. For American liberals the growth of federal power meant the chance to complete the racial reforms begun by Reconstruction and the economic reforms begun by the New Deal without a fundamental restructuring of American society. But for many others, those who "understood the American creed, not as a common set of national values, but as a justification for their particular set of local values," the Great Society proved to be deeply unsettling. Their fears, however, were never fully aired, nor was Johnson given the chance to build a national consensus for the Great Society, because Barry Goldwater, his opponent in 1964, gave LBJ the enormous advantage of running as a social reformer while still seeming to be the less radical of the two.

Johnson's Republican opposition came from a group of youth activists deeply opposed to American policies in Vietnam and bitterly hostile to what they called the "Establishment," symbolized by Nelson Rockefeller. Their movement was directed by Stephen Shadeg, who had been heavily influenced by the thought and tactics of Chairman Mao. Their candidate, described by conservative William Buckley as one of "the few genuine radicals in American life," was Barry Morris Goldwater, junior senator from Arizona.

The Goldwater movement was built on the strength of the old Taftite right, the "veterans of the thirty years' war with the New Deal." Like Taft, Goldwater would say, "Yes, I fear Washington, more than I fear Moscow." But most of all Goldwater feared what he saw as Moscow's influence in Washington, so that as a first-term senator he was one of the diehards who opposed the censure of McCarthy after almost the entire Senate had turned against the demagogue from Wisconsin. The old right had been repeatedly defeated, in its struggle to control the Republican Party, by what it called the Eastern establishment, otherwise known as the "two-bit New Dealers" or "me-too Republicans." But in 1964 the Goldwater movement defeated the Rockefeller Republicans by mobilizing two new political elements: nouveau riche anti-union oilmen and aerospace men of the Southwest, and ideologically charged conservative youth.

Like their left-wing counterparts, these young conservatives disdained the soft society of welfarism with all its compromises and government paternalism. They complained of a "sickness in our society and the lack of a common purpose" that might "restore inner meaning to every man's life in a time too often rushed, too often obsessed with petty needs and material greeds." Contemptuous of businessmen who placed profit before free market ethics, they dreamed of a world made whole by the heroic deeds of rugged individuals untrammeled by the heavy hand of the state. Their allies, the Texas oilmen and aerospace entrepreneurs, however, were beneficiaries of vast government subsidies such as the oil-depletion allowance. But both were united in their hostility to the Rockefeller wing of the Republican Party. And both subscribed to the notion that only a laissez-faire economy could create the disciplined individuals with the character and fortitude necessary to sustain democracy. Politics for the activists was not so much a matter of pursuing material interests as a national screen on which to project their deepest cultural fears. They were part of a mood, a mood of deluxe puritanism, as much as an ideology, and in the words of Richard Whalen, "Barry Goldwater was the favorite son of their state of mind."

But even with his activists and oilmen, Goldwater, like Taft before him, might have lost the nomination if it hadn't been for the first nationwide stirrings of a white backlash against the civil rights movement. Interest in Goldwater was flagging when Alabama's Governor George Wallace, a flaming segregationist, made a surprising showing in liberal Wisconsin's Democratic primary. The Wallace showing revived interest in Goldwater, who was seen as the Republican most opposed to federal intervention on behalf of Afro-Americans. When Goldwater was nominated, Wallace's candidacy collapsed, suggesting a considerable overlap in the two men's donors and constituencies. Tall, trim, and handsome, the altogether affable Goldwater was not personally a bigot. A member of the NAACP, Goldwater was the kind of terribly sincere fellow everyone likes to have for a neighbor or fraternity brother. He came to popular attention by spearheading congressional criticism of Walter Reuther and by his outspoken calls for a holy crusade against Communism in general and Castro in particular. But as Goldwater told reporter Joseph Alsop: "You know, I haven't really got a first-class brain." And it showed. His combination of bland and outrageous statements alienated all but the right wing of the Republican Party from his candidacy. He could in the same speech assert that "where fraternities are not allowed, Communism flourishes" and then, warming to his message, suggest that nuclear weapons be used against Cuba, China, and North Vietnam if they refused to accede to American demands. Goldwater was unafraid of voicing unpopular views. He called for the abolition of the TVA, an end to the graduated income tax, and the elimination of Social Security, while campaigning forthrightly for the elimination of the union shop. "My aim," he said, "is not to pass laws but to repeal them." Here, in the words of Phyllis Schlafly, was "a choice and not an echo."

There was really no need for Johnson to criticize Goldwater's campaign for being too radical. Goldwater did it for him, proclaiming on national TV that "extremism in the defense of liberty is no vice." When the Goldwaterites adopted the slogan "In your hearts you know he's right," Democrats responded with "In your guts you know he's nuts." Johnson replied to Goldwater's "no substitute for victory" rhetoric on Vietnam with a proclamation of restraint. "We are not," LBJ told the American people, "about to send American boys nine or ten thousand miles from home to do what Asian boys ought to be doing for themselves." It is a virtual replay of the Truman-MacArthur struggle, with the same outcome.

With the successful focusing of the campaign on Goldwater's artless "shoot from the lip" pronouncements—"The child has no right to an education; in most cases he will get along very well without it"—Johnson's own measures at home and abroad went undebated. It was a curious consequence of the 1964 campaign that the fundamental issues raised by both Johnson's social innovations and Goldwater's ideological thrust went almost unnoticed, producing a curiously empty campaign which ironically denied Johnson the opportunity to build support for the Great Society. The consensus that emerged instead was that Barry Goldwater was unfit for office. The reaction to Goldwater was so broadly negative that the party which once denounced "economic royalists" now found Wall Street and big business flocking to its banner. Johnson attracted the nation's corporate elite in creating what Oscar Gass has called a Grossblock, a coalition of upper-middle-class professionals and lower-middle-class blue-collar workers, big business and labor, Catholics and Protestants, blacks and whites outside the Deep South, in a national replication of the Texas Democratic Party's "one big tent."

LBJ swept to victory with 61 percent of the vote, only 5 points short of doubling Goldwater's total. The Democrats gained 2 seats in the Senate and 37 in the House, creating enormous Democratic majorities.

LBJ's victory was so overwhelming that commentators openly speculated about the impending death of both conservatism and the Republican Party. We are left, said one observer, with a "one and a half party system." But an analysis of local voting patterns revealed something very different. On a host of social issues, ranging from prayer in the public schools to calls for cutting federal expenditures and reducing welfare spending, the electorate was far closer to Goldwater than to Johnson. Goldwater the candidate was repudiated, but on a local level conservatism was intact and even thriving. In California, for instance, areas which went strongly for LBJ also voted to repeal the state's anti-discriminatory fair housing laws by a better than two-to-one margin. Similarly, in Maryland, areas which had supported George Wallace when he made his strong showing in the Democratic primary there went overwhelmingly for LBJ in the general election. These Maryland voters were in favor of the civil rights bill even as they feared black militancy.

Goldwater's defeat was of such proportion that ironically it served to break the hold conservative Democrats held over their own party. So many Northern liberals triumphed in congressional races against Republicans "dragged down by Barry" that for the first time the Democrats had clear majorities in both houses without having to rely on their Dixiecrat allies. On the other hand, Goldwater, by piggybacking his right-to-work rhetoric on George Wallace's states' rights racism, had carried the Deep South, breaking the Democrats' century-long hold over that region. And while the Goldwater campaign rhetoric was most noted for its fire-eating foreign policy, it was Goldwater's appeal to the white backlash against black militancy that had garnered most of his votes North and South.

Lyndon Johnson was keenly aware that the American political system's balance of powers had been designed for stalemate. As a young congressman, he had seen FDR, at the height of his power, humbled when he tried to pack the Supreme Court. Johnson realized that unless he moved quickly to take advantage of his landslide victory, the naturally parochial tendencies of the Congress would block his Great Society initiatives. Johnson moved rapidly to circumvent the established interests in Congress. Instead of asking congressmen for legislative proposals, he organized task forces composed of administration aides and social reform academics to draw up legislation which would then be presented to the sachems as a fait accompli. Or as LBJ put it to his aides, "I want to see a whole bunch of coonskins on the wall."

The programs Johnson deemed most important were Medicare to protect the elderly from catastrophic losses and aid to elementary education to upgrade the schooling for both black and white poor. Legislation for Medicare and aid to elementary education had been proposed by Democrats ever since the mid-1940s but had always met fierce opposition from the American Medical Association and proponents of states' rights. Johnson knew that if he won on these two issues, "the momentum," as historian Jim Heath has put it, "would carry over, making it relatively easy to enact the rest of his legislative program." As before, the powerful AMA put up a tenacious fight against any form of federally guaranteed health insurance for the elderly, portraying it as a step on the road to socialized medicine. But Johnson, aided by the wily Wilbur Mills, of the House Ways and Means Committee, not only got Medicare passed; in a little-noticed maneuver, Medicaid, health care for the indigent, was tacked on. LBJ flew to Independence, Missouri, to sign the bill in front of a smiling Harry S. Truman. On January 12, 1965, only five days after the Medicare legislation was approved, LBJ sent the politically explosive aid to elementary education bill to the Congress. Part and parcel of the War on Poverty, the bill was opposed by Protestant fundamentalists who wanted to deny federal money to the Catholic schools and by segregationists who saw Washington's money as the beginning of federal control over local schools. Here Johnson, aided by Senator Wayne Morse, achieved what the senator called a "back-door victory," by overtly ignoring racial and religious questions in order to target money regionally on the basis of population below the poverty level in a given area.

With Medicare and aid to education passed, Johnson moved quickly to complete what critics called his "revolution from above." If the word "revolution" was overblown, the critics were right to see that LBJ made unprecedented use of the federal budget. "No previous budget had ever been so contrived to do something for every major economic interest in the nation." But LBJ offered something for almost all his supporters: tax cuts for big business; billions of dollars for Appalachian social and economic development; the first major additions to our national parks and the first comprehensive air and water pollution standards for environmentalists; truth in packaging legislation for consumers; federal aid for mass transit for city dwellers; a subsidy boost for farmers; a National Arts and Humanities Foundation for academics; and, in LBJ's own words, "the goddamnedest toughest voting rights act" and Model Cities, low-cost housing, job-training programs, and slum clearance for blacks. At the end of this spate of legislation, the Democratic leadership on the Hill spoke jubilantly of the "fabulous 89th" Congress as "the Congress of fulfillment," "the Congress of accomplished hopes," "the Congress of realized dreams."

In the words of liberal policy analyst Sar Levitan, a great deal of LBJ's agenda involved "unabashedly class legislation. . . . designating a special group in the population as eligible to receive the benefits of American law." Class legislation was nothing new in American politics—federal insurance for overseas corporate investments and the mortgage tax deduction for homeowners are examples. What was different about the Great Society was that it extended such special benefits to those who were least well off. Johnson's left-wing critics complained that in order to aid the poor, his legislation provided a windfall for a multitude of contractors and middlemen who ultimately were the greatest beneficiaries. There is a good deal of truth to this charge. The doctors who fought Medicaid so bitterly were to number among its prime beneficiaries. Building contractors often became wealthy through Model Cities renewal efforts. This said, however, it is unlikely that any of the legislation directed at alleviating poverty could have passed a Congress composed of men representing American business and middle-class interests unless they too were cut in on federal largess.

Johnson, the adventurous conservative, was denounced as a "Red" by fiscal conservatives and simply a pork-barrel New Dealer by leftists, but both charges were wide of the mark. The New Deal was designed to aid widows, orphans, and the indigent; in short, it represented help for those worst off without addressing the underlying issues of social fairness. The Great Society, without being socialist, tried to partially redefine the structure of opportunity in America. Its aim was not simply to provide handouts to the poor; rather, it attempted to make the competitive race of life a bit fairer. The Great Society had a dramatic effect in relieving poverty. From 1964 to 1968 more than 14 million Americans moved out of poverty as the proportion of the impoverished was halved from 22 to 11 percent of the nation. Just as FDR's New Deal had incorporated working-class immigrants and organized them into the mainstream of American life, LBJ's Great Society tried to do the same for blacks and the poverty-stricken.

By 1945 black demands for civil rights had become undeniable. The reasoned and dignified struggle for full citizenship, pursued with great courage and nobility, evoked widespread admiration. The black leadership and particularly Dr. King came to be revered by liberals eager to atone for past failings and awed by King's combination of shrewdness and moral grandeur. With formal freedoms attained, the focus shifted to the equivalent of the nineteenth century's "forty acres and a mule"—that is, to economic citizenship, and in particular to the problems of the Northern ghettos, where, in the words of Martin Luther King, there was the threat of "social catastrophe."

In June 1965 Lyndon Johnson was an uncrowned monarch at the height of his power. Respected, if not idolized, by liberals who found him too vulgar, he enjoyed an extraordinary sway over Congress, and the country enjoyed an unprecedented prosperity. The initial agenda for the Great Society had been nearly completed, and amid projections of greater budget surpluses to come there were promises of even more sweeping social programs. It seemed that the small war raging in Asia could be brought to a successful conclusion. On June 4, 1965, Johnson, responding to fears about the social disintegration of the black city slums, gave a memorable address at Howard University, an address that records the high-water mark of the possibilities for an American social democracy. Referring to the Voting Rights Act, which was generally taken to be the keystone of civil rights legislation, Johnson declared that it was not an end but a beginning: "Freedom is not enough. You do not wipe away the scars of centuries by saying, 'Now you are free to go where you want, do as you desire' . . . You do not take a person who for years has been hobbled by chains and liberate him, bring him up to the starting line of a race and say, 'You are free to compete with all the others,' and still believe that you have been completely fair." "The country," he said, "had to move beyond opportunity to achievement. . . . This is the next and more profound stage of the battle for civil rights. We do not seek just freedom, but opportunity. Not just equality as a right and theory, but equality as fact and as result."

On August 6, LBJ signed legislation for a comprehensive voting rights bill whose sweep and enforcement powers were barely dreamed of a decade earlier. On August 9, large-scale rioting broke out in Watts, the black section of Los Angeles. Remarkably enough and unrealized at the time, Johnson's kingdom had begun to crumble.

There had been large-scale race rioting in 1919, 1935, and 1943 and some minor civil disturbances in the summer of 1964, but it was widely assumed that the reforms of the Great Society had made such outbursts a thing of the past. Watts shook that complacency. The issue of race was far more intractable than had appeared. Watts was not a typical ghetto. Despite its poverty—30 percent of the adult males were unemployed—Watts was better off than other ghettos. Its neat rows of small freestanding houses were a far cry from the crowded crumbling tenements of most of the nation's big cities. Blacks in Los Angeles held a quarter of the jobs in the city government; there were black councilmen, assemblymen, and congressmen. A largely black organization, the National Urban League, just a year earlier had rated Los Angeles the best major city for blacks to live in. In short, Los Angeles was considered a model of racial progress yet a bloody riot had erupted there. Thirty-five people were killed, six hundred buildings were looted, thousands were arrested, and fires blazed everywhere during the five days of turmoil.

The liberals who had supported the civil rights movement were thrown off balance by Watts and the riots that followed in Chicago, Philadelphia, Newark, Cleveland, Detroit, and other cities. In Detroit, the home of relatively well-to-do black auto workers, the rioting lasted for a week and more than forty people, almost all of them black, were killed. Like a river which overflows its banks and cuts a new channel, the emotions that filled the civil rights movement overflowed their original forms. Young rioters in Watts talked about the extraordinary sense of power and liberation they had enjoyed, in much the same manner that civil rights workers earlier had talked of a "Freedom High."

The prophet of regeneration through violence was Malcolm Little, a former convict turned Black Muslim, whose eloquence rivaled that of King himself. While March on Washington organizer Bayard Rustin spoke of the need for a grand coalition of blacks and whites to seize the moment and begin remaking American society, Malcolm X (he rejected his family's slavery-derived surname) talked of a rage and a chasm between whites and blacks so great as to be unbridgeable by white goodwill.

"The best accuser of the white man," Malcolm X insisted that brutalized blacks wanted, not justice, but revenge. Too much had been done to talk of forgiveness. Liberal reformers, he said, might provide bread, but they could do nothing to restore the manhood that had been stripped from blacks. Africans, he advised, had freed themselves physically and spiritually through violent struggle; Afro-Americans should do no less. Placing a Trotskyite twist on the invocations of earlier generations of black nationalists, he called on the Third World to redress the injustices of the First. In this struggle, blacks were not a groveling minority petitioning humbly for the relief of their grievances, but part of an aroused world majority whose struggle would reshape the globe. Less grandiloquently, he told his followers: "If someone puts a hand on you, send him to the cemetery." In February 1965, Malcolm X was assassinated by rival Black Muslims.

Until Watts, harsh voices like Malcolm X's were drowned out by the sweet melodies of the conspicuously middle-class civil rights marchers. The disciplined and dignified fight against Jim Crow was carried on in the name of liberal fair play. Demonstrations and protests were aimed at anachronisms, those segregated facilities in hotels, libraries, and terminals that impeded the mobility of the middle-class black. In the South, activists used a moral jujitsu to turn the violence of the "Bull" Connors to their advantage, but in the North, the march, the demonstration, the sit-in were useless in the face of the sometimes subtle web of repressions which ensnared inner-city blacks. Watts seemed to break through all that. The riots brought quick results: TV attention, ministrations and money from numerous social agencies, and promises of jobs and "consultantships" from worried businessmen.

Older leaders like Rustin and A. Philip Randolph and the leaders of main-line civil rights organizations like the NAACP and the Urban League warned blacks that the riots were a false dawn. But for young militants intoxicated by pictures of the black masses seemingly taking power, however briefly, into their own hands, the riots promised personal and political rebirth. For increasing numbers of angry young blacks, it now seemed possible to reject not only middle-class leadership but integration as well. For would-be Castros and their white supporters who saw the black masses as the "suffering servants of humanity," the riots read not merely as rough retributive justice but as the opening act of a revolutionary scenario. In the overheated words of LeRoi Jones, the rioters were the "fellaheen of modernity," the propertyless dispossessed whose anger would overthrow the ancient regime and cleanse the world. In this view the unwitting guardians of the old order were the liberals, the modern-day Girondists and Mensheviks who would have to give way before the revolutionary tide. This was, to say the least, a fanciful scenario in a country where only 11 percent of the population was black and where the heirs of the former slaves were divided by a double consciousness which made them both deeply American and African.

A large number of black leaders, however, independent of their position on the question of revolution, saw the riots as a chance to escape the demeaning rhetoric designed to show that black people were fit to join American society. They now turned the question around and asked stunned liberals "whether American middle-class society was fit for them." Or as James Baldwin put it: "Do I really want to be integrated into a burning house." The saccharine harmony of the civil rights movement ("We—meaning black and white together—shall overcome") was replaced by a call for black autonomy, or what came to be called Black Power.

◦ Loosely speaking, Black Power was the social therapy of self-assertion. Black, not white, was beautiful. In its exotic forms it glorified the untrammeled sexuality of the black hipster and denounced the uptight morality of a sexually shriveled middle-class America. In its most extreme forms, people like former civil rights leader Stokely Carmichael talked of wanting "to smash everything Western civilization had created." More modestly, Black Power simply meant that blacks should cultivate their own garden. Instead of working toward integration, its advocates wanted blacks to take control of their own neighborhoods and schools and forge a black nation within a nation. This was a declaration of independence from traditional coalition politics. "We don't need white liberals," Carmichael told his followers. "We have to make integration irrelevant."

Radical in rhetoric—Black Power militants like Roy Innis, Carmichael, and H. Rap Brown became famous for talking about nonnegotiable demands and "white capitalist pigs"—Black Power proved surprisingly compatible with white corporate interests.

A.T.&T. funded the first national Black Power conference in the summer of 1967, and the Ford Foundation backed numerous Black Power demonstration projects, including the educationally disastrous and socially divisive decentralization of the New York City school system. While middle America was aghast at the "Look out, whitey, Black Power's gonna get your mama" rhetoric, corporate America saw that the "expressive" politics of cultural self-assertion posed no real threat to established business practices. The psychodrama of threat and accommodation captured the public eye, and corporate leaders were roundly criticized for symbolically caving in to extremist blackmail. What wasn't obvious was the enormous disparity between the volume and grandiosity of the rhetoric and the modesty of the specific demands being made. For the price of "consultantships" and the promise to do more in the future, corporate leaders were able to soothe their consciences and present themselves as courageous, socially concerned citizens, while militants, continuing to drone on about all the awful things that would happen if their demands weren't met, could produce patronage and a stream of small victories for their followers. Thus was the momentum of a great social movement dissipated by pretension, nationalist fantasies, and a thinly disguised paternalism. "It was one of those fascinating alliances into which the parties stumble, half consciously and half by design, and which are the stuff of a major turning point in politics."

The friendship with the "Princes of Power" called for by such respected black leaders as Kenneth Clark was glued together by an implicit agreement that racism—that is, white American middle-class culture—was both the historical and contemporary source of most black problems. This emphasis on white racism, ratified by the presidential commission which studied the riots and whose report was trumpeted with great force and enthusiasm by the major media, came at a time when, by almost any measure, racism was declining dramatically. The appeal of racism as the all-purpose explanation for black problems was that it promised so much to so many at so small a cost. For corporate leaders, proposals for major economic changes were displaced by those aimed at changing attitudes, something that comes easily to the well educated; similarly, upper-middle-class Democrats found it a marvelous club to use on their old-line political enemies who hadn't yet caught on to the new racial etiquette. For ministers and social workers, "soul doctors" in the "helping professions," the emphasis on white racism as something akin to a social disease was a boon to their hopes for ministering to a "sick" society. But perhaps most important, for the increasingly "nationalist" black middle class, it served the purpose of obscuring the broad class differences within the black community, while it freed black Americans of any responsibility for their own plight.

The officially endorsed fight against racism, highly laudatory in and of itself, tended to reduce deep-seated social and economic problems to a question of false consciousness on the part of lower-middle-class whites. And just as important, it redefined the broad anti-poverty thrust of the Great Society initiatives solely in terms of black problems. The initiatives against discrimination in housing and employment, cut off from a broader policy, came to be looked on as exclusively matters of black self-interest or, even worse, special privilege. Rather than representing a revolutionary extension of the Great Society, Black Power and its accompanying emphasis on racism, proved the source of its unraveling. By directing the currents of reform into narrowly defined "black only" channels, it undercut its own popular and moral basis of support while laying the foundation for a broadly based attack on social reform.

The further irony of Black Power is that the therapeutic struggle against white racism derailed the possibility of New Deal-style public works projects which might have provided honorable employment for unskilled blacks while rebuilding the infrastructure of the economically moribund cities they were trapped in. Campaigns against discrimination in employment and housing and make-work job-training programs had little effect on the lives of the bottom 60 percent of the black population. In the postwar years the black community was increasingly divided between a slowly rising lower middle and middle class and the vast number of former migrants from the Deep South who never managed to get an economic toehold in the city.

The migration to the city, with its sometimes illusory freedoms and rearrangements of traditional social patterns, produced a high rate of family and social breakdowns for virtually all ethnic groups, from the Irish of Dublin and Boston to the Russian Jews settling in London and New York. But unlike the earlier immigrants, for whom the city provided the first step up on the ladder of mobility, the black peasantry which had been brutally driven off the farms of the South by mechanization and depression in the 1930s, 1940s, and 1950s arrived in cities where the demand for unskilled labor was fast disappearing. "Perhaps never in history," said Richard Wright, "has a more unprepared folk wanted to go to the city."

What made the black migrants to the city so sharply different was that only they faced the probability of long-term inter-generational unemployment. The consequent social breakdown of those families unfortunate enough to be headed by continually unemployed fathers produced family dissolution on an unprecedented scale. In Watts, for example, the proportion of children under eighteen living with both parents dropped from 56 percent in 1960, already a low figure, to 44 percent in 1965 and it continued to fall. Temporarily obscured by the rhetoric of "black is beautiful," this process of family dissolution began to feed on itself, laying the basis for the long-term social catastrophe King had warned about.

The 1966 mid-term congressional elections revealed just how much the nation's anti-poverty effort owed to the Goldwater debacle which allowed LBJ to ram major reforms through the Congress. The grass-roots opposition to statism and extensive social welfare programs was undiminished even when the Great Society rode high in the Washington saddle. When the moral logic of civil rights and the political pressures produced by the riots led the government to impose itself on the organization of life at the local level through fair housing and school integration measures, home-town conservatism moved back into the national arena and the groundwork was laid for a right-wing revival.

The Republicans, implying that Johnson's poverty programs

were largely responsible for the riots, turned the election into a referendum on the Great Society and "crime in the streets." House Republican leader Gerald R. Ford captured the tone of the campaign when he asked, "How long are we going to abdicate law and order—the backbone of civilization—in favor of a social theory that the man who heaves a brick through your window is simply the misunderstood and underprivileged product of a broken home?" It was a theme that played brilliantly on the resentments of white urban ethnics who were angered by the way the riots, which often took place on the edge of their neighborhoods, produced more financial rewards than arrests. But it was the "theories" that Ford referred to, the tendency of guilt-ridden reformers to rationalize all black demands, which infuriated urban ethnics most and threatened to divide the Democratic Party between low-income "bread and butter" white Democrats trapped in the burning cities and the New Politics heirs of the Stevensonian tradition of high-minded reform.

The elections were a disaster for the Democrats. Forty-five members of the House who had supported the poverty programs lost their seats, "an emphatic message to the survivors." The GOP gained 47 seats in the House and 3 in the Senate, while the balance in the statehouses shifted from a 33–17 Democratic advantage to an even split. Most unnerving for liberals was that longtime civil rights advocate Senator Paul Douglas of Illinois was defeated by a "determined" white rebellion against "open occupancy housing." The election brought forth a panoply of new conservative spokesmen, including Ronald Reagan, who became governor of California in a landslide. Reagan had directed his campaign against welfare chiselers and big government.

The political meaning of the election was obscured, however, because it was soon overshadowed by the increasingly unpopular war in Vietnam and the spectacular efflorescence of the "youth culture."

9

Vietnam at Home and Abroad

I knew from the start that I was bound to be crucified either way I moved. If I left the woman I really loved—the Great Society—in order to get involved with that bitch of a war on the other side of the world, then I would lose everything at home. But if I left that war and let the Communists take over South Vietnam, then I would be seen as a coward and my nation would be seen as an appeaser and we would both find it impossible to accomplish anything for anybody anywhere on the entire globe.

—LBJ

THERE IS NO DOUBT where Lyndon Johnson's priorities lay. Unlike Kennedy, who had a fascination with foreign policy and a fondness for the martial virtues, Johnson, the "fixer," the aficionado of "wheeling and dealing," was firmly rooted in domestic politics. From the start Johnson recognized that the post-election honeymoon with Congress and the American people would be short. So he was constantly exhorting an already pliant Congress to move even faster on his legislative proposals while doing as much as his wooden speaking style would allow to create popular support for his programs. This urgency and public volubility on domestic matters stood in sharp contrast to his stand on foreign affairs. In his first two state-of-the-union addresses he barely mentioned Vietnam. With the support of the New York *Times* and the Washington *Post*, he effectively ridiculed Goldwater's proposals for escalating what was still very much a back-burner affair. In private Johnson's views on Vietnam were not much different than Goldwater's, but determined above all to buy time for the Great

Society, he avoided making the war into an issue which would derail his reform plans.

Johnson, though less interested in foreign policy than Kennedy, was no less a believer in the doctrine of containment. To the lessons of Munich he added those of China and Korea. Truman, as he quite correctly understood it, had been destroyed by McCarthyism after the fall of China, because he had refused to apply the universal message of his anti-Communist doctrine to Asia. It was a mistake Johnson was determined not to repeat. "I am not," he told his ambassador to South Vietnam, "going to be the President who saw Vietnam go the way China did." "In the forties and fifties," said Johnson, "we took our stand in Europe to protect the freedom of those threatened by aggression. Now the center of attention has shifted to another part of the world where aggression is on the march. Our stand must be as firm as ever."

Committed to the war against Communism but fearful of the political consequences of escalation, Johnson, faced with a serious decline in the position of America's South Vietnamese ally/puppets, consciously imitated the example set by FDR in leading the United States into World War II. LBJ "took the nation into war by indirection and dissimulation," not to say outright lies. In order to buttress the faltering position of South Vietnam, he stepped up the bombing of the North and directed commando raids against the enemy's coastal installations. It was the North Vietnamese response to one of those commando raids which led to the 1964 Gulf of Tonkin incident, in which Johnson claimed that American ships had been wantonly attacked by the North Vietnamese in an unprovoked assault. Johnson ordered air strikes on the North and placed before Congress a loosely worded resolution giving the President the authority to "take all necessary measures to repel any armed attack against the forces of the United States and to prevent further aggression." The Gulf of Tonkin resolution, which received overwhelming support in the House (416–0) and Senate (88–2), was not, as is constitutionally mandated, a declaration of war. But it was, as a critic would put it later, a blank check for presidential power. Subsequently it was discovered that Johnson had been carrying the resolution in his pocket for months before the Tonkin affair and was only looking for the excuse to present it.

Johnson never chose to cash the check in for all that it was worth. He never tried to stir the country's deep and abiding anti-Communist passions in support of a major war because he feared that such passions could either push him into a conflict with China or, as he himself put it, give "all those conservatives in Congress . . . a weapon against the Great Society." Instead of following the advice of Kennedy's technologically oriented crisis managers, he ordered a bombing escalation against North Vietnam in what was intended to be "the most carefully calibrated military operation in recent history." This "slow squeeze" strategy was designed not to win the war in any conventional sense but simply to deny Hanoi a victory. For advisers like Robert McNamara, who had earlier argued that "every quantitative measurement we have shows that we are winning the war," it seemed inconceivable that the most powerful nation on earth could be denied such limited objectives. Or, as another adviser, Walter W. Rostow, put it, the certain success of the "slow squeeze" strategy "flows from the simple fact that we are the greatest power in the world—if we behave like it." Faced with this slow, inexorable growth of overwhelming American military might, threatening great destruction in the North, so that argument went, Hanoi would decide to cease its military activities in the South and come to a negotiated settlement. In the words of McGeorge Bundy, the idea was "to keep before Hanoi the carrot of our desisting as well as the stick of continued pressure . . . Once such a policy is put into force, we shall be able to speak in Vietnam on many topics and in many ways with growing force and effectiveness."

The logical force of simultaneous escalation and offers of negotiation was undeniable, but history is not logic and there was no way for McNamara and company, who were ignorant of Vietnamese history, to quantify the extraordinary nationalist élan of the North Vietnamese. (Commenting on the strength of tribal affinities, Murray Kempton quipped, "When the history of the postwar world is written it will be discovered that there were only two superpowers, North Vietnam and Israel.") While the Americans engaged in what was intended to be a passionless war of limited aims, the North Vietnamese, who had been fighting against colonial rule for half a century, were waging a total war in which they were willing to make sacrifices far beyond the rational expectations of the most sophisticated Pentagon computer models. The more we bombed, the more North Vietnamese troops infiltrated the South.

The bombing was designed to limit American casualties by making the dispatch of ground troops unnecessary. But the failure of the bombing to bring the North Vietnamese to the bargaining table and the instability of the South Vietnamese government produced the need for more and more American troops. In late 1965 the new South Vietnamese government of General Thieu and Air Marshal Ky requested 200,000 more American troops (there were already 75,000 in South Vietnam). LBJ reluctantly agreed and he slowly began to increase American troop levels until there were 385,000 by the end of 1966, 486,000 by the end of 1967, and 536,000 by the end of 1968.

Dismayed by the failure of escalation to bring the North Vietnamese to the bargaining table—for their part, the North Vietnamese, insisting on the 1954 Geneva Accords guaranteeing a unified Vietnam, refused to accept the independence of South Vietnam and thus thought there was nothing to negotiate about —Johnson turned to his advisers, who, with few exceptions, insisted that there was no choice but to stay the course. The alternative, American withdrawal, would, Johnson correctly saw, lead to "Communist carnage," a slaughter which would be projected into every living room in the country and which, like the fall of China and the Korean stalemate, was bound to produce, he thought, a powerful right-wing backlash. Rather than move to full-scale war or retreat, Johnson tried to position himself in the middle between what he thought were two politically unacceptable extremes. To prove that his was the only moderate and therefore prudent course, he displayed a mountain of polls which showed that as many as one-third of the American people were in favor of using nuclear weapons if they would shorten the war. Similarly, students, those most likely to have to fight, were not only highly supportive of the war; a majority wanted escalation if it would guarantee victory. In short, the dominant attitude in 1965 was: "End the war as soon as possible, but don't let South Vietnam go Communist."

Roosevelt's New Deal and Truman's Fair Deal had objectives that were mundane if difficult to attain. They were directed at reforming the nation's political and social economy. But beginning in the late 1950s with the "crisis" of national purpose, Presidents and presidential candidates began to speak of something far more ambitious, such as Kennedy's call for national "excellence" as part of the New, spiritually infused, Frontier. Presidential candidates like Goldwater and Johnson talked not merely of organizing the government but of making the society moral or magnificent as part of a national mission which aimed at providing an increasingly technocratic society with a sense of purpose and élan. The Great Society, said Johnson, was to be "a place where the city of man serves not only the needs of the body and the demands of commerce but the desire for beauty and the hunger for community." The idea of the Great Society, then, was not just a campaign slogan; it was a substitute for the older set of political and moral ideals which had been displaced by the corrosive power of technical rationality and by the immediate pleasures of affluent living. In short, the private virtues essential for the public life of a democracy, now eroded, were to be supplied by the state, an extraordinary departure in American political thought. (Shortly the New Left would mimic the moral claims of the Great Society by offering itself as a replacement for those same lost virtues.)

In the new order of things presidencies would no longer be administrations so much as reigns in which the leader was expected to make his mark on the national culture and psyche as well as the budget. But for all its moral rhetoric, the Great Society relied, not on a new reformation, not on popular fervor or individual virtue, but on social scientists and the multiplication of professional/client relationships to achieve many of its ends. And social science, whatever its value, was committed to being just that, a science of society: the objective study of men and women free of moral overtones. The irony, then, of the Great Society offering moral guidance is that the people it unleashed to make the world right were, whatever their personal predilections, themselves committed to the belief that there were no enduring ethical truths. This left the modern citizen without a compelling reason to accept the guidance of the state. It remained a set of institutional arrangements imposing "a bureaucratic unity on a society which lacked a genuine moral consensus, or sense of community."

In pre-modern society, wrote Lionel Trilling, the individual's public and private lives are ordered by a unifying hierarchy of relationships. The compulsions of life, however painful, are seen as part of the natural order of things. But in America of the 1950s the dislocation, uprootedness, and affluence made possible by economic growth severed, for some, the connection between "our local normalities and the inevitable necessities of existence." In the new order, as Walter Lippmann explained, "the compulsions are painful, and as it were accidental, unnecessary, wanton and full of mockery." Specifically then, the inability of the modern techno-cratic state to command assent and respect was exacerbated by the "tension between the extraordinary freedom of choice" enjoyed by the members of the educated middle class in their private lives as consumers and "the seemingly arbitrary and fixed, hence illegiti-mate structures of public institutional life." The state, in the words of one rebel, was like "a giant bell jar which drops overhead and smothers you." "I want," he said, "to determine my own destiny." This search for identity and authenticity, this preoccupation with a continuous geometry of psychic self-placement, provided much of the emotional energy which suffused the 1960s. Youth's simul-taneous and often contradictory search for both moral authority and individual autonomy found a temporary haven in the anti-war movement, which offered the children of the educated upper mid-dle class the promise of personal fulfillment through political re-demption.

In late 1963 and early 1964, pacifist groups led by A. J. Muste, Bayard Rustin, and Dave Dellinger, some of the World War II conscientious objectors who had helped bring the civil rights movement to the fore, responded in kind to the state's claims to moral leadership. They began to protest and demonstrate against what they described as an immoral war in Vietnam. Initially their impact was very limited, so limited that Johnson barely took notice of them even as he fretted about the danger from the hawks while pursuing his policy of "moderation." As late as the spring of 1965 the New York *Times* could baldly state that "no one except a few pacifists here and the North Vietnamese and the Chinese Commu-nists are asking for a precipitate withdrawal. Virtually all Americans understand we must stay in Vietnam at least for the near future." The Washington *Post*, not as yet the political force it was to become, was if anything more hawkish. In its pages David Halberstam, later a major critic of the war, captured the establishment sentiment when he insisted that Vietnam was "vital to U.S. interests." But at the same time, in the spring of 1965, the first sizable demonstrations against the war erupted. Twenty-five thousand attended a Washington rally to applaud speeches by Senators Morse and Gruening, the only members of the Senate to vote against the Tonkin resolution, and radical historian Staughton Lynd, while being entertained by folk singers Joan Baez, Judy Collins, and Phil Ochs.

The demonstration in Washington was preceded by a new type of protest, the teach-in. Begun at the University of Michigan, the teach-ins quickly spread around the nation's universities, drawing large and devout audiences for two- and three-day (and sometimes all-night) academic camp meetings. Often Vietnam was as much the occasion as the reason for these political prayer meetings, where many of the talks were not about the war at all but instead were loosely philosophical discussions touching on the personal experience and sensibility which had drawn the participants together. The students gathered were, in the words of the Port Huron Statement (the founding document of Students for a Democratic Society), "bred in at least modest comfort," but looked with unease on the world they inherited. That comfort, the speakers insisted, had been purchased at an inordinate price. They argued that everyone had been diminished by the comforts that almost all had enjoyed. In the fairy-tale 1950s, it was said, America had won luxury and lost its soul. In the spirit of Wadsworth and the Romantics, they insisted that the mechanical progress which seemed to have benefited the whole of society had impoverished the individual.

The talks which drew the greatest applause were generally those in which the speaker began by announcing that he knew little about the war except that it was evil and then went on in stock existential language to decry a "universe bereft of purpose and moral law," a universe in which man was adrift in an adventure which, as Camus's Rebel had foreseen, "was bound to have an unhappy ending." Those gathered were urged to overcome "the

inner alienation" that was said to define American life. In 1953
Norman Mailer, writing about alienation, seemed to hunger for a
visible enemy when he said: ". . . the artist feels most alienated
when he loses the sharp sense of what he is alienated from. . . .
Today the enemy is vague, the work seems done, the audience more
sophisticated than the writer . . . Really the history of the 20th
century seems made to be ignored." In the Vietnam War, Mailer
found both the visible enemy and the larger audience for his rumi-
nations that he had yearned for. In a speech ostensibly devoted to
the war, he told an attentive crowd that the mind-numbing nature
of modern society was behind both the war and "that particular
corrosive sensation so many of us feel in the chest and the guts so
much of the time, that sense of the body grown empty within,
and of the psyche pierced by a wound whose dimensions keep
opening." This sense of being "part of the living dead," as one
student from an ostensibly privileged background put it, was explained by Daniel Boorstin as a by-product of the contemporary
world: "Everything about our lives becomes more attenuated
[because] as central heating and air conditioning assimilate winter
and summer, as canning and deep freezing homogenize the diets
of the seasons, as television reduces the difference between being
here and being there . . . our whole world is flattened out." For
anti-war students the symbol of that flattening was the way they
had "become wrapped in numbers, statistics, reduced to standardized digits for social security, student IDs, test scores . . ."

✦ Trapped in what Hegel called the "unhappy consciousness" of
alienated souls whose skepticism has cut them off from the past
without providing a path to the future, the anti-war students
turned to the "redemptive" communities created in the civil rights
struggle as models for their own salvation. A Rutgers professor
drew cheers when he quoted T. S. Eliot, asking, "What life have
you, if you have not life together? There is no life that is not in
community." Similarly the historian of American foreign policy
William Appleman Williams drew the loudest cheers at a Wisconsin teach-in, not when he talked of American imperialism, but
when he proclaimed that "we have the makings of a community
here." In the midst of this quite literally desperate desire for fel-
lowship and legitimate authority, some of the more enthusiastic participants proclaimed that the teach-ins themselves were liberated

said, that "the *Reader's Digest* and Lawrence Welk and Hilton Hotels are organically connected with the Special Forces napalming villages." In a similar vein, Norman Mailer made white bread, as Charles Reich would later make homogenized peanut butter, the symbol of psychic repression at home and murderous imperialism abroad. White bread, said Mailer, was the embodiment of the demonic corporate power "which took the taste and crust out of bread and wrapped the remains in waxed paper and was, at the far extension of the same process, the same mentality which was out in Asia escalating, defoliating . . . White bread," he added, "was also television."

Lyndon Johnson's ambitious temperament and resolutely pragmatic intelligence cut him off from the world of the anti-Vietnam protesters. He was bewildered by their view of the world and stunned by the ferocity of their protests. To his dismay he found that the protests in the streets were escalating apace with the heightened bombing. Students publicly burned their draft cards despite the threat of jail and a five-thousand-dollar fine. And when the buildup of ground forces required the drafting of more students, demonstrators blocked the entrances to army installations and draft headquarters as the anti-war protest coalesced into something like a mass movement. But perhaps most upsetting of all was the marchers' taunt of "Hey, hey, LBJ, how many kids did you kill today!" By the end of 1966, at the very time that his civil rights program was coming under heavy attack, Johnson was unable to leave Washington without first having his aides carefully check to see if his appearance would set off firestorms of protest. Almost imprisoned in the White House, Johnson complained that he was "in the position of a jackrabbit in a hailstorm, hunkered up and taking it."

Faced with a deep split in the Democratic constituency between old-line Democrats supportive of the war but critical of Great Society civil rights ardor and New Class, New Politics Democrats heartily in favor of even stronger civil rights measures but bitterly critical of the war, Johnson chose not to choose between "guns and butter." Instead he characteristically tried to reconcile the two by offering the Vietnamese a version of the

Great Society. Promising a billion dollars in American aid and investment, he called upon the North Vietnamese to lay down their arms and join him in building a TVA on the Mekong. He was baffled by the North Vietnamese refusal to accept American generosity. "I don't understand," he said. "George Meany would've grabbed at a deal like that . . ." At home leaders of the Mobilization Against the War were only further enraged, describing the offer as "welfare state imperialism." Frustrated, Johnson lashed out at the elite media, the networks, the New York *Times*, and the Washington *Post*. He accused them of glamourizing the protesters while vilifying our almost forgotten allies, the South Vietnamese government.

The prestige press's coverage was shoddy from its pro-war beginnings to its anti-war end, but by themselves neither the media nor the anti-war protesters were the source of the President's difficulties. The obvious disgust with which many of the protesters looked upon Amerika, as it was spelled in demonstrations, produced more rather than less support for rallying around the President in time of war. But the protesters did succeed in pushing the war to the forefront of American politics, forcing the Administration to provide a convincing justification for the fighting. This was Johnson's real problem, for it was something he was unable to do. Like Truman during the Korean War, he was unable to provide a satisfying rationale for limited war. Hawks wanted to know why he was holding back. Surely if hostilities against North Vietnam were justified, a constitutionally mandated declaration of war and then an all-out assault would quickly settle the issue. But if North Vietnam was only a shadow opponent, then why not go after the real enemies, Russia and China? But if the Russian empire was a mortal foe, why had Johnson announced a policy of "bridge-building to the East," a forerunner of détente, in the midst of the war? And if it wasn't Russia or China per se that we were fighting but something called world Communism, how could the sharp Sino-Soviet split be explained and why were we continuing to trade with the Communist countries of Eastern Europe, including the Soviet Union? In the end the Administration was left with the unconvincing specter of the "Asiatic hordes" or what Secretary of State Dean Rusk described as a "militant, and riots in August, "it was as if the future waited on the first of each month to deliver events completely unforeseen the month before." The second of those events following Tet was Eugene McCarthy's "victory" in the New Hampshire primary.

In the months before Tet, Allard Lowenstein, an energetic New Politics liberal, former national chairman of Students for Stevenson who had been prominent in the civil rights movement, hastened back and forth across the United States looking for a prominent fellow liberal willing to lead a "dump Johnson" movement. His own choice was Robert Kennedy, who made no bones about his distaste for the "usurper" in the White House, but Kennedy refused to risk his career by opposing a sitting President. In the end Lowenstein found that only Eugene McCarthy, the poet-politician from Minnesota, was willing to take on the fight. A quixotic figure, culturally in the mold of Adlai Stevenson, McCarthy was in effect a "back bench" senator without substantial influence. A latecomer to the anti-war cause, he was more conservative than Johnson on social policy; his view of politics flowed from an almost Tory bemusement with American mythology. When he spoke of the "limits of American power" he referred not so much to military and strategic realities as to a consumer culture whose citizens were so self-absorbed as to be unwilling to make the sacrifices empire demanded. Kennedy would eventually offer himself as the leader who could "redeem" America. But for McCarthy "the public spirit of America [was] so decayed as to not be worth trying to lead." From early January 1968, when he announced his candidacy, to late January and Tet, his campaign languished.

With the broad and bitter reaction to Tet, McCarthy's fortunes soared. In New Hampshire, the setting for the crucial first Democratic primary in March, he taunted the Administration. "Only a few months ago," he said, "we were told [by LBJ] 65 percent of the [South Vietnamese] population was secure. Now we know that even the American Embassy is not secure." Still shunned by established politicians, he reached out to a "coalition of conscience" —a counter-establishment of scientists, academics, educators, the mobile post-World War II college class—by proclaiming: "Whatever is morally necessary [that is, ending the war] must be made politically possible." His supporters included folk singers Peter, Paul, and Mary, poet Robert Lowell, the editor of the *Harvard* the size and power of the surprise attack the battle had resulted in a victory for his forces. He was again half right. As the Washington *Post*'s Don Oberdorfer explained it, the Vietnamese and their Vietcong/NLF allies "lost the best of a generation of resistance fighters, and . . . because the people of the cities did not rise up against the foreigners and puppets at Tet . . . the Communist claim to a moral and political authority in South Vietnam suffered a serious blow." A high NLF official later explained that the military losses suffered at Tet had been catastrophic. The Vietnamese later admitted to losing 600,000 men between 1965 and 1968, the equivalent of 6 million in American terms. Then why was Westmoreland only half right? Because through a set of double ironies the military defeat for the North Vietnamese was also, in the words on one military expert, the "most disastrous strategic military defeat ever suffered by the United States." Other calamitous defeats, like the surprise Japanese attack on Pearl Harbor, strengthened American resolve, but the North Vietnamese ability even to launch Tet after the government's claims of imminent success acted "like a delayed time fuse" igniting all the doubts that had been smoldering for the past three years. LBJ himself "was to some degree psychologically defeated by the . . . onslaught on the cities of Vietnam," and in the Senate Tet set off "a critical reaction against the validity as well as the credibility of the Administration's policies," so that not even the hawks were able to provide enthusiastic support for Johnson's policies. Walter Cronkite, once a hawk, summed up the prevailing sentiment on the evening news: "It is increasingly clear," he said, "that the only rational way out . . . will be to negotiate . . . not as victors but as an honorable people." If the first irony was that the Vietnamese military defeat was also their great strategic victory, the second was that the offensive designed to set off a rebellion in South Vietnam set one off in the United States instead.

All years are not equal. There are periods when a gathering of events transforms what will come after them. In the history of the Cold War, 1946 was such a year. For the Vietnam War, the year was 1968. In 1968, in the period between the Tet offensive in January and the crescendo of the Democratic national convention

Crimson, and the president of the Dreyfus Fund. They were, in the words of one exuberant reporter, "probably the most intelligent and highly educated group of people who had ever joined together politically in the history of civilization." Their uphill campaign against the Democratic "establishment" in the snows of New Hampshire was a "festival for democracy," a signal event in their lives, and in the life of the nation as well.

McCarthy's anti-war message, self-assured style, and barely concealed sense of natural superiority brought in 5,500 unsolicited votes in the Republican primary, but the real shock was that on the Democratic side this Tory maverick totally bereft of organized party support drew 42.4 percent of the vote to only 49.5 percent for the sitting President. McCarthy's supporters and people in the anti-war movement everywhere were elated. But a closer look at the election results by the Michigan Opinion Research Center found that only 40 percent or about 9,000 of 23,000 McCarthy voters were doves who favored an American withdrawal from Vietnam. Sixty percent of the McCarthy voters were hawks who favored escalating the war but voted for the senator because of their impatience with Johnson's limited-war policies. But for the moment the size and composition of the vote meant far less than that so many Democrats had been willing to vote against the incumbent. It was McCarthy's genius both to expose Johnson's vulnerability and to demonstrate the emerging power of the New Class,* a class Robert Kennedy believed rightfully belonged to him. Within three days Kennedy announced that he too was an anti-war candidate for the presidency.

Robert Kennedy's reluctance to run may have stemmed from a fear that LBJ would use his access to the FBI and CIA to expose the political skeletons in the former Attorney General's closet. Some of the unsavory aspects of Robert Kennedy's past—his committee work for Joe McCarthy, his fanatical, rule-bending pursuit of Jimmy Hoffa, and his would-be warrior's fascination with the grisly business of counterinsurgency (when he worked in his brother's administration he kept a Green Beret on his desk)

---

* I use the term New Class as an example of Max Weber's notion of the *Stand* or status group—that is, "an amorphous but exclusive community distinguished by a common," in this case semi-bohemian, lifestyle. The barriers to entry are barriers of style and standing not wealth per se.

—were known, but what was not as yet public knowledge was his role in Kennedy Inc.'s use of Mafia Inc. to try to rub out Fidel Castro, whom RFK wanted to "get" as badly as Hoffa. And perhaps most damaging, given his transformation into a champion of civil rights, was his illegal wire tapping as Attorney General of Martin Luther King. But for all he had to hide, not least of which was his seminal role in a war he had come to oppose, Kennedy had, in the years since he left LBJ's administration in 1964, become a symbol of hope and encouragement for blacks and Mexican-Americans. Pushed from power by his brother's death, he began to cultivate the politics of morality and moralism seeded by the civil rights movement. It was a measure of how much America had changed in a short half decade, that, as Ronald Steel points out, while brother John hoped to use American power to secure "a grand and global alliance . . . that can assure a more fruitful life for all of mankind," Robert was faced with the task, as he saw it, of trying to save America from itself. The passions he had once reserved for the Green Berets and getting Castro were now directed at eliminating poverty and racism. His new sentiments, which he conveyed so brilliantly, drew the dispossessed, the braceros and ghetto dwellers of America, to him in a way that McCarthy could never hope to match. McCarthy's candidacy represented the growth and coming to self-consciousness of a new political class which, like the rise of labor in the 1930s, was to transform American politics, so in the long run it was the McCarthy and not the Kennedy campaign which was significant. But Kennedy, by dint of his personality, his family aura, and a program combining a tough law-and-order appeal with calls for more social justice, promised, if only briefly, to heal the breach in the Democratic Party and the nation between white ethnics and the New Class and between white ethnics and blacks. "Bobby Kennedy didn't ask them to love one another. He simply asked them to work for what both equally needed: jobs, houses, opportunity —and not at each other's expense." In the short run it was in Kennedy, whose "liberal faith in progress was combined with his Catholic faith in power," that both anti-war and main-line politicians found a candidate through whom they could express their opposition to what had become LBJ's war.

McCarthy and Kennedy threatened LBJ with the humiliating prospect of having to fight to hold on to the presidency, and they accelerated the process of reappraisal already under way at the White House. Shaken by the weakness of the dollar due to the way Vietnam expenditures exacerbated inflation, tensions with the European allies critical of the war, and the breakdown of Soviet-American discussions, Johnson called upon one of the architects of containment, Clark Clifford, to step in and replace Robert McNamara as Secretary of Defense. Sworn in as Secretary on March 1, Clifford, a hard-liner, was quickly dismayed by the doubt and confusion over Vietnam that beset even the inner circles of government and the Pentagon. Clifford prevailed upon Johnson to convene the "Wise Men," "quite literally a Who's Who of the American Establishment," drawn from Wall Street, the big banks, and former administrations. These included Dean Acheson and Averell Harriman, two of the men most responsible for initiating containment, as well as a host of "Best and Brightest" luminaries like McGeorge Bundy, George Ball, Cyrus Vance, and William Bundy. Unsettled by the way the war was dividing the establishment from its own wives and children, many of whom were passionate doves, and shaken by the way war had threatened the dollar and undermined business confidence in the economy, "the establishment made a characteristic decision not to send good money after bad." The war, said Acheson, had undermined our most critical priority, "the home front."

Johnson, annoyed at the way the "Wise Men" had made their decision to recommend deescalation on the basis of elite sentiment, growled about how "the establishment bastards have bailed out." But he too recognized that the "menace" of Red China had diminished significantly since the Sino-Soviet split and the Cultural Revolution, which had thrown China into chaos. It was the Soviet Union which was delighted to see the United States tied down in a strategically insignificant war in Asia, which benefited from the war's continuation.

On March 31, LBJ's positive standings in the Gallup poll fell to an all-time low of 35 percent. That night Johnson, fearful that his presidency was dividing the country and possibly delaying peace, went on the air with a pair of startling announcements.

First he proclaimed a partial bombing halt in the hope that it might encourage negotiations with Hanoi; then he told the American people that he was not a candidate for reelection.

Before the nation could absorb the shock of Johnson's decision to withdraw from the presidential race, tragedy struck. On April 4, four days after Johnson's speech, Martin Luther King, Jr., returned to Memphis, Tennessee, for a second try at aiding the city's striking sanitation workers. Increasingly frustrated in his efforts to use nonviolent methods to tackle the thorny problems of economic opportunity and de facto Northern segregation, King had begun to broaden his efforts by seeking coalitions with both labor and the anti-war movement. Disturbed by the growth of black violence in general and the Black Panthers, a slogan-shouting paramilitary group, in particular, King had come to believe that a new, wider movement was needed to transform the basis of American society. He never had the chance to give it a try. That night he was killed by a white racist.

In the wake of King's assassination riots broke out in over 100 American cities. In Chicago, Mayor Daley, angered by looting, ordered the police to "shoot to kill." By the end of the week thirty-seven people were dead. Washington, the scene of some of the worst violence, looked like an occupied city, with smoke hovering over the monuments and sandbags surrounding the Capitol. It seemed for a moment that the slogan of the left wing of the anti-war movement, "Bring the war home," was coming true. The old regime might just topple after all. It was this spirit of great possibilities, created by Johnson's withdrawal, the riots, the growing criticism of the war by militant and sometimes armed black organizations, that suggested America was entering into a revolutionary situation. When student radicals at Columbia University took over campus buildings in part to protest university policy toward neighboring Harlem, New York Mayor John Lindsay initially refused to send in the police for fear that such actions might produce a black uprising in support of the students.

A quarter of a century earlier, Henry Luce, founder and editor of *Time* magazine, surveyed America's prospects in the midst of war and proclaimed an American Century in which American ideas and values would conquer the globe. Surveying America in the aftermath of the spring fury of 1968, he bemoaned "the loss of a working consensus, for the first time in our lives, as to what we think America means." The usually sober and somber Richard Rovere put it more succinctly; "we were," he said, "half out of our trees."

Congresswoman Shirley Chisholm gainsaid counsels of despair and announced that blacks and college students would save America from its own wickedness. But these two groups were themselves politically and culturally divided by the Kennedy and McCarthy campaigns. The King assassination and its aftermath only served to heighten the bitter rivalry as each candidate insisted that his leadership was the only alternative to violence and despair. The candidates fought through a series of bruising primary battles as the prelude to the climactic California contest. In California, Kennedy fought a classic fight, tailoring his message to whatever constituency he was put in front of. Not so McCarthy. Increasingly contemptuous of the whole process, he refused to modify his positions to suit his audience. "I am what I am," he told his followers, "and I won't be changing."

McCarthy's hubris, which he shared with his followers, was part and parcel of the 1960s quest for authenticity. In classic 1960s —that is to say, aristocratic—style, the campaign became for him a matter, not of winning, but of making a personal statement. The electorate, he seemed to be saying, was unfit to pass judgment. It was McCarthy's hauteur that linked him with some of the student radicals who were appalled by bourgeois politicians but nonetheless shared McCarthy's feelings: not only that were they too good for American society, but that they could afford to be radical because their inherent worth guaranteed them a successful place in life if they deigned to so choose. Kennedy's victory in the June 4 California primary seemed to settle the issue between the two men politically if not culturally. But then on the very night of his victory Kennedy was killed by a Palestinian assassin enraged by the senator's strong support for Israel. Kennedy's death left Vice-President Hubert H. Humphrey, Johnson's chosen successor, as the sole rival to McCarthy's nomination.

It is highly unlikely, even if Kennedy had lived, that Hubert Humphrey could have been denied the Democratic nomination. Most convention delegates were selected, not in the primaries which received maximum media attention, but in state caucuses dominated by party regulars, most of whom supported Humphrey. And Humphrey, as local Democratic leaders pointed out, was the candidate most representative of rank-and-file Democrats. But the broad support for Humphrey meant little to those with deep anti-war feelings. With the war dominating the attention of the political class, Humphrey's often obsequious support of Johnson's Vietnam policies made him an object of hatred and ridicule for the anti-war movement. Humphrey's old-time American optimism, his politics of joy, cut him off from the anger that infused so many. Even Lyndon Johnson described his Vice-President as "just too old-fashioned, he looks like, he talks like he belongs to the past." And it was a measure of how much the war had scrambled old loyalties that Humphrey's long service to liberal causes was forgotten along with McCarthy's mediocrity as a senator and Kennedy's past reputation for ruthless ambition. Vietnam, it seemed, was all that mattered. Vietnam was, as one anti-war leader put it, "the liberals' war," and Humphrey represented the old liberalism. When Humphrey was asked, "Whatever happened to the liberal program you stood for?" he responded, "It passed. Does that upset you?" In truth it did upset many. Humphrey's New Deal policies, addressed as they were to the "old" politics of scarcity, were at once too tepid and too bureaucratic for the youthful reformers.

For radicals, student and otherwise, the proper response to a public relations war was a public relations anti-war movement. The great demonstrations like the October 1967 March on the Pentagon were grand outdoor dramas where protesters placed flowers in the muzzles of soldiers' rifles while "far out" counter-culture figures tried to levitate the Pentagon with Hindu mantras. The August 1968 Democratic national convention was to provide the occasion for the most important of these psychodramas. When it became clear that Humphrey had the nomination sewn up, Allard Lowenstein, the original organizer of the "dump Johnson" movement, tried to encourage as many as possible of the "clean for Gene" middle-class "kids" to come to Chicago to stage a peaceful protest against the Humphrey "coronation." They were joined by a smaller and far more colorful contingent of radicals, and the radicals' cultural cousins, the self-proclaimed crazies, mutants, and Yippies. Updated version of the 1920s cult of the unspoiled child, the Yippies depicted life as a struggle between the hard machine of government and adult life and the soft vital organs of sensuality which offered a path to happiness and salvation. The path to salvation, moreover, was to be quick and easy, according to Yippie leader Abbie Hoffman. Hoffman, a former crack SNCC organizer and would-be stand-up comic, mocking the traditional middle-class quest for character, pronounced marijuana and LSD as the sure paths to insight and the higher consciousness. "The radical and the get-rich-quick artist," said Louis Adamic, "are brothers under the skin." While Hoffman talked about drugs, his fellow racketeer in radicalism, Jerry Rubin, promoted "free love." The birth-control pill had hastened the breakdown of the once sharp distinction between the "good girl" and the "whore" and the Yippies jumped into the breach shouting, "Do it!"—the title of a book by Rubin. Free Love was a moral duty because if people could only be made to feel nice about each other, "war, racial injustice, economic exploitation, and poverty could be abolished." The staged manners of the Yippies, in everything from their bohemian dress to their casual public use of four-letter words, conveyed not only a hostility to the imperialist war in Vietnam but to "racist," "uptight" blue-collar and middle America in general. The Yippies and the radicals went to Chicago to use the television forum provided by the national convention to force a confrontation with the authorities, which would "unmask the repression which lay beneath the veneer of liberal tolerance" and thus halt the process of cooptation begun by the Kennedy and McCarthy campaigns. Unfortunately for many concerned, the authorities in this case were not timorous, liberal university officials, many of whom sympathized with the protesters, but that most unenlightened fellow, the Honorable Mayor Richard J. Daley, "Boss" of Chicago. In an age of urban breakdown, Daley, one of the last of the old-time Democratic machine chiefs, looked upon the convention as tribute to his "stewardship" of the "city that works." And part of what made it "work" was the head-knocking Chicago police, who helped see to it that in rigidly segregated Chi-town black people were kept in their "place." Hollywood couldn't have better cast the symbolic clash between the hip and the square.

While the confrontation between the police and the Yippies

was shaping up outside the convention, a different but interesting drama was playing itself out inside. Just as the way seemed clear for Humphrey's victory a new champion entered the lists. Rallying the Kennedy loyalists who had refused to swing over to McCarthy, George McGovern raised a stern challenge by forcing a floor debate on the issue of Vietnam. McGovern called for a total bombing halt, negotiations with the National Liberation Front of South Vietnam, and American troop withdrawals. Humphrey, caught between his desire to appease the Kennedy people and his debt to Johnson, balked, insisting, as did Richard Nixon, that he could support a total bombing halt only when it would not endanger American troops. In the midst of this verbal conflict, the delegates were horrified to discover that the passions separating the two sides were being violently played out on the streets of Chicago in clashes between the police and the demonstrators. As in the earlier symbolic confrontation between Hiss and Chambers, both looked past the other to the ever-present symbols of the twentieth century, "Communism" and "fascism." That division was re-created en masse on the streets of Chicago, where in a televised face-off the "fascists," or in 1960s jargon the "pigs," were the cigar-smoking potato-faced bigots of the Chicago Police Department, while the "Communists," or in 1960s terms "radicals," were spoiled brats of affluence, who at a time when the brothers and cousins of the cops were fighting in Vietnam betrayed their country by carrying the Vietcong flag.

The "kids" taunted the police with provocative sexual slogans and gestures and threw bags of feces and urine at them. The verbally maladroit police responded with their own language, physical violence. They launched an indiscriminate attack, a "police riot," not only against their taunters but against other demonstrators, innocent bystanders, and media people, most of whose sympathies for McCarthy and Kennedy were abundantly obvious. As riots go, it wasn't particularly bloody. No one was killed. At the Republican convention five weeks earlier, three black people had been slain without great public comment. What gave the melee its enormous impact was not just that it was televised, though that was important, but that the people being beaten up by the lower-middle-class cops were either the colleagues or culturally the kith and kin of professional upper-middle-class America. Or as Tom

Wicker of the New York *Times* put it: "These were our children in the streets of Chicago." The frenzied anger of the police who went "berserk," pursuing their targets into hotels in order to be sure to pummel them, confirmed the worst fears of liberals and the New Class about the "fascist" potential of "middle" America.

In 1965 Martin Luther King's attempt to march in Cicero, a suburb of Chicago, had produced a violent response by the jeering, rock-throwing residents of the blue-collar town. The incident helped transform some civil rights sympathizers into radicals willing to write off the North as well as the South as hopelessly bigoted. The 1968 riot produced a similar response among members of the liberal media. Miraculously, as one *Newsweek* reporter put it, "no one was killed by . . . Daley's beefy cops who went on a sustained rampage unprecedented outside the unreconstructed boondocks of Dixie." Similarly angered, the leaders of the prestige press and other editors and publishers demanded an explanation from Daley, who became the symbol of what had gone wrong in America. The network executives, proud of the way their crews had continued filming despite the intimidation, were outspoken in their criticism of Daley. But they were soon dismayed to discover that the pictures they had transmitted created overwhelming public support for Daley and his police. The issue, much to the surprise of journalists, had become, not the war, but the protesters' response to it. By their tactics the protesters had made themselves the issue and the contempt they felt for middle America was being repaid with support for Daley and his police.

10

Kulturkampf

With us the people are national, from affection, and a consciousness of living under a system that protects their rights and
interests. But true nationality is very much confined to the
mass . . . The higher classes, restrained in their activities, repress
these feelings.

—JAMES FENIMORE COOPER

THE VIETNAM WAR NEVER BECAME an immediate issue in the
1968 race among Humphrey, Richard Nixon, and George Wallace
because to some degree all the candidates supported the anti-
Communist crusade which had sent us there. But while the war
itself was not an issue, the politics of the war—that is, the anti-war
movement—was very much in question. As Andrew Greeley explained with understatement: "If the white ethnic is told in effect
that to support peace he must also support the Black Panthers,
women's liberation, widespread use of drugs, free love, campus
radicals, . . . long hair, and picketing clergymen, he may find it
very difficult to put himself on the side of peace." While radicals
and liberals insisted there was a connection between the violence
rained down upon Vietnam and the social injustice and hence
violence of American cities, ethnic Democrats turned the connection around and asked why liberals, so sensitive to death and
destruction in Vietnam, were so insensitive to the rising murder
rate and social destruction inflicted on their neighborhoods.

In the 1966 congressional elections which brought the Great

Society to a halt, the chief issues were rising crime rates and ghetto riots. In the years that followed, both got worse. Many blacks saw no alternative; as one black man explained: "To the white man the solution to the racial crisis means the absence of tension. To me it is getting my rights." Even had there been no racism, the arrival of vast numbers of newcomers into declining cities, abandoned by both the affluent whites and numerous companies, would have produced sharp tension between those recently arrived and older settled immigrants who had to bear the brunt of absorbing the newcomers. As it was, the problem of racism and urban adjustment was compounded by the New Politics alliance between upper-middle-class, often surburan cultural liberals and inner-city blacks. In 1968 the issue was not only the violence but "radical chic," the white liberal justifications for it. Liberals penitent for the country's past behavior toward blacks insisted on seeing every sign of white ethnic discontent as a cover for racism, which, although still formidable, was on the decline.

White ethnics, whose relative success made them imagine "that they stood near the center in the American scheme of things," and who believed that their work, self-reliance, and responsibility earned them a measure of esteem, felt themselves pushed, crowded, and cornered. Ridiculed by campus radicals, assaulted by unemployed black youth, many turned ferociously on the establishment that despised them. In the prestige press and political magazines of the period, the central conflict centered on the so-called generation gap that divided along the lines of the New Politics versus the old liberalism. But many more youths were busboys, apprentices, factory workers, clerks, and cops than students at the top schools, and for these white working-class youths both the New Politics and the old liberalism were part of the same establishment that was aligning itself with the black rebellion and threatening their neighborhoods. "Browbeaten" from above and "threatened" from below, the working-class young adults, who tended to be more disaffected than their parents, looked upon integration as part of "an organized effort within which the agents of government, the mass media, and even the church are conspirators. Thus, he too becomes anti-establishment, but for him it is a liberal establishment, and before it he feels increasingly powerless."

The man who most effectively played upon those feelings of

powerlessness was a revolutionary ascetic who neither drank nor smoked nor indulged in hobbies, Governor George Corley Wallace of Alabama. Wallace, accused of being a "pink" as a young man, had come on the national scene shouting, "Segregation now, segregation forever." But by 1967 he seized upon the resentments engendered by the counterculture to talk about "pointy-headed, intellectual morons" who "don't know how to park a bicycle straight." Playing to his audience, who responded to his animadversions the way the counterculture reacted to a rock star, Wallace declared: "If any demonstrator ever lays down in front of my car, it'll be the last car he'll ever lay down in front of." This impresario of grievance disgusted his cultural betters far more than he frightened them. "Wallace in his plastic-like, ill-cut suits, his grey drip-dry shirts," wrote *The New York Review of Books*' Elizabeth Hardwick, wore "the scent of hurry and hair oil: if he were not a figure, a star, he would be indistinguishable from the lowest of the crowd." Hardwick went on to verbally bash a substantial portion of the country; "the pity and sorrow and guilt of the times," she exclaimed, "lies in just this terrible trashiness of the lives of ordinary people." Wallace battened on such feelings.

In the 1950s the CIO's Operation Dixie had planned to remake the South in the image of Northern liberalism by forging an alliance of black and white workers. The civil rights movement similarly tried with greater success to bring the twentieth century south of the Mason-Dixon line. But Wallace, whose rise fed off and was parallel to that of Martin Luther King, turned the tables. A scavenger of reform, he showed that Southern racial politics could be brought North. Glimpsing Wallace's intent, NBC correspondent Douglas Kiker explained: "It is as if somewhere, sometime a while back, George Wallace had been awakened by a white blinding vision: They all hate black people, all of them. They're all afraid of them. Great God! That's it. They're all Southern! The whole United States is Southern!" (Kiker and his friends excepted of course.) Kiker's sentiments, once the exclusive purview of radicals, became standard liberal fare. But Kiker was more than half wrong.

Wallace supporters, who made up only about a quarter of the electorate, were far more likely than Nixon or Humphrey supporters to harbor racist sentiments. But even among the Wallace supporters more than half did not feel that black progress had been "too fast." They recognized the rough justice of the civil rights movement, but flocked to Wallace anyway because after Bobby Kennedy's death he and he alone spoke to their grievances, real and imagined.

Most Wallace voters, said Edward Kennedy, "are not motivated by racial hostility or prejudice." "It is they," he explained, "who bear the burdens of a draft that defers the better off, are unable to afford higher education but are not poor enough for scholarships." They are the ones, he went on, who carry the brunt of the taxes for an "established system [that] has not been sympathetic to them." "We cannot," he warned, "expect our citizens to pay taxes to solve other people's problems . . . when their own problems are not being met."

The Democratic Party Humphrey inherited was a "mutinous rudderless hulk." Hubert Humphrey would have liked to reach the dissidents to his cultural left and right. He tried bravely to talk about how liberals were not afraid to say the unpopular things, by which he meant speak out against crime without catering to racism. But Humphrey was as cut off from the froth of the Wallace people as he was removed from the diatribes of anti-Amerikanism. For the Wallace Democrats, he was just another example of a big government politician who trampled on their interests; for the New Politics Democrats, he was LBJ's "toady" and "doormat," and in truth Humphrey was so mesmerized by LBJ's accomplishments and personality that he swallowed his doubts about Vietnam policy in silence. In September, while support for Wallace surged in the North, particularly among union members, New Politics liberals debated whether to endorse Humphrey. "To some it seemed absurd to depose the monarch and then crown his buddy; to others it seemed masochistic not to vote against Nixon." Meanwhile Humphrey trailed Nixon, the Republican nominee, by as much as 20 points in the polls while at times leading Wallace by a scant 7 or 8 percent.

In October, Humphrey rallied a lukewarm endorsement from McCarthy and his own modifications on Vietnam softened the New Politics hostility while a sustained campaign by the AFL-CIO brought older unionists leaning toward Wallace back into the Democratic fold. But some younger unionists, many of whom held working-class views which kept them from voting with Nixon, stayed with Wallace and even talked of his heading "a real labor party."

In what the prestige press billed as the year of the New Politics, the major beneficiary of the turmoil was the awkward man of the old politics, Richard Milhous Nixon. The New York *Times'* Tom Wicker wrote of how Nixon had run a masterful campaign, while conservative ideologues like Kevin Phillips, who worked for Nixon's campaign manager, John Mitchell, were excited by the prospect of creating a New Republican majority. That new majority, Phillips hoped, would be built on the booming South and West, both of which were increasingly Republican as they came into their own, and the disaffected ethnics of the Northeast. Wicker was mistaken and Phillips was to be disappointed.

Herbert Klein, Nixon's director of communications, tried to create a new Nixon. (This was the second new Nixon; the first new model had been designed in 1956.) This new new Nixon was a "strong leader, the cool confident winner to whom the public could turn in trust." Klein succeeded in his image-building because Nixon was never tested. Everything fell into his lap. First of all, Nixon got an almost free ride in the Republican nomination process. His support from Strom Thurmond, the South Carolina Democrat turned Republican, staved off the charge of Ronald Reagan, the California conservative who had been elected governor only two years earlier, while on his left Nelson Rockefeller self-destructed as he had so many times before. As with Jack Kennedy, Nixon's chief concern was foreign policy, but he had very little to say on Vietnam. After a long delay, he was finally scheduled in late March 1968 to give his own views, which, however rhetorically hedged, would have made him vulnerable to criticism. But he was saved at the very last moment by Lyndon Johnson's resignation. Subsequently, Nixon hid behind the chaos of the Democrats to announce, like Eisenhower on Korea in 1952, that he had a plan to end the war. There was no plan.

Nixon enjoyed similar luck on race and domestic issues, where he comfortably positioned himself between the "kids and crazies" of the left and Wallace's racism on the right. Statesmanlike, he talked about the need for everyone to lower their voices, adopting "Bring us together" as his slogan. He made a few tough speeches on lawlessness, but he didn't have to say much. Race and crime were the topics in nearly every bar and tavern in the nation, so he could quietly reap what Wallace had sown. Nixon did talk about the "forgotten American," "the silent majority," an image borrowed from Edmund Burke's description of quiet cows grazing in a meadow of noisy impudent crickets. That silent majority, he said, loved its country and the freedom it offered; and respected the family, individual initiative, and the personal decorum trampled on by radicals. But for all the press discussion of Nixon's Southern and silent majority strategies, Nixon never reached out to the silent majority; he talked about them but not to them. The harsh words, when spoken, were from the lips of his little-known and lightly regarded vice-presidential choice, Spiro Agnew, governor of Maryland, who, like the press, was struck by "the improbability" of his nomination. But Agnew, referring to Nixon's days as designated Red-baiter for Eisenhower, was to be Nixon's Nixon. It was a shrewd choice. His vulgarity and crudeness ("If you've seen one slum you've seen them all") provided what little fire the Republican campaign possessed. Nixon's low-key strategy had its risks and was widely criticized by Republicans at the time, but in light of Nixon's response to pressure in 1972 it was probably a wise choice. In the end, Samuel Lubell explains, the voters "saw Nixon as little more than a convenient collection basket, the only one available"—the argument being that a vote for Wallace was a wasted vote—"into which they were depositing their numerous discontents with the Johnson administration."

In 1964, when the GOP was pronounced dead, 61 percent of the voters cast their ballots against Barry Goldwater. Four years later, unhinged by riots, muggings, radical rhetoric, and a veritable *Kulturkampf*, 57 percent of the electorate voted against Hubert Horatio Humphrey, heir to the 1964 victory. The 57 percent was composed of Nixon's 43.4 percent and Wallace's 13.5 percent, half of which came from states outside the Old South. Nixon's popular majority was a bare half million votes over Humphrey, but the Republican won 302 electoral votes to the Democrat's 191 and the Alabamian's 45, all from the Deep South.

Wallace had come within 43,000 votes of denying the winner an electoral majority, which would have created a crisis by throwing the election into the House, where both parties would have to bargain with the gamy governor. It was nearly a belated victory for Strom Thurmond's 1948 Dixiecrat campaign. The Democrats had collapsed in the South and the border states, where the election was a two-way contest between Nixon and Wallace; they were almost as weak in the West, where Nixon carried all but four of the trans-Mississippi states. Humphrey held on to the Democratic strength in the Northeast, capturing almost 60 percent of the crucial Catholic vote, but this champion of the laboring man garnered only half the union ballots. In 1960 Nixon carried but one of South Philadelphia's 131 largely Italian white ethnic precincts, in 1964 Goldwater carried 12, and in 1968 the Nixon total rose to 45. Together Nixon and Wallace captured a majority of the South Philadelphia ethnic vote. The Democrats experienced similar declines in most major cities, losing 20 or more percentage points from their 1960 showing. Nationwide, Humphrey carried only 38 percent of the white voters and it was only overwhelming black and Jewish support which kept him in contention. In city after city, racial conflicts had destroyed the old alliance. The New Deal had unraveled block by block.

> In our age there is no such thing as "keeping out of politics."
> All issues are political issues, and politics itself is a mass of lies,
> evasions, folly, hatred and schizophrenia.
> —GEORGE ORWELL

Richard Nixon, it is important to remember, was a wartime President. America's blessed geographic position has meant that there has never been an external threat so unambiguous as to unify the country. The War of 1812 produced the threat of New England's secession, while the Mexican War generated widespread opposition in the Northeast. In the Civil War the Copperheads of the North and the Unionists of the South split their respective camps. World War I produced fierce opposition from the socialists, and World War II and the Korean War evoked strong hostility from isolationists. Only the brief and "glorious" Spanish-American War was different. The war Nixon inherited, however, was the first (with the arguable exception of 1812) which had "fundamentally divided the ruling classes."

Richard Nixon became President as many Americans were losing the ahistorical birthright that endowed them with a self-evident sense of their own inherent goodness and invincibility. The crises of foreign policy, race, and culture which had all burst together filled the nation with unaccustomed fears for its future. Rather than culminating in the Chicago turmoil, these fears and the conflicts behind them grew and intensified during the first two years of the Nixon presidency.

The concurrent crises had subjected the nation's institutions to intense criticism that revealed the often ugly disparity between our professed principles and our actual practices, between, that is, professions of equality and the reality of racial inequality, between the rhetoric of a foreign policy based on freedom and the support of right-wing dictatorships friendly to American investment. Conservatives like Edmund Burke had always feared that the shattering of collective illusions would reduce society to mere dust. And in the late 1960s the delegitimation of national institutions meant that the larger national loyalty was replaced by many lesser ones which divided people by race, sex, ethnicity, and region.

If the American political tradition had been built on the Protestant injunction of "every man his own priest," the new mood carried this much further, so that every man and woman, black or white, straight or gay, was given the possibility of becoming a dissenting heretic. It is unlikely that any new President could have succeeded under those conditions, conditions that helped destroy the master conciliator Lyndon Johnson, but Richard Nixon, a past master of divisive politics, was particularly ill equipped to handle the challenge.

In the first year of Nixon's presidency, the New York *Times*, his old adversary from the McCarthy era, moved quickly from favoring a mutual American and North Vietnamese pullout from the South to calling for complete and unconditional withdrawal. The *Times* was joined by the Washington *Post* and the Council on Foreign Relations, two more of Nixon's old "Eastern establishment" adversaries. Those who had done so much to support the war originally turned against it with an intensity born in part of a desire to obscure their earlier errors. For Nixon and the middle Americans who supported him, the students chanting, "Ho, Ho, Ho Chi Minh, NLF is going to win," and their more restrained counterparts in the press were little more than traitors "giving aid and comfort" to an enemy who was shooting at American boys.

Nixon was unwilling to bend to "establishment" pressure. He was unwilling to end the war on even its moderate opponents' terms of a gradual timetable for complete withdrawal. Nixon, like JFK, conceived of the presidency as a platform for foreign policy leadership. Domestic policy, he said, cavalierly ignoring the domestic turmoil of the 1960s, could be taken care of by the Cabinet. Nixon and his chief adviser, Henry Kissinger, saw foreign policy, in the French expression, as "the King's secret." Domestic pressures could not be allowed to interfere with the grand designs of war and statesmanship. This is not because Nixon did not recognize a link between foreign and domestic issues. On the contrary, he saw a close connection between the political will he thought necessary to keep racial and domestic dissent under control and the will necessary to keep American force credible abroad. Nonetheless, Nixon recognized that the American involvement in Vietnam had to be reduced, although he was never willing to reduce it so fast or fully as to threaten South Vietnam. "Prestige," he said, is not an empty word. "A great nation," he insisted, "cannot renege on its pledges" without losing its standing. What he was unwilling to do was to withdraw in such a manner that his policy could be seen as a concession to an anti-war movement that, by questioning not only Vietnam but the Pax Americana based on freedom of presidential action, threatened, as he saw it, to undermine American military credibility around the globe. Rather than give public recognition to the reality of democratic dissent, Nixon chose to try to move foreign policy out of the arena of democratic decision making.

But even if Nixon had been willing to engage in a dialogue with the massive anti-war movement, it is unlikely that calm would have returned to the country. The anti-war and civil rights crusades had already given birth to a whole new range of movements of inclusion and social protest. These new movements, of which feminism and environmentalism were the most important, were animated and organized by the people shaped by both Kennedy-like appeals to national greatness and the New Left–New Politics traditions of social criticism. The energy and drive of these movements was supplied by the balance they struck between apocalyptic fears and the individual efforts, inspired by earlier movements of dissent, which were mobilized to counteract the impending doom.

David Bazelon captured the spirit of these new movements when, speaking in the voice of the educated reformer, he wrote: "We are a great society, or we are nothing any of us can bear to think of. A great society must entertain great projects. If we are not going to rule the world, then we must remake ourselves."

Feminism, like the student movement, was initially a reaction to the "sterility" of the consumer culture. In *The Feminine Mystique*, a powerful polemic published in 1963, Betty Friedan described the plight of the college-educated woman trapped in the daily routine of housework and child care, who was supposed to take pleasure from the insipid commercials instructing her how to utilize the latest cleaning discovery. Friedan reached beyond hyperbole when she described the middle-class home as a "comfortable concentration camp" for women, but there was considerable truth to the quip that isolated suburban women seemed endlessly consigned to deliver children, "obstetrically once and by car forever after." Friedan's pronouncement, "I want something more than my husband, my children and my home," had an enormous resonance for the rapidly growing number of women graduating from college in the 1960s. In a society in which affluence and the pill had begun to free people from traditional sexual constraints and in which blacks were freeing themselves from oppression, it seemed only natural for educated women to rethink their own place in the scheme of things. And just as involvement in the anti-slavery movement had led an earlier generation of women to discover their own oppression, the participation of activist women in the civil rights movement stirred a new feminist awakening in the 1960s. These feelings were quickened when, in the often tense struggle to assert black dominance in the movement, the participation of "pushy" white women was dismissed with sexist comments like Stokely Carmichael's "The position of the women in the movement should be prone." Shunted aside by the thrust of black power, activist white women began to organize on their own behalf. In 1966 the National Organization for Women (NOW) was founded. Led by Friedan, NOW's initial program was in the best American individualist tradition, a clarion call for equal rights, equal opportunity, and an end to discrimination. NOW's appeal was, in the words of a male academic, "compelling to all men of goodwill." "We all knew suburban housewives stuck with inferior husbands who no longer loved them; we all knew underpaid women who worked for overpaid men." But these rhetorical gestures of goodwill were of little effect until in 1968 feminists began a series of symbolic assaults on male bastions, including the revered Miss America pageant, where radical younger women from WITCH (Women's International Terrorist Conspiracy from Hell) disrupted the proceedings by symbolically discarding their undergarments.

Feminists had a two-track attitude about sex. On the one hand, many of the younger feminists were attracted to an open "liberated" sexuality, the democratization of desire, already available to men raised on the *Playboy* "ethic." On the other hand, they were appalled by the way women's sexuality in advertising reduced them to the status of playthings. "Our legs, busts, eyes, mouths, fingers, hair, abdomens, and vaginas," observed a group of Boston feminists, "are used to sell stockings, bras, fashions, cosmetics, hair coloring, and a multitude of birth-control products that men would not consider using in any form."

The central message of feminism, that "the personal is the political," came as a revelation to women who had never before thought of how the plight of individual women was linked to the larger structures of society. Feminism made public all the private assumptions of life. It politicized sex by metaphorically presenting the bedroom as the battleground for change. "The initial feminist understanding," said writer Vivian Gornick, "came as a kind of explosion: shattering, scattering, everything tumbling about, the old world within splintering even as the new one was collecting."

The new world Gornick looked forward to encompassed far more than the original feminist demands to outlaw discrimination in pay and employment, demands which received legislative sanction in the early 1970s. Radical feminists launched a fierce attack on male supremacy—that is, patriarchy and, by extension, the traditional family. In a continuation of the great reversal which began the 1960s, marriage was defined as a concubinage, in which a woman traded regularized sexual favors for security, and prostitution was glorified as an honest independent exercise of a woman's true position in a society said to be dominated by male imperialism.

The critique gave new meaning to the phrase "A good man is hard to find," as when best-selling author Susan Brownmiller argued that rape was "nothing more or less than a continuous process of intimidation by which *all men* keep *all women* in a state of fear." Not surprisingly, Brownmiller went on to note tartly that it was "hard to find a women's liberationist who is not in some way disaffected by the sound of wedding bells." Or in the words of the feminist bumper sticker: "Don't cook dinner tonight, starve a rat today." It is interesting that the rejection of traditional male values often failed to include a rejection of the gospel of individual success. While being a housewife was derided as "nothingness, total nothingness" and motherhood was mocked as "breeding," career success was extolled. But women could be freed for competition with men and career success, the argument continued, only if they were liberated from their role as "breeders" of children. Carrying the point to its logical conclusion, Shulamith Firestone declared pregnancy barbaric and urged women to seize the technology of reproduction, to create artificial wombs, and so end female subordination to biology. Biology, to contravene Freud, would no longer be destiny.

Firestone's proposals were impractical at the time, but many feminists seized upon the importance of reforming the country's archaic abortion laws as a step toward sexual autonomy. Their efforts bore quick results. In mid-1971 the Supreme Court, in *Roe* v. *Wade*, legalized abortion on the grounds of a woman's "right to privacy" and by declaring that a fetus had no standing as a person under the Fourteenth Amendment. The campaign against patriarchy and for abortion dovetailed smartly with another middle-class reform movement of the period: Zero Population Growth (ZPG).

The postwar baby boom responsible for a good deal of the institutional chaos which characterized the 1960s had yet another ripple effect in the late 1960s, a population explosion scare. Between 1945 and 1970, the American population grew by an enormous 42 percent, from 140 to 200 million people. Between 1950 and 1960 alone, the population grew by 28 million, a figure as large as the entire population increase of the seven decades from 1790 to 1860. This population boom, accompanied by a high level of mass consumption, heightened the unpleasant side effects of economic growth. America, Paul Ehrlich pointed out in his influential *The Population Bomb* (1969), accounted for only 6 percent of the world's population but 40 percent of its consumption and 50 percent of its pollution. The problem, as Ehrlich saw it, was that the newcomers to mass consumption, the unenlightened proles who "insisted on breeding excessively," mucked "up the environment with their plastic spray cans and electric baubles." The growth of this tasteless sort of throwaway consumption made life unpleasant for the more cultured members of the middle class, who found beaches and country lakes, which can't be mass-produced, becoming crowded and less pleasurable as more and more new people could afford access to them. If voluntary measures failed to halt this erosion in the quality of life, Ehrlich insisted, compulsory government population controls would be necessary. One of Ehrlich's colleagues, Martha Willing, suggested making it a crime to have more than two children, while another proposed inoculating both males and females against fertility at puberty. Ehrlich and the people associated with his upper-middle-class organization, ZPG, conveyed a Malthusian sense of doom about the plagues that would follow unless we repented and repudiated the false gods of economic growth and mass consumption. By 1983, predicted Ehrlich, steak would be just a memory after a billion people had starved to death around the globe, while the use of dangerous chemical pesticides would lead the United States into a nuclear confrontation with Japan and the U.S.S.R. Fortunately, trend is not destiny and 1972 saw the beginning of a sharp and continuous drop in the American birth rate.

The population bomb fears were a case of a recurring middle-class panic, but the accompanying fears about pollution and the environment were not so easily discounted.

Many of the hopes of the late 1940s and early 1950s were tied to the high-technology, high-energy methods of production developed during the war, which first promised to raise and then succeeded in raising the American standard of living. Until the early 1960s both scientists and lay public were generally unaware of the hidden costs imposed by vastly increased fluorocarbon consumption and the use of plastics and pesticides. But, beginning with the 1962 publication of Rachel Carson's pathbreaking *Silent Spring*, which exposed the malign effects of the wonder pesticide

DDT, which had greatly increased crop yields, the nation became increasingly aware of the underside of high-tech productivity. High-tech mass production had raised living standards and vastly increased the number, type, and quality of goods available to Americans of limited means, but it also poisoned the nation's air, water, and soil. DDT killed off not only harmful insects but birds and wildlife as well, while petrochemical fertilizers "created vast nitrogenous wastes that drained into rivers and lakes," literally killing them. At the same time oil and strip-mined coal used increasingly to produce energy left the soil barren and the air filled with a smog which in Los Angeles and other cities became a direct threat to public health.

In "The Sources of Public Unhappiness," written for the upscale *New Yorker*, former Johnson, McCarthy, and Robert Kennedy aide Richard Goodwin talked of how the awareness of environmental dangers had produced a sense of foreboding. For the "average citizen," said Goodwin, public life seemed to be running out of control. "The air around him is poisoned, parkland disappears under relentless bulldozers, traffic stalls and jams, airplanes cannot land . . . Yet he cannot remember having decided that these things should happen, or ever having wished them. He has no sense that there is anything he can do to arrest the tide."

By 1968 the growing awareness of the pollution and a muted version of the counterculture's anti-modernism created a response to the malaise Goodwin had identified. In the summer and fall of 1969, while the ghettos were quiet, the environmentalist movement became the new rage, receiving blanket coverage from the networks and top news magazines. "Suddenly, it seemed that every journalist in New York had turned with relief from worrying about 'the war and the cities' to worrying about the environment."

The environmental activists were drawn from the ranks of upper-middle-class whites who had filled the anti-war and civil rights movements, but environmentalism, as a plea for clean air and water, drew broader popular support. By April 1970, the date of the first Earth Day, environmentalism was so broadly popular that Congress adjourned for the day and 10 million schoolchildren took part in events to mark the occasion. "Ecology," cracked California Democrat Jesse Unruh, "has become the political substitute for the word 'mother.'" Responding to the popular outcry,

Congress not only passed clean air, clean water, and safe waste disposal legislation; it also, with President Nixon's approval, created an Environmental Protection Agency in 1971, with the power to bring suit against the corporations or municipalities which violated the standards in the environmental legislation.

Like John Kennedy in 1960, Nixon, who focused on foreign policy, came to office with a set of attitudes but without a domestic program. Again like John Kennedy, "the marketing managers of Nixon Inc." had the "pragmatic" ideology of non-ideology. Nixon's position in the Republican Party had always been as a broker between the provincial wildmen, the Brickers, McCarthys, and Goldwaters, and the Eastern establishment. Elected by a narrow margin, Nixon began thinking about reelection almost as soon as he entered office. Governing became an extension of campaigning. Or as one aide put it, referring to Nixon's closest advisers, most of whom were public relations men, this administration gives "the impression of a four-year sales meeting." While searching for a salable domestic policy, he confided to Daniel Patrick Moynihan that the "real reason Hubert lost was not Vietnam"; he lost because the New Deal was over. Knowingly or not, he was echoing the words of the first Eisenhower administration. The New Deal, it seems, has been a long time dying. With his ball-and-socket flexibility, Nixon initially saw some of the left-liberal attacks made by Richard Goodwin and others on the efficacy and legitimacy of federal power as an opening for a moderate conservatism that lowered expectations while providing responsible government. To the surprise of many liberals, then, Richard Nixon took up a position at the head of the environmentalist parade. In signing environmental legislation, he caught the spirit of the moment when he proclaimed: "It is now or never for us to pay our debt to the past by reclaiming the purity of . . . our environment." Nixon went even further. In paying homage to the swelling feeling for the sanctity of nature, he struck a "radical" note, intoning that "we must learn not how to master nature but how to master ourselves, our institutions and our technology."

The broad consensus on conservation began to dissolve when environmentalism was used to challenge unchecked corporate power. The first challenge came from a young Harvard Law School graduate, Ralph Nader. In 1965 Nader published *Unsafe at Any*

Speed, a devastating critique of the way the lack of competition in the auto industry allowed the three giants to engage in a mock rivalry over car styles while producing autos which, ignoring safety design, were unable to protect passengers in even a low-speed accident. Rewarded for his efforts by having General Motors turn its private spies on him, Nader went on to become a leading advocate of environmentalism. His basic message was simple. At a time, he argued, when giant economic concentrations are able to dominate markets, the free play of competition could no longer be relied on to protect the consumer. "Air pollution," wrote Nader, "is a new way of looking at an old American problem, concentrated and irresponsible corporate power." An age of monopoly required consumer organizations and government regulation designed to guarantee a minimum of social responsibility from organizations so large as to in effect be public but which were run solely for private profit. Nader's Raiders, task forces staffed by the veterans of social reform, studied topics ranging from air and water pollution to the depredations of agribusiness. The Nader task force on agriculture found that nearly half the land in America's most important agricultural state, California, was comprised of just forty-five farms, which received huge federal water subsidies of dubious legality. Agribusiness, the report noted, relied on machine harvesting and pest control methods which made food more expensive and threatened the land's ecological balance. "Corporate economic, product and environmental crimes," concluded Nader, "are part of a raging corporate radicalism which generates technological violence, undermines the integrity of government, breaks laws, blocks needed reforms, and repudiates a quality competitive system with substantial consumer sovereignty."

Nader's hopes that consumerism and environmentalism would spawn a mass reform movement were never fulfilled. In part Nader's trenchant criticism of corporate practices mobilized a political counter-response on the part of business, exemplified by Nixon's fierce assertion: "We are not going to allow the environmental issue to be used, sometimes falsely and sometimes in a demagogic way, basically to destroy the system." But Nader's hopes also received a blow from an unexpected source, the parallel and overlapping countercultural and ecological challenge to corporate business practices.

Though drawn like the Naderites from the sons and daughters of people who had already "made it," the ecologists, believers in the wilderness as a semi-sacred terrain threatened by the ravages of timber companies and snowmobiles, were an even wealthier group, sprinkled with "old money." Their vanguard organization, the Sierra Club, which had once preached a conventional brand of conservationism, turned increasingly during the turmoil of the 1960s to a religious view of nature that challenged traditional Western notions about the character of human existence. Where the Greek Protagoras had argued that "man is the measure of all things" and Christianity emphasized man's immortal soul, the ecologists' pantheistic view of nature was a mix of beat and Orientalist quietism and romantic aestheticism which preached a naturalist piety that seemingly rejected anthropocentric materialism.

The Sierra Club theology, one logical culmination of the revolt against mass society, was given its widest hearing in Charles Reich's best-selling *Greening of America*. Reich, a forty-two-year-old graduate of prep school and Yale, who described himself "as just like everyone else," was a former clerk to the backpacking civil libertarian Supreme Court Justice William O. Douglas and a member of a prestigious law firm before he joined the faculty at Yale. His book, which took pleasure in dividing the nation into warring cultures of grubby materialists on one side and bell-bottomed Beatles-humming lovers of peace and nature on the other, featured an endorsement from Senator George McGovern calling it one of the most profound books ever written about America. *The Times* of London, which serialized the book, caught its appeal in the subheads it gave to the sections. These read: "The Men with the Grey-Flannel Minds" . . . "A Generation Betrayed" . . . "Plastic Lives in Plastic Homes" . . . "The Flowering of America." As the subheads indicate, the book was a virtual recapitulation of the countercultural litany. We live, said Reich, "in a society no one created and no one wants," but if "the most thoughtful and passionate of our youth" are given their heads, he foresaw an environmentalist-oriented revolution which promised "a higher reason, a more human community, and a new and liberated individual." The "new consciousness" promised "a new and enriching relationship of man to himself, to other men, to society, to nature, to land." But, warned Reich, if this new consciousness was denied, if the mechanized exploitation of nature which linked corporate profits to mass consumption was not halted, a terrible fate would befall the earth and all its inhabitants.

In 1970 it was predicted that by 1980 "urban dwellers would have to wear gas masks to breathe," and that by 1985 new scientifically unleashed diseases that people lacked natural antibodies for would inflict the world with a plague of vast proportions. For some, like leftist environmentalist Barry Commoner, the coming catastrophe was an opportunity for "the radical reorganization of national economies and international commerce along lines that make ecological sense." But for the well-to-do bored with the homogeneity of modern life and the ugliness of industrial society, there was a "wish, barely disguised as a fear, that the era of economic growth may really be finished, and that a New Dark Age may be upon us." For the California mystic Theodore Roszak, living that New Dark Age promised an end to "the absurd affluence of middle-class America" and a return to a Paleolithic future of shamanistic spirituality and true community.

The stained-glass radicalism preached by Roszak and Reich, who complained about America's lack of "culture, tradition," and "social order," produced an angry response from middle America, which reacted to the attack on its position in society the way business responded to Nader. "Some people," wrote black leader Vernon Jordan, "have been too cavalier in proposing policies to preserve the physical environment for themselves while other poor people pay the costs." A popular labor union bumper sticker read: "If You're Hungry and Out of Work, Eat an Environmentalist." Like the first protest against consumption exemplified by John Kenneth Galbraith in the late 1950s, in which people driving Volvos told people driving Chevies to mind their social manners, environmentalism, despite its solid core of genuine concerns and often broad support, turned into a movement of "$20,000-a-year men telling all the $7,500-a-year men to simply stay where they are so we can all survive."

11

Nixon and Kissinger:

Deception, Dollars, and Détente

My fellow Americans, we live in an age of anarchy, both abroad and at home.

— RICHARD M. NIXON

THE GNOMIC QUALITY OF the new administration's statements about the most divisive issue of all, Vietnam, raised initial hopes for a brilliant De Gaulle-like stroke that would bring the war to a rapid end. Skillfully packaged by Henry Kissinger, the essence of the Nixon message was as follows: Vietnam will go down in history as "one of America's finest hours," but one such war is enough and there won't be any more. Kissinger amplified the message for a bedazzled press corps with studied opacities and delphic "off the record" comments about a "realistic" policy which recognized the "limits" of American power. The effectiveness of the Nixon-Kissinger opening public relations blitz bought some time and goodwill for the new administration while obscuring the continuity of policy.

The talk of a new modesty, however, did not signal any change in the aims and interests of American foreign policy. The maintenance of global credibility and containment still governed. The North Vietnamese had to be denied victory, according to Nixon, not because they were Communists (he was already aware of the growing importance of the Sino-Soviet split), but because a defeat for the United States would undermine American prestige and credibility around the globe. Ruling out nuclear escalation as counterproductive, Nixon also eschewed a long-term conventional escalation on the grounds that "there was no way I could hold the country together" for a long period of time "in view of the number of casualties we would be sustaining." The solution, as he saw it, was the same one the Johnson administration had come to in its closing phase: he would reduce American commitments by Vietnamizing the war. The ensuing Nixon doctrine enunciated in July 1969 said that America would maintain its "commitments" but future wars in Asia would have to be fought by Asians. It was a low-profile version of containment.

Nixon differed from LBJ in what he was willing to do to make Vietnamization work. Updating Eisenhower's New Look foreign policy which proposed to prevent "brushfire" wars with the threat of massive nuclear attack, Nixon proposed to combine the withdrawal of conventional forces with massive conventional bombing far exceeding anything Johnson had been willing to contemplate. For Nixon, displays of firepower were also displays of guts and determination. "What distinguishes me from Johnson," he wrote Kissinger, "is that I have the *will* in spades." And to show the North Vietnamese just how dangerous he could be, despite withdrawing troops, Nixon insisted on cultivating an air of unpredictability. Acting on what some called the Madman Theory of War, he told his top aide, H. R. Haldeman, "I want the North Vietnamese to believe I've reached the point where I might do anything to stop the war" on terms favorable to the United States. Nixon's hope was that the random brutality of massive bombing would lead the North Vietnamese to make the diplomatic concession necessary for an American withdrawal that could at least avoid looking like a desertion. Like Johnson and Rostow, Nixon and Kissinger were convinced that the North Vietnamese had a "breaking point." The game, as they saw it, was a race to see which would break first, the North Vietnamese under the pressure of bombing or the Administration under the pressure of a still-building domestic opposition to the war, an opposition which had come to the fore even in the normally conservative Senate.

In October 1969 the largest anti-war demonstrations to date, involving over a million people, took place in Washington and around the nation. The demonstrations, accompanied by a flurry of books and polls which claimed to show that "the system" was either tottering on the brink of destruction or invulnerable but so corrupt as to be beyond redemption, heightened the political mood of confrontation. Vietnamization, however, took the wind out of the sails of mass protests. By rapidly reducing the number of ground troops from a high of 543,000 in April 1969 to 60,000 by September 1972, Vietnamization dramatically reduced the student draft, which had mobilized the bulk of the demonstrators.

Vietnamization all but ended the mass protests against the war, but its baffling mixture of escalation and withdrawal served, along with still-smoldering racial tension, to ignite a panoply of ugly incidents. Shouting matches between black and white students erupted into fistfights on half a dozen campuses, and at Cornell armed black students seized the student union and won concessions from the school's president. In Vietnam, young, often black soldiers were involved in a number of highly publicized "fragging" incidents, in which troops sometimes shot their commanding officer rather than follow him into combat. It was in the spirit of "fragging" that the Black Panthers tried to "bring the war home" by engaging the police in low-level guerrilla warfare. Bombs were set off at the Manhattan offices of IBM, General Telephone, and Mobil Oil, while followers of H. Rap Brown and students involved in the Columbia strike and the Weatherman conventicle were killed in separate premature bomb explosions. New York City alone faced 1,000 bomb threats a month during 1969–70. To the White House, the "threat" to its authority and hence its policies was exemplified by the speech given by Black Panther leader David Hilliard at the October 1960 anti-Vietnam demonstrations in San Francisco. "Richard Nixon is an evil man," said Hilliard. Then, drawing an analogy from Vietnam, he accused Nixon of unleashing counterinsurgency teams on the Black Panthers. "We will kill Richard Nixon," he said. "We will kill any motherfuckers that stand in the way of our freedom." Hilliard was arrested for threatening the life of the President.

In the midst of this already supercharged atmosphere, Nixon announced the unconstitutional American invasion of Cambodia. The reactions to the Cambodian invasion set into play a chain of events which led to genocide in Southeast Asia and unprecedented constitutional and political crisis at home. As with Tet, a body blow delivered in Asia was received in America.

Cambodia was formally neutral in the war, but a weak government in Pnom-Penh under the leadership of Prince Norodom Sihanouk was unable to prevent the Vietnamese from using Cambodian territory as a sanctuary to attack the South. In March 1969, before the enunciation of the Nixon doctrine, the President ordered the bombing of the Vietnamese positions in Cambodia, both for straightforward military reasons and as a signal to the North Vietnamese that a new hard-nosed player had entered the game. It was a sign of the weakness of Nixon's position, however, that he was forced to keep the bombing secret for fear of the public reaction if it was revealed that the American Air Force had extended an already unpopular war by bombing a neutral country without a constitutionally mandated declaration of war. When General Thieu's regime was slow in adapting to Vietnamization, the still-secret bombing was intensified. In order to keep the B-52 raids secret, military documents were falsified and Kissinger repeatedly lied to the Senate Foreign Relations Committee about American activities in Cambodia. In the midst of all this secrecy, Nixon was furious when someone in the Administration leaked information on the Cambodia operation to William Beecher of the New York *Times.* The story was printed, some eyebrows were raised, but the Administration's denial continued to be effective and the sorties continued. Nixon and Kissinger, however, ordered FBI director Hoover illegally to wiretap prominent government officials, including members of Kissinger's own National Security Council staff, to find the source of the leaks.

In early April 1970 Sihanouk was ousted in a right-wing coup led by General Lon Nol. Sihanouk's departure paved the way on April 9 for a largely unsuccessful American invasion of North Vietnam's Cambodian sanctuaries.

The Cambodian invasion was consistent with the underlying military logic of the Nixon-Kissinger policy, but it came as a rude shock to journalists and politicians, who, lulled by the troop withdrawals, had failed to notice the continuity in policy. Senator Kennedy denounced the invasion as "madness," while the New York *Times* described it as "a virtual renunciation of the President's promise of disengagement from Southeast Asia."

Anticipating the hostile reaction, Nixon went on television on April 30, just a day after the invasion had been made public. Claiming that an American defeat in Vietnam would unleash the forces of totalitarianism around the globe, he insisted that the invasion of Cambodia was a guarantee of American "credibility." "The most powerful nation in the world," he said, replying to his critics, could not afford to act "like a pitiful helpless giant." Appealing to national pride, he asserted that "it is not our power but our will and character that is being tested tonight." "We will not be humiliated, we will not be defeated."

The invasion temporarily revived the nearly moribund student anti-war movement. From coast to coast, campuses erupted in passionate anti-war marches and protests. During one of those demonstrations at previously little-known Kent State University in Kent, Ohio, National Guardsmen initially called out because of a violent truckers' strike were sent to the campus to quell disturbances which had included the bombing of an ROTC building. The National Guardsmen panicked after some rock throwing by the students and they fired indiscriminately into the crowd, killing four white students. On May 14 two black students were killed in a less publicized incident at Mississippi's Jackson State College. The killings, coming on the heels of the invasion and the February 1970 revelation of the My Lai massacre, produced what one college president called "the most disastrous May in the history of American higher education." Protests broke out on more than 400 campuses, 250 of which had to be shut down before the end of the semester. A Harris poll in May found that 76 percent of the students felt that there had to be "basic changes in the system."

Student anger was met, as it was after the Chicago riots, by the outrage of middle America. "The score is four," ran a gleeful Kent, Ohio, jingle. "And next time more." A *Newsweek* poll found overwhelming support for the Guardsmen and a strong plurality in favor of the Cambodia invasion.

In New York, the city's "silk stocking" Mayor John Lindsay's call for conciliation and reflection served instead to highlight the depths of the national divisions. "The country," said Lindsay, "is virtually on the edge of a spiritual—and perhaps physical—breakdown." Senate dove J. William Fulbright agreed. Alarmed at growing alienation from U.S. foreign policy among the business community, Fulbright spoke of a change from mere social and moral conflict to a "condition indicative of social disintegration." Fulbright's fears were played out in Wall Street, where a demonstration of students and some businessmen against the war was met by a charging, chanting band of 200 to 300 "hardhats," marching not so much in favor of the war as against the protesters. Enraged by the Lindsay administration's lowering of the American flag in mourning for the Kent State dead, the construction workers charged into the "longhairs," leaving 70 people wounded in their wake. A few weeks later, on May 20, 1970, a hundred thousand workers from the building trades and the docks marched and burned Lindsay in effigy.

The Senate debate on Cambodia, the most important since that on the Truman Doctrine, was only slightly less heated. On April 28, the day before the invasion of Cambodia, South Dakota's Senator George McGovern, a leading dove, introduced a resolution which called upon the President to terminate all U.S. military activity in Southeast Asia by December 31, 1971. A long-standing critic of the Vietnam War, he had already denounced it as a "moral and political disaster—a terrible cancer eating away the soul of the nation." But on April 28 McGovern went even further. Addressing his fellow senators in tones rarely heard in their gentlemanly surroundings, he exclaimed, "Every senator in this chamber is partly responsible for sending 50,000 young Americans to an early grave." "This chamber reeks of blood . . . And if we do not end this damnable war, those young men will someday curse us for our pitiful willingness to let the executive carry the burden that the Constitution places on us." The resolution was defeated 55–39. By the time Senator Vance Hartke spoke to his colleagues about Southeast Asia, shortly after the Cambodian invasion, the mood of the Senate had changed. The President's actions in Cambodia, said the middle-of-the-road senator, were "a declaration of war against the Senate."

"American democracy," wrote historian Henry J. Ford in 1898, "has revived the oldest institution of the race, elective kingship." From Franklin Roosevelt on, the President was more than just the chief administrator. In liberal eyes he was the man "on whom an impatient world waited for miracles," a "magnificent lion roaming the political landscape preying on injustice, isolationism, stand-pattism, and all the other enemies of reform at home and internationalism abroad." The extraordinary foreign policy powers FDR attained in an era of war and dictatorship were perpetuated for his successors by the Cold War and containment. War-making powers are granted solely to the Congress by the Constitution. But only the President could respond rapidly to brushfire wars and he alone had control of nuclear weapons that might have to be launched on a moment's notice.

The presidency, as Charles Beard put it, was the "Dark Continent of constitutionalism," but liberals who associated Congress with union busting and McCarthyism had been willing to place their faith in the White House as the only way of surmounting the crabbed provincialism of Capitol Hill. Until Vietnam called into question the "imperial presidency's" foreign policy judgments, it never occurred to liberals that the President's symbolic powers, his ability to embody the national ethos, could be turned against them by conservatives. In the congressional debates on containment, Truman had insisted that the nation speak with only one voice in foreign policy. Politics had to stop at the water's edge. In the second great reversal, it was the conservative supporters of global containment who took this position while liberals, converted to constitutionalism, insisted on the need for free and open debate.

The Cambodian invasion goaded the Senate into support for the Cooper-Church amendment. Sponsored by a Republican moderate (John Sherman Cooper) and a Democratic liberal (Frank Church), it called for prohibiting the use of American funds for military operations in Cambodia after July 1, 1970. It was designed as a first step in limiting the President's war-making discretion. The amendment was passed in the Senate 58–37, but was defeated in the House 237–153. Then Senators George McGovern and Mark Hatfield (a liberal Republican), convinced that the crisis engendered by the Vietnam War was threatening what amounted to civil war, introduced another amendment; this one would commit the President to the removal of all combat personnel from Southeast Asia by December 31, 1971. The amendment was defeated 55–39, but the White House responded with a sharp counterattack.

Taking a dignified stand, the Administration and its senatorial spokesmen, such as Robert Dole of Kansas, insisted that the McGovern-Hatfield amendment would undercut the U.S. position at the ongoing but largely futile Paris peace talks between the United States and North Vietnam. Other, less restrained Republicans, like Michigan's Robert Griffin, implied that liberal senators were part of those malign forces manipulating public opinion who would stab America's troops in the back, while the far-right Senator George Murphy of California, a former movie song-and-dance man, conjured up McCarthyite images of leftists undermining authority at home by underwriting American defeat abroad. The "inner message" being sent by the Republicans was, as historian Gordon Levin put it, that "if pressed by anti-war elements the Administration would not hesitate to politicize middle America to defend Nixon's foreign policy." In return for order, the liberals would have to accept the fact that the ambiguous policy of Vietnamization was the most improvement they could achieve over President Johnson's approach to the war.

The debate over the specifics of Cambodia was generalized first into a debate about the broad aims of American foreign policy and ultimately a struggle over the nature of American society. For liberals, the war was a threat to American democracy. Popular internationalism had its birth at the time of World War II, in the fear that American democracy could not survive in a world of dictators and desperadoes. The United Nations and free trade had been designed to produce an open world, a liberal capitalist international order that would absorb dictatorial command economies in a rising tide of wealth and interdependence. But much to their shock, liberal internationalists discovered that the war in Vietnam was producing the very sort of garrison-state mentality they had always warned against. Secondly, where previously an activist presidency abroad had been seen as a prerequisite to an activist reforming presidency at home, the vast post-World War II growth in both military and social spending meant that the two were constantly competing for federal funds. Without an end to an interventionist foreign policy, liberals thought, it would be impossible to give the pressing problems of race, poverty, and urban decay the resources and attention they required.

Underlying the fears of a garrison state and the competition between social and military priorities was a crucial but often undiscussed loss of certainty about the purposes of American policy. U.S. foreign policy, it seemed, was trying to reshape the world in the image of a nineteenth-century America, complete with its small-town certainties that were fast disappearing. "Why," asked David Riesman, "should we ask the Asians and Africans, who had not yet fatally succumbed to the modern virus, to live through the worst of the 19th century merely to arrive at the state we are trying to leave?" This was the foreign policy analogue of the domestic race issue. How could middle-class America insist that black America adopt middle-class virtues when so many educated Americans were desperately trying to shed those "hangups"?

Conservatives were eager to pick up the argument. Pointing to the economic failures of the Soviet sphere, they insisted that America still had lessons to teach the world. While "progressives" held that Vietnam was responsible for the drugs and violence and racial conflict afflicting America, conservatives turned the argument around. They claimed that permissivism produced the social ravages of drugs and violence at home which were exported to Vietnam in the form of rape, mutiny, and marijuana. It was the welfare state, conservatives insisted, which produced decadence at home in the form of an anti-war movement which succored Hanoi. Firmness in Vietnam was essential, they argued, if firmness and certainty at home were ever to be restored.

Despite their differences, both sides feared that, no matter how the war ended, there would be "bitter recriminations," like those after the "loss" of China. They were wrong. Unlike China, where there were deep and passionate ties, Vietnam had no strong cultural connections with the United States. The right-wing radicalism Nixon threatened to unleash was a response to the counterculture and the anti-war movement, not a defense of the American involvement in Vietnam per se. This distinction is probably best highlighted by the remarks of a middle-aged Massachusetts middle American. "The war in Vietnam," she complained, was started by a "bunch of Harvard professors who run the State Department." These men were squandering the blood and money of people like herself in a pointless foreign involvement. What about the Harvard students who were, at the time, sacrificing their own blood to stop the war? "It's disgusting," she replied. "They're worse than the professors."

"Kent State," said Nixon's top aide, H. R. Haldeman, "marked a turning point for Nixon, a beginning of his downhill slide toward Watergate." In the weeks following Kent State the nation seemed to be reeling out of control. Dissent erupted not only on the campuses but within HEW and other departments of government, where an organization, Federal Employees for a Democratic Society, modeling itself on Students for a Democratic Society, had issued the "Potomac Statement" calling upon government workers to resist illegitimate authority. From the Administration's point of view, "these people" were conducting "a kind of internal guerrilla war against the President . . . trying to frustrate his goals by unauthorized leaks" to the press in order, as John Ehrlichman put it, to "create hostility in the Congress and abroad and to affect public opinion."

Dissent even seeped into the White House itself, seemingly infecting everyone but Nixon's immediate entourage, the Palace Guard. "Cambodia isn't black or white," said a second-level White House aide, "it's shades of gray." Speaking as though he were an outsider, the aide went on: "Now the Administration has turned a psychological corner and retreated into itself." "Cambodia," he said, "was being made a black-or-white, all-or-nothing test of our loyalty to RN."

Nixon's Cabinet contained a mix of moderate and conservative Republicans. Its Goldwaterite political operatives and Chicago School Friedmanites were balanced by "liberal" Republicans like Nixon's old friend Robert Finch at HEW and Walter Hickel at Interior. But when Finch criticized Vice-President Agnew directly and Nixon indirectly for "heating up the climate in which the Kent State students were killed," and when Hickel insisted that Nixon had to make an effort to talk with the protesters, they were dismissed as being insufficiently loyal. For Nixon loyalists, the Cambodian demonstrations and the bombings were all part of the same "extra-parliamentary" forces which had destroyed Johnson and which, if left unchecked, would destroy not only the Nixon administration but the country as well. Convinced of a secret revolutionary "conspiracy," Nixon drew his inner circle into a holy mission to combat the enemies of the Administration and thus America. That inner circle consisted of the men he trusted most, the men who stayed with him when he was down and out after his defeat in the 1962 California gubernatorial race. They included Attorney General John Mitchell, top aides advertising man H. R. Haldeman and lawyer John Ehrlichman, and political adviser Murray Chotiner, Nixon's tutor in political hardball.

Nixon was cut off from day-to-day contact with most members of his administration, let alone Republican moderates in the Senate. He had his daily activities monitored by the "Berlin Wall" of Haldeman and Ehrlichman, the so-called Prussians who provided a protective cocoon in which the leader could concentrate on the foreign policy matters closest to his heart. On domestic matters the power in the Administration was Attorney General John Mitchell. Like the "Prussians" a man of no prior political experience, Mitchell had made his mark in public life by devising "authority financing" for Nelson Rockefeller, an ingenious means of circumventing constitutional limitations on a state's bonded indebtedness. Mitchell, or "El Supremo" as he was sometimes known, established himself as the Administration's domestic hard-liner. He enraged blacks and appealed to Southern racists by opposing the extension of the landmark 1965 voting rights act, denouncing it as "essentially regional legislation." On Kent State he instructed the Justice Department not to call for a grand jury to investigate the killings. His sense of legal procedure, however, was best exemplified in his proposals for wiretapping without court order, no-knock searches, and "preventive detention" for repeat criminal offenders, plans as inventive in their own way as his bond sale innovations.

Nixon's aides, without sharing a common affection for each other or their chief (Haldeman referred to Nixon privately as "Rufus, the leader of the free world"), partook of Nixon's Us vs. Them view of things. Theirs was a "thieves' kitchen of intrigue and mutual suspicion," bound together by personal ambition and a genuine distaste for the liberal media and the counterculture. Nixon's enemies were their enemies and Nixon was quite specific as to who his enemies were. The Hiss case, Nixon wrote, "brought me national fame, but it also left a residue of hatred and hostility toward me—not only among the Communists but also among substantial segments of the press and the intellectual community . . . who have subjected me to a continuous utterly unprincipled and vicious smear campaign." Those old enemies had been joined by a new enemy, the student radicals. The radicals demonstrating against the Vietnam War were, argued Henry Kissinger, a threat to the nation, because their protests undermined American credibility in his secret negotiations with the North Vietnamese. "What was important," wrote Leslie Gelb, an editor of the Pentagon Papers, "was not so much what was going on in Vietnam but what was happening in America." Concurring on this point with Nixon and Kissinger, Gelb, a liberal, went on: "The war could be lost only if the American public turned sour on it. American public opinion was the essential domino. U.S. leaders knew it. Hanoi's leaders knew it." The importance of U.S. public opinion produced an inverted replay of the 1945 Yalta debate between Roosevelt's aide Harry Hopkins and Stalin, with Kissinger echoing the Soviet dictator's "We'll take care of our public opinion and you take care of yours." Xuan Thuy, the North Vietnamese negotiator, replied: "Since your public opinion speaks on the situation, therefore we must give it an interpretation." To which Kissinger responded: "I won't listen to it at these meetings." The peace negotiations, then, put Nixon in the enviable position of being able to identify his old foes in the liberal media as near-treasonous enemies of American diplomacy.

Nixon decided to mount a two-pronged attack on his domestic enemies, one secret and the other public and overtly political. When both the FBI and the CIA reported that they could find no connection between American radicals and foreign powers, the White House tried to set up a new special national security agency composed of people from the FBI, CIA, and DIA (Defense Intelligence Agency) led by J. Edgar Hoover, who turned the job down as an unjustified encroachment on FBI prerogatives. Rebuffed, Nixon decided to establish his own White House security operations. Following plans outlined by White House lawyer Tom Huston, a former student president of Young Americans for Freedom (YAF), the new security operation was given the job of both plugging leaks to the press and monitoring or disrupting, through means fair or foul, Nixon's political enemies. A liberal think tank, the Brookings Institution, for instance, was to be the target of a break-in and bombing. Never fully carried out, the Huston plan came to life as the "Plumbers," a "special" investigative unit designed to plug "leaks." In 1971 "Plumbers" burglarized the psychiatrist Daniel Ellsberg, a former defense analyst suspected of leaking the "secret" Pentagon Papers on the mishandling of the war to the New York *Times*. The "Plumbers' " fame, if not their fortune, came when during the presidential campaign of 1972 they were caught breaking into the Washington offices of the Democratic National Committee.

The key player in the openly political side of Nixon's offensive was Vice-President Spiro Agnew. Agnew had earlier been elected to the Maryland statehouse as a liberal Rockefeller Republican with black and Jewish support. He made a name for himself as a hard-liner and drew the attention of the Nixon entourage during the rioting in Baltimore set off by the assassination of Martin Luther King. Angered by the looting, he lashed out at the "circuit-riding, Hanoi-visiting, caterwauling, riot-inciting, burn-America-down type of [black] leader." For the first eleven months of the Nixon presidency, Agnew had little to do other than fantasize about palling around with his idol Frank Sinatra. Agnew, who came to ideas late in life, was taken by Irving Kristol's book of short essays *On the Democratic Idea in America*. Agnew discovered in Kristol's neo-conservative polemics intellectual rationalizations for his growing hostility to liberals and the anti-war movement, and he had his staff boil down the already brief essays in preparation for the day when he could use their ideas on the stump. His opportunity came after Nixon responded to the October 1969 anti-war demonstration with his famed "Silent Majority" speech. Its message, like Kristol's on the danger to democracy posed by activist zealots, was borrowed from Burke. The public response to Nixon's praise for the great mass of middle Americans and criticism of radicals led the President to tell his staff that "we've got those bastards on the run," and Agnew was given the job of keeping them there. In a series of speeches in October and November 1969, Agnew, who appeared to have become a demagogue out of boredom, delivered the most celebrated denunciatory speeches since Senator Joe McCarthy's famous Wheeling, West Virginia, escapade of 1950.

Agnew's speeches attacked national self-criticism as "a spirit of national masochism," liberal academics as "an effete corps of impudent snobs," and the television network executives as "a small and unelected elite," a "tiny and closed fraternity of privileged men" totally unrepresentative of the nation. The liberal media, and there is no doubt that the media was liberal, became the new devil of conservative demonology. It was now the media and not the Great Society or FDR or the bankers who were a conspiratorial threat to the American way of life.

When Agnew told an Ohio State commencement audience that "a society which comes to fear its children is effete," he was attacking campus radicalism, but when he said that "a sniveling, hand-wringing power structure deserves the violent rebellion it encourages," he was taking a potshot at both the liberal establishment and the Brahmins of the Republican Party, men who insisted that the Republican Party had to reach out to disaffected students. The story of the Republican Party in the 1960s was a tale of defeat and humiliation for its bluebloods, such as Rockefeller, Scranton, and Romney. But, as the theory went in the White House circles, the problem with the Republican Party was that it was still simply a vehicle for Yankee Wasps and if the party was ever to attract Baptist and blue-collar America it would have to purge itself of its mandarins. Nixon even toyed for a moment with the idea of a new party.

The 1970 mid-term elections held out the tantalizing prospect of building, if not a new party or even a Republican majority, then an ideological majority for Nixonism. "This country," said John Mitchell with eager anticipation, "is going so far right you are not going to recognize it." For his part, Agnew issued a clarion call for undisguised political warfare. If in attacking effete liberalism "we polarize the American people, I say it is time for a positive polarization." "It is time to rip away the rhetoric and to divide on authentic lines." "The time has come," he declared, "for someone . . . to represent the workingman of this country, the tax-paying patriot," who, he claimed, in a perverse echo of FDR, had become "the Forgotten Man" of American politics.

"Most voters," wrote Humphrey's political adviser Ben Wattenberg, speaking of rising crime rates and student radicalism, were "downright fearful" of many of the new facets of American life, and "given the chance they would vote against fear." Nixon and Agnew took Wattenberg's words to heart and campaigned for a new majority solely by appealing for "law and order." Nixon, said John Mitchell, "is running for sheriff." And in the summer of 1970 Spiro Agnew became a virtual one-man road show for toughness and traditionalism. But the avenging angels of the silent majority had neglected to read all of what Wattenberg had written, for Wattenberg also pointed out that while the mass of the voters who were "unpoor, unblack, and unyoung" were deeply worried by the adversary culture's assault, they were also troubled by the economy and rising unemployment.

Nixon had made a point of honoring the hardhat leaders who had attacked New York anti-war demonstrators, and Agnew promised that workingmen would be "the cornerstone of the New Majority," but unemployment had risen sharply over the summer of 1970 to 5 percent, the highest it had been in six years, and for construction workers it was over 12 percent. When AFL-CIO president George Meany, who had been wined and dined by the Administration for more than a year, failed to get any concrete proposals from the White House on unemployment, he backed off from the Republicans and denounced their "phony issues" and "inflammatory rhetoric." For their part, Democratic candidates effectively countered the Republicans by coming out to campaign with American flags in their lapels, emphasizing, in a more muted way, the law and order issue.

When the votes were counted, the Republicans had a net loss of eleven governorships and nine seats in the House while picking up two Senate seats. It was better than incumbent parties generally do in off years, but given the initial expectations, it was a great disappointment. By and large, Baptist and Catholic blue-collar America stuck with the Democrats. There was as yet no "Emerging Republican Majority."

Richard Nixon was an unusual "conservative" President. He was neither personally friendly with the leading corporate businessmen nor particularly interested in the principles of the market economy. The chairman of his Council of Economic Advisers found that Nixon's attitude toward his economic responsibilities was "somewhat like that of a little boy doing required lessons." What Nixon wanted from his economic advisers and the economy was, above all, the freedom of action to be an activist, pathbreaking President in the mold of Kennedy and Johnson. He believed that he had lost the 1960 election because of Eisenhower's refusal to stimulate the economy during an election year. It was a "mistake" he was determined not to repeat.

"The period of 1945 to 1970" was, in the words of Michael Harrington, "the time of the Keynesian euphoria," when a gently controlled inflation provided relatively full employment and "it seemed that the business cycle had been conquered." In the prosperity of the 1960s the work force increased by 19 percent but the economy's output jumped by 47 percent, producing a 35 percent increase in disposable income (adjusted for inflation). The American economy appeared to be a wondrous self-perpetuating machine which could simultaneously make us all wealthier and happier while financing an attack on our social problems. U.S. economic power made for utopian visions at home and awesome power abroad. In 1966 U.S. industry was so dominant that the profits of General Motors for that year equaled the combined profits of the 30 largest German, French, and British firms. Of the 87 companies in the world doing a billion-dollar business or more, 60 were American. The continued growth of American power seemed inevitable, alarming Europeans, who feared they would be "overtaken and dominated by a more advanced civilization."

The European fears were grossly exaggerated. By 1970 there were distinct signs of trouble for the American economy. Postwar prosperity had been fueled by cheap oil. But after a century of steadily increasing American production we had run out of "easy oil." The older American wells were played out and the new oil was in areas like Alaska's North Slope, which posed serious environmental problems. In the future, America would have to either raise the price of oil to pay for the cost of drilling deep into the earth's crust, open our doors to a dependency on cheap imported oil, or engage in energy conservation. Nixon chose the second option, with the White House expectation, blind to the turmoil of the Middle East, that foreign oil would remain cheap. By depending increasingly on foreign oil for our rapidly expanding energy consumption, the government gave the Arab oil-producing nations the means to blackmail the American economy.

In the 1950s the United States was producing half the world's cars and oil and about 40 percent of all manufactured goods. But in the years between 1964 and 1971, while American exports increased by 69 percent, imports, primarily from Europe and Japan, increased by 144 percent. In 1970, for the first time since World War II, the United States, the world's most powerful economy, was actually running a trade deficit. Arthur Burns traced the problems of the American economy to what came to be called stagflation, simultaneous inflation and high unemployment. "The rules of economics are not working in quite the way they used to," said Burns. "The nation must recognize," he explained, that we are dealing, practically speaking, with a new problem. Here he looked out across the political horizon. "The classical remedies" may not work "well enough or fast enough . . ."

In the post-election winter of 1970, Nixon was both dismayed by the election returns and disturbed by the damper the economy so thoughtlessly threatened to throw over his presidency. Nixonomics, gloated Democratic chairman Larry O'Brien, means that "all the things that should go up—the stock market, corporate profits, real spending income, productivity—go down, and all the things that should go down—unemployment, prices, interest rates —go up." Nixon responded with a daring move that symbolized the political realignments of the period. He appointed a conservative Democrat, former Texas governor John Connally, Secretary of the Treasury. Handsome, forceful, supremely self-confident, Connally, who commanded any room he entered, was everything Nixon wasn't but wanted to be.

The trade and treasury problems Connally faced were formidable. The liberal capitalist economic world order established by the United States at the end of World War II was based on a system of fixed exchange rates between world currencies. The system, established at the Bretton Woods Conference of 1944, was technically called the gold-exchange standard. The major currencies were tied to the dollar in fixed ratios and "the convertibility of dollars into gold at $35 an ounce was the system's theoretic anchor." In practice, the war-decimated economies of America's major trading partners held on to the dollars they earned or borrowed, because they needed the dollar to trade with the United States or third parties, so that the gold reserve was rarely drawn upon.

America's enormous productivity advantage over Europe was based on its standardized mass production made possible by standardized mass credit. As Europe recovered from the war, the creation of the Common Market and the modernization of its financial institutions allowed it to adopt those same techniques and reduce the enormous trade surplus the United States had once enjoyed. But as the U.S.-European trade gap narrowed, Europe, beginning in the early 1960s, was flooded with dollars sent there to support the Pax Americana. The enormous cost of maintaining an American army in Europe as a counter to the Soviets meant that by the 1960s, although the United States still had a favorable balance of trade with Europe, its current accounts, the sum of all monies sent back and forth, was in constant deficit.

The current-accounts deficit grew worse through the 1960s, because in the midst of extraordinary prosperity the United States was losing its competitive position. The loss was based on a decline in productivity and the growth of inflation, both of which made American goods more expensive. "Between 1965 and 1970, output per man-hour in manufacturing . . . rose on the average 14 percent each year in Japan, more than 6 percent in France, and even in Britain, plagued with industrial trouble, 3.6 percent. In the United States it rose 2.1 percent." American productivity declined because the baby-boom bulge in the labor force was unmet by investment in new plants and equipment and in part because American multinational corporations were exporting capital abroad to set up manufacturing based on low-cost labor. Between 1950 and 1970 the value of American manufacturing investment abroad grew from $12 to $78 billion. To make matters worse, a great deal of the capital expended in the United States was lost to productive uses. While businessmen often mocked hippies, they too were caught up in the Aquarian expectations of the period and vast sums were expended Peter Pan-like on projects which were never to produce a return. At the same time an increasing proportion of the nation's talent was directed not toward creating wealth but toward taking it away from someone else, through corporate takeovers and medical malpractice, libel, and damage suits. A proliferation of corporate lawyers, consultants, brokers, lobbyists, and speculators added to the GNP while reducing the sum of human happiness.

Inflation was a worldwide problem of Keynesian economies, but it was more severe in the United States than in Europe and Japan, primarily because of the cost of financing the Vietnam War. Johnson's advisers had urged him in 1965 to pay for the war through a tax increase. He refused, fearing this would endanger popular support for the war. Instead, he simply printed more money. Inflation rose from 2 percent in 1965 to 6 percent in 1970. The inflated, overvalued dollar was increasingly less competitive, and markets both at home and abroad were lost to the Japanese and Europeans. Cheaper foreign cars, for instance, which commanded less than 6 percent of the American market in 1960, had 16 percent by 1970–71. And along with German cars, Americans were buying Italian shoes, French wines, and Japanese TVs.

In sum, then, while the American percentage of manufacturing production declined, there was less and less need abroad for dollars to buy American goods, while Americans were spending more and more money overseas both to buy foreign goods and to support our far-flung military colonies. As dollars piled up overseas, the United States reached a gentlemen's agreement with our allies that those dollars would not be cashed in for gold. The French, however, contending they were not going to allow American paper money to buy up Europe, insisted on cashing in the dollars out of America's dwindling gold supply. If others chose to follow their example, Fort Knox would soon be bare.

Nixon and Connally were left with a series of tough choices. One way to reduce inflation would have been to cut government spending, but the military budget was already on the decline and a drop in social spending could endanger Nixon's '72 reelection. Monetarists like Milton Friedman proposed a sharp cutback in the money supply, which would, hopefully, deflate the dollar and make American exports more competitive in the long run, but deflation also risked creating unemployment, which would backfire at election time. Finally, Nixon could devalue the dollar by breaking the Bretton Woods Agreement and cutting the tie between the dollar and gold at $35 an ounce. But in 1931, when the British had cut sterling, then the world's major reserve currency loose from gold, the international monetary system collapsed and exacerbated the Depression, which had already put a quarter of the American labor force out of work.

Faced with the limits of American power in Vietnam, Nixon and

Kissinger chose to scale down the American role in order to buttress the policy of global containment which underlay it. Faced with the decline of American competitiveness, Nixon and Connally chose to redefine the role of the dollar rather than reorganize the managerial state capitalism which underlay it. Connally exemplified the corporatism of managerial state capitalism: "The days are past," said Connally, "when we could enjoy the luxury of an antagonistic relationship between business and government." Current conditions, he argued, referring to growing international competition from government-supported Japanese and European cartels, required a partnership between big government, big business, and big labor. Or, as Nixon sugarcoated it, "there are times when economic freedom must be protected from its own excesses."

Nixon's announcement that "I am now a Keynesian in economics" was greeted by incredulity by those who wrongly thought of him as a conservative ideologue and with anger by those Republicans who were free-marketeers. But his announcement of his Keynesianism was little more than a reflection of the realities of the modern mixed economy, in which government inevitably plays a major role in organizing the economy. In 1929 government spending amounted to a mere 8 percent of the GNP; by 1970 it was 30 percent. The government, through its fiscal and monetary policies, regulations and guidelines, affected every aspect of the national economy. Connally, for one, understood that, and the former protégé of Lyndon Johnson proposed to use the activist presidency created by FDR for conservative corporate goals, much as Nixon was using the foreign policy powers FDR and Truman had created for conservative ends in foreign affairs.

Connally brought aggressive, table-pounding economic nationalism to the Treasury. He was blunt in his criticism of both the free military ride that the Europeans and Japanese were getting and their trade barriers against American goods. "It isn't a question of cutting the number of American troops in Europe," he explained. "It's a question of who the hell is going to pay for them." Connally, said Richard Whalen, "had not the slightest economic or cultural affinity for Western Europe. His world view was that of a land-locked Texan, who recognized neighbors and strangers. Foreigners fell into two categories: cooperative and uncooperative." Insofar as the same Western European countries which relied on the

United States for their military defense had refused to come to America's aid during the Vietnam War, he felt no obligation to consult with them on the American economic decisions which would affect them all.

On Sunday, August 15, 1971, a month after the startling announcement of Henry Kissinger's hitherto secret contacts with Red China, Nixon shocked both Europe and America with the announcement of his "New Economic Policy." "We found ourselves confronted," said Nixon, "with intense and increasing competition from other major industrialized nations. As one measure of this, between 1960 and 1971 Japan's exports increased 242 percent." At the same time "our total [gold] reserves dwindled from 21 billion dollars in 1946 to roughly 12 billion at the end of 1971 . . ." This "means that the old days, in which we were willing to accept arrangements which put as at a competitive disadvantage with respect to our trading partners, are gone—and the old policies must go with them." The upshot was that the United States reneged on the Bretton Woods Agreement and ended the convertibility of dollars into gold. Henceforth, currencies would "float" against one another without the benefit of an anchor. The monetary system which had provided international trading stability for a quarter century was simply abandoned. Further, to aid the American balance of trade, there was to be a 10 percent surcharge on imports. There would also be a 10 percent tax credit for business investment in new plants and equipment, and, most startling of all, in light of Nixon's earlier statements, a ninety-day freeze on wages and prices, but not profits, to slow down inflation. The immediate public reaction was overwhelmingly favorable. Nixon's economic nationalism had put him in a good position for the 1972 election. And to ensure the best possible conditions for the campaign, "every effort," recalls Defense Secretary Melvin Laird, "was made to create an economic boom for the 1972 election." "The Defense Department, for example, bought a two-year supply of toilet paper." And at the Federal Reserve Bank, the monetarist chairman Arthur Burns compromised himself by sharply increasing the money supply to stimulate a preelection prosperity. The combination of all these measures was to create a runaway inflation well before the 1973 oil-price shock, which would have to be cooled off after the election. In pursuit of his own power Nixon was creating a stop-and-go political business cycle to match the economic one which was already plaguing capitalist economies.

In his memoirs Henry Kissinger describes his surprise at a comment made to him by Anatoly Dobrynin early in the Nixon presidency. The Soviet Ambassador spoke of the "great opportunities that had been lost in Soviet-American affairs, especially between 1959 and 1963." This was the period, in retrospect, not only of two Berlin crises and the Cuban missile crisis but also of the Sino-Soviet split. Though far less visible to the Americans, the rivalry and resentment between Russia and China was undermining the unity of the "Communist bloc." The ancient animosities between the Russian and Chinese empires, animosities similar in their twentieth-century ideological form to the internal wars of Islam and Christendom, reached a new level of tension when the Chinese exploded their first atomic bomb in 1964. The loose talk in Bejing of how China could take several hundred million casualties in a nuclear exchange and still come out the winner frightened the Soviets, who feared a Chinese attempt to instigate a nuclear confrontation between themselves and the United States. LBJ, hemmed in by Vietnam and domestic turmoil, moved cautiously to exploit the situation. In vain, he repeatedly sought Russian mediation to end the war in Vietnam and he was on the verge of signing a strategic arms limitation agreement with the Soviets when Moscow in 1968 invaded Czechoslovakia, which had grown too liberal for the Kremlin to tolerate.

In March 1969, just three months after Nixon had taken office, the increasingly undisguised hostility between the rival leaders of the "socialist camp" briefly burst into border warfare. The alarmed Soviets secretly sounded out Washington about how the United States would respond to a preemptive Soviet nuclear strike against the Chinese. Nixon and Kissinger, who were already floating rumors of a rapprochement with the Chinese, were cool to the possibility. What they wanted was, not a defeated China, but a situation in which the continuing rivalry between Russia and China could be used first to extricate the United States from Vietnam and then to build a new world order based on balance-of-power diplomacy.

The Sino-Soviet split opened the road to what Hans Morgenthau called "the ideological decontamination" of American foreign policy. The American emphasis on ideology, argued Kissinger, had led to wild fluctuation between "poles of euphoria and panic." Cloaked in the robes of Old World cynicism, Kissinger proposed to purge American foreign policy of its idealist sentimentalities. The emotional fluctuations of anti-Communism would be replaced by the stability and enduring coherence of power and interest. We "have no permanent enemies," Kissinger explained in December 1969, "we will judge other countries, including Communist countries . . . on the basis of their actions and not on the basis of their domestic ideology."

The new diplomacy, like the New Economic Policy, seemed to recognize the limits of American power. But the recognition of limits did not, for Nixon and Kissinger, lead, as it led with many liberals, to a withdrawal from America's international position. Instead, it produced a reformation based on an updating of Roosevelt's concept of the "Four Policemen" and classic nineteenth-century balance-of-power assumptions.

In Nixon's grand formulation of the new American realism, which he presented to a conference of media executives in July 1971, it was taken for granted that Russia and the United States were stalemated militarily. After the initial American lead, both sides had approximately an equal number of ICBMs (about 1,050), so that neither could hope to gain a decisive nuclear advantage. In the future, said Nixon, "economic power will be the key to other kinds of power." "As we look ahead five years, ten years," explained the President, "we see five great economic superpowers: The United States, Western Europe, the Soviet Union, Mainland China, and of course Japan" (the only newcomer to FDR's Four Policemen). With military domination rendered obsolete by the dangers of Mutually Assured Nuclear Destruction, these five powers would, in the manner of Adam Smith's invisible hand, balance each other off, producing an equilibrium beneficial to all.

In effect, this new condominium of the great powers would jointly police the world while relations among them would be kept in harmony by the shifting alignments of interest. It was an alluring but flawed vision. To start with, neither Russia nor China was an economic superpower. Far from it. It was in part their economic backwardness that made them interested in a rapprochement with the West. A fragmented Western Europe, moreover, was incapable of acting coherently. But most importantly, the harmony depended solely on a fragile mechanical balance unsupported by shared authority or common moral purpose.

Kissinger recognized the problem and insisted: "We must identify interests and positive values beyond security." Like FDR, Nixon and Kissinger wanted to draw the Soviets into a web of mutually beneficial and hence mutually restraining relationships. It was to be an exercise in behavior modification, or as one critic sarcastically put it: "The bear would be treated like one of B. F. Skinner's pigeons." "The Soviets," said Kissinger, "want a predictable administration. And in a curious way, I think they want one that puts limits on them. Their system is not capable of operating under the principle of self-restraint." The carrots Kissinger held out included our acknowledgment of the equality of the two superpowers, which the Soviet leadership seemed to crave. That full acceptance of Russia's military status, which was designed to reassure and soothe the Russians, was epitomized, FDR style, by Nixon's self-advertised "personal relationship with Brezhnev." But there were more concrete benefits as well. The Russians were granted badly needed trade credits and trading status as a most favored nation along with promises of technological help for the Soviets' retarded industries. Most important of all, Nixon and Kissinger gave what FDR had refused to give and what neither Stalin's blockade of Berlin nor Khrushchev's Cuban adventure had been able to gain—unequivocal American recognition of Soviet hegemony over Eastern Europe, including East Germany. The path was opened for greatly expanded trade between West Germany and the Soviets, which in time would undercut the American relationship with Western Europe.

The stick with which Nixon and Kissinger hoped to push the Soviets into a "structure" of peace was China. The Chinese, in their own words, hoped "to fight the near barbarian with the far barbarian." When Chinese Foreign Minister Zhou Enlai told the Americans: "One should not lose the whole world just to gain South Vietnam," and when Nixon decried the U.S. tendency "to obscure our vision almost totally of the world because of Vietnam," both men were saying that their common enemy (the U.S.S.R.)

made them friends of a sort. America, said LBJ's Secretary of State, Dean Rusk, was in Vietnam because of the dangers of Chinese imperialism, but in February 1972, Richard Nixon, who had made his political career by denouncing Truman's sellout of "Free" China and had fought ever since to deny Mao's Red China legitimacy, traveled to Bejing to shower praise and concessions on his old enemies. On his arrival, timed to coincide with prime-time TV viewing in the United States, Nixon struck the tone that would characterize his meeting with the Chinese leaders: "What we do here can change the world."

Nixon and Kissinger insisted that the United States had to deal with the Russians even if we found them boorishly crude. By contrast, there was for both men, as for many Americans, a genuine affection for the Chinese, their leaders, and their culture. Nixon the Quaker and John Kenneth Galbraith the Scotch Calvinist both admired what they saw as the "spiritual and spartan life" of China, a life which reminded them of America before it had been corrupted by material pleasures. "The leader class in the United States," Nixon told his Cabinet, "lack the backbone, the strength" that the Chinese leaders have. "Whatever the failures of their system," he exclaimed, "there is in their leader class a spirit that makes them formidable." But for those who cared to look, China was probably the society that has come closest to Hannah Arendt's ideal-typical totalitarianism.

Symbolically, Nixon offered the Chinese the words on Taiwan they, like the Russians on Eastern Europe, had waited so long to hear. Sounding much like Truman, Nixon announced: "The ultimate relationship between Taiwan and the Mainland is not a matter for the United States to decide." Substantively, he offered economic credits and badly needed technical assistance, with the clear implication that if the relationship proved mutually beneficial, military aid could be forthcoming. The "linkage," to use a favorite Kissinger word, Nixon wanted in return was for the Chinese to pressure the North Vietnamese to accept the American terms being offered in what until just before the China trip were secret U.S.-North Vietnamese negotiations. Those negotiations were stalled because, while the United States was willing to withdraw, it still hoped that the Thieu government might survive. So it refused North Vietnamese proposals for forming a "coalition" government between the Thieu forces and the North Vietnamese-controlled Viet Cong.

Nixon and Kissinger greatly overestimated China's influence on Vietnam. In the period between Nixon's February visit to Peking and his scheduled May trip to Russia, the North Vietnamese demonstrated their independence by sharply escalating the military struggle in Vietnam to forestall any possible big-power deal. Nixon responded with a dramatic escalation of his own, placing his Moscow trip and emerging understanding with the Soviets at risk. Nixon ordered a restoration of the B-52 attacks on North Vietnam suspended by Johnson in 1968, and when the Vietnamese offensive across the so-called demilitarized zone continued, he ordered the mining of North Vietnam's chief port, Haiphong. Haiphong was the Vietnamese port for Soviet supplies, so it was feared that the Russians would be forced to cancel the scheduled Moscow summit rather than allow their merchant marine to be endangered by American mines. Nixon won his gamble. The Soviets, unnerved in part by the China visit and in the process of purchasing badly needed American grain supplies, remained silent as their own and their allies' shipping came under American attack.

In May, Nixon traveled to Moscow as planned to conclude agreement on the Strategic Arms Limitation Talks (SALT). "The talks were based on a rare conjunction of technological and military trends." Improvements in spy satellites made it possible, for the first time, to monitor an arms limitation agreement. At the same time, the reduction in American military spending under Nixon and the rapid growth of the Soviet ICBM forces made a missile agreement an attractive alternative to a new American buildup at a time when no new American weapons systems were being developed. "In traditional diplomacy," explained Kissinger, "the aim was, through an accumulation of small advantages, to gain a qualitative edge over your major rivals. In the nuclear age, the most dangerous thing to aim for is a qualitative edge over your major rivals," because the very act of trying to achieve that edge could encourage an enemy's preemptive strike. The concept of American nuclear "superiority," upon which the defense of Europe had been based, was to be replaced by "sufficiency." Nixon, who insisted on negotiating without his technical advisers present, defined sufficiency as a SALT agreement which limited the Soviets to 1,618 missiles and the United States to 1,054. The rationale for the disparity was the American qualitative superiority.

In addition to SALT, Nixon and Brezhnev signed a statement of "Basic Principles" which called upon both sides to "do their utmost to avoid military confrontations" and to "recognize that efforts to obtain unilateral advantage at the expense of the other, directly or indirectly," are inconsistent "with the objectives of the agreement." "The historians of some future age," enthused Nixon, "will write of the year 1972 . . . that this was the year when America helped to lead the world out of the lowlands of constant war to the high plateau of peace." For the time being Nixon had every reason to be pleased with the agreement. At a point when Americans were badly divided on foreign policy and Russian military power was growing rapidly, he seemed to have secured an agreement which exchanged American economic aid for Soviet military restraint. As in 1945, the hope was that American economic aid would become so indispensable for the well-being of Soviet society that the Russian leadership would think twice before jeopardizing it. It was to be no more successful the second time around.

In the long run, by promising far more than they could deliver the agreements with the Soviets increased rather than decreased mutual suspicions. To begin with, the assumptions behind the economic carrot were flawed. Western technical and economic aid, it was argued, would lead to an internal liberalization and thus to an external mellowing of Soviet policy. But, in fact, modernization through Western aid was an alternative to internal liberalization, while is was the capitalists who became dependent on sales to the Soviets rather than the other way around. Even more important, by overselling détente to suggest that it represented a cessation of hostilities everywhere, while the Soviets made it clear that their support for "liberation" struggles in the Third World would continue, Nixon laid the groundwork for a tremendous disillusionment. The Russians, it would be argued by Ronald Reagan and other conservative critics, could never be trusted. Similarly, Nixon's miscalculation on the missile numbers, in which the Soviets were allowed more missiles in the expectation that it would take a long time for them to match the American qualitative edge, was quickly exposed when the Russians soon developed their own MIRVs (Multiple Independently Targetable Reentry Vehicles)—that is, multi-warhead missiles. Here again the reaction was to question the value of negotiations. After having insisted that their goal was to free American foreign policy from its cycles of euphoria and disillusionment, the Nixon-Kissinger initiatives set off a new round of disillusionment.

In the short run, however, Nixon's televised trip to Moscow, which *Newsweek* dubbed "the Moscow primary," was a tremendous political success for the President. Nixon had used his control of foreign policy to dominate the 1972 presidential campaign season. Nixon was the first American President to travel to China; his proclamations of peace and détente on prime-time television overshadowed the continuing conflict in Vietnam and guaranteed an avalanche of public acclaim. "A lot of things are coming together at a point," said a visibly pleased John Ehrlichman. "And it is a point, frankly, which we selected as a target time as a matter of enlightened self-interest."

12

Coup and Counter-coup

I always used to be sure reform would sweep the country, that is, I used to be sure until I talked to the man next to me on the streetcar.

—RAY STANNARD BAKER

THE DEMOCRATS ENTERED THE 1972 presidential nomination season more divided than ever by the schisms of 1968. A host of candidates, their place on the political compass defined by their stand on the war and their relationship to the New Politics, fought as much to humiliate their party enemies as to defeat the Republicans. The spirit of the campaign was captured by McGovern admirer Hunter Thompson, who in unconscious parody argued that "the only way to save the Democratic Party is to destroy it." Remade, the Democratic Party would be a fit vehicle, said Thompson (purposely echoing Allen Ginsberg's "Howl"), for those who were "the most committed, the most idealistic, the best minds of my generation."

On the left, as redefined by the events of the late 1960s, the candidates fighting to inherit the Kennedy-McCarthy legions of 1968 were New York mayor and former "silk stocking" Republican John Lindsay and former World War II bomber pilot and college professor George McGovern, the Senate's most outspoken critic of the Vietnam War. In the not so vital center stood the early front-runner, the Democratic 1968 vice-presidential candidate, Edmund Muskie, and the once Happy Warrior, Hubert Humphrey. Humphrey, the Democrat New Politics liberals loved to hate, was dogged both by his record on Vietnam and by the blue-collar reaction to the Johnson-Humphrey record on civil rights. To their immediate right stood Washington's Senator Henry Jackson, a Vietnam hawk and economic liberal, who was big labor's second choice after Humphrey. Beyond the pale of respectability was George Wallace, the man who won the most votes in the primaries.

In the spring of 1972, Muskie's middle-of-the-road campaign faltered before a highly polarized electorate. Assisted by some dirty tricks from CREEP, Nixon's Committee to Re-Elect the President, he was pushed from the race. In one of the many ironies of the campaign the Nixonites were doing all they could to help nominate the choice of their archenemies, George McGovern, a man they correctly sized up as unelectable.

As late as March 1972, McGovern was the choice of only one Democrat in twenty. But he had the advantage of running under the rules he and his allies had designed to minimize the representation of party leaders and traditional Democrats while maximizing the impact of the New Politics activists who were the driving force behind his campaign. McGovern's core supporters, drawn from the anti-war, feminist, and environmental movements, were less interested in politics than in the mental hygiene of raising the nation's consciousness to their own exalted levels. For his part, McGovern recognized that ethnic Democrats viewed him with suspicion. Addressing the party's ritual of unity, the annual Al Smith Dinner, he joked that "I feel a little like Al Smith addressing the Baptist League of East Texas." McGovern came to resent the ethnics and the Southerners as people trapped in the false consciousness of opposing the good things he was going to bring them, but he made an effort, albeit on his own terms, to reach out to Wallace supporters.

In the Florida primary, Wallace, running on the issues, swept to an overwhelming victory, carrying every county in the state. In April 1971, the Supreme Court, led by Nixon appointee Warren Burger, had ruled 9–0 that cities could bus children out of their neighborhoods to improve the overall racial balance in the municipalities' school systems. The decision, which blacks greeted tepidly, produced outrage and the firebombing of buses by lower-middle-class whites in some of the cities affected. Whites were confused as well as angry. On the one hand, black leaders loudly and forcibly denounced "forced integration," calling instead for black control of black schools financed from the public treasury. On the other hand, the Court imposed a "forced integration" that stripped people of control over their children's education.

Wallace made busing and, to a lesser extent, school prayer the central issues of the primary and forced all the other candidates to define themselves in relation to his attacks on the federal government. "What did these so-called lib'rals bring us?" Wallace asked rhetorically from the podium, and then answered: "Drugs. Riots. Bureaucrats. Contempt for the average citizen, taxes that crush him and leave no freedom. Wars that can't be won. . . . That's what they brung us." The problem, Wallace explained in blazing the trail for what would come to be called the New Right, was that "as a result of the growing power of Washington, we have already become a government-fearing people instead of a God-fearing people. . . . I have accepted Christ as my personal savior, and that is one important reason why I have pledged my life to opposing tyranny wherever I find it."

Thrown off balance by the success of Wallace's crusading right-wing moralism, Humphrey, the most popular candidate among blacks, flirted with attacking busing but finally backed off, whereas Muskie responded with outrage and denounced Wallace for what he was, a racist. Even the Republicans were drawn into the fray. Nixon, who had spent a good deal of time looking over his shoulder at Wallace, came out with a ringing condemnation of busing and called for legislative circumvention of the Court's decision. Nixon, whose record on civil rights was mixed—desegregation advanced rapidly during his administration—had earlier tried to neutralize Wallace's strength in Dixie by attempting to appoint two undistinguished Southern conservatives to the Supreme Court.

The most interesting response to Wallace came from George McGovern, who refused to condemn Wallace and instead, acting on a theory supplied by pollster Pat Cadell, tried to sympathize with and appeal to the "alienation" of the Wallace voters. Alienation, according to Cadell, "cut across all ranks and classes of Americans." It was a matter, not of issues, but of psychic well-being, and McGovern could, the argument went, win over those voters by reaching out to them and expressing an interest in their problems. Left- and right-wing moralism were to be fused in a therapeutic campaign against the flabby, pragmatic center.

On March 15, 1972, the eve of what was to become his greatest electoral triumph, Wallace was critically wounded by an assassin during a speech in which he attacked Humphrey and McGovern for backing the Gulf of Tonkin resolution. "Those liberals got us into the war," he charged, "and then they wouldn't let us win it." Wallace had already run a strong second in two Northern states, Indiana and Pennsylvania, and now he won both the Maryland and Michigan primaries, partly on the strength of the busing issue. Forced to withdraw because of his serious wound, Wallace had 3.35 million votes but only 323 delegates. McGovern, master of the rules he had helped design, had 2.2 million votes but 409 delegates. With Wallace eliminated, the contest was reduced to a two-man race between Humphrey and McGovern, with the outcome hinging on what was to be a bruising California primary.

In California, Humphrey's uncharacteristically tough attack on McGovern exposed the electoral weaknesses of the social gospeler's campaign. Picking up where Jackson had begun, Humphrey attacked both the smug self-righteousness of McGovern's style and his stand on "Acid, Amnesty [for Vietnam draft evaders], and Abortion," the last two of which McGovern supported. Humphrey also ridiculed McGovern's "demogrant" proposal, a rehashed version of the guaranteed minimum income proposals of the Nixon administration, which would have given $1,000 to everyone "from the poorest migrant workers to the Rockefellers." The money for these proposals, said Humphrey accurately, would come out of the pockets of the workingmen who paid the taxes. By campaign's end a badly weakened McGovern won a narrow pyrrhic victory, as a substantial number of Humphrey voters indicated that they would switch to the Republicans in the general election.

The revenge of the New Politics on the old was completed at the McGovern-dominated Democratic national convention. The new rules for selecting delegates on the basis of numerical quotas (initiated by the McGovern Commission on Party Structure and Delegate Selection) succeeded in sharply increasing the representation of blacks and women, whose numbers tripled from 1968. And youth (delegates between eighteen and twenty-nine), a key element in the McGovern electoral strategy since the passage of the amendment giving eighteen-year-olds the franchise, increased eightfold from less than 3 to 23 percent. Looking over her own California delegation pledged to McGovern, actress Shirley MacLaine exulted that it "looked like a couple of high schools, a grape boycott, a Black Panther rally, and four or five politicians who walked in the wrong door." Some politicians weren't able to get in by any door. Excluded from the convention were the Bronx and Brooklyn chairmen of the Democratic Party and the New York State Democratic chairman, Joe Crangle. The increased representation for McGovern's constituencies came at the price of excluding local party leaders and representatives of white lower-middle-class "ancestral" Democrats. Iowa's delegation, for instance, hadn't a single farmer, while New York, the nation's most unionized state, had only three members of organized labor but nine members of Gay Liberation organizations. They've "reformed us out of the presidency, and now they're trying to reform us out of the party," complained Ohio congressman Wayne Hays, later driven from Capitol Hill in a sex scandal.

The most dramatic reversal came with the Illinois delegation, traditionally led by the archvillain of 1968, Chicago mayor Richard Daley. Daley and his entire delegation were unseated and replaced by unelected delegates led by the black preacher Jesse Jackson and a reform alderman. The new delegation was virtually bereft of ethnic Democrats from a stronghold of ethnic Democratic voters. "Anybody who would reform Chicago's Democratic Party by dropping the white ethnic," wrote Daley critic Mike Royko, "would probably begin a diet by shooting himself in the stomach." McGovern and his supporters did not so much capture the Democratic Party as displace it. "They have got their own party going," said an old-time Democratic leader, "and they have not invited me."

Early in the Nixon presidency speech writer William Safire received a request from H. R. Haldeman: "Few seem aware of the Nixon political philosophy. . . . The President feels that this general subject . . . would be worth some work and effort by our PR group. Would you please follow up?" "Strange," Safire responded, "fitting a philosophy to the set of deeds, but sometimes that is what has to be done." The lack of consistent perspective allowed Nixon to engage in the "spectacular" economic and diplomatic departures which earned applause at the price of conservative disaffection. Nixon's support for a guaranteed minimum income bill (which failed congressional approval) and his sharp reduction in spending on military hardware led, along with "détente," to a "suspension" of support for the Administration by a prominent group of conservative intellectuals led by William F. Buckley. But whatever Nixon's meanderings, and they were considerable (as the New York *Times* put it: "Seldom in Western politics . . . has a national leader so completely turned his back on a lifetime of beliefs to adopt those of his political opponents"), he was faithful to his hatred for the federal bureaucracy, a hatred which formed the very marrow of Republican politics.

Nixon became obsessed with his inability to control the bureaucracy. Safire records Nixon's despairing handwritten note in the margin of a memo: "government doesn't work." What led to the note and numerous outbursts was Nixon's discovery that low-level civil service appointees were able to block his initiatives with impunity. As Ben Heineman explained in a secret report prepared for LBJ: "Top political executives—the President and the Cabinet Secretaries—preside over agencies which they never own and only rarely command. Their managerial authority is constantly challenged by powerful legislative committees, well-organized interest groups, entrenched bureau chiefs with narrow program mandates, and the career civil service." Given these realities, even the presidentially appointed members of the Cabinet tend to become dependent on civil service employees, most of whom are Democrats, and switch their primary loyalties to the department they are administering. As John Ehrlichman put it, speaking of the high-level appointees: "We only see them at the White House Christmas party; they go and marry the natives."

The request for Safire to design and package a Nixon political philosophy led to Nixon's proposals for a "New Federalism." Nixon's frustrations with the bureaucracy, combined with his awareness that everyone from "pointyheads to peckerwoods" was losing confidence in governmental authority, led early on in his administration to the theme of government itself as the source of the country's problems.

The war aside, the growing frustration with government had three primary sources. First, there was the long-term "Weberian" shift of power from the sometimes capricious personal authority of local officials to the bureaucratically rational but distant power of national institutions. The political world which revolved around the local notable, the political ward heeler, the priest, or powerful proprietor was displaced by the burgeoning power of the federal courts and regulatory agencies. The new rules were much fairer in that they recognized the rights of blacks and other minorities. But the new forms of power lacked authority; unavoidably, if they were to impose racial justice, they lacked the stamp of local consent.

The shift in the locus of authority was accompanied by a change in the range and function of government tasks. In the 1930s the New Deal pioneered social aid for the temporarily destitute. The New Deal extended its aid to those who, in nineteenth-century language, could be called the "worthy poor," widows, orphans, and normally stable workingmen temporarily thrown out of work by the business cycle. The Great Society was far, far more ambitious. It extended a helping hand to those "unworthy poor" once considered beyond the pale. It promised not merely to rehabilitate people down on their luck but to raise up from the underclass people, often black, who had never fully participated in the economic life of the country. These were people who needed long-term, possibly permanent government aid if they were to be freed from endemic poverty. Theories aside, however, the government knew very little about how to extend such aid effectively.

Finally, the Great Society's expansion of government services had produced a welfare-state version of tribalism, in which ethnic and social groups organized to compete for government monies. Here too there were frustrations as the expectations of government support far outran the monies available, producing new disappointments, while heightening old ethnic conflicts.

Nixon, allowing his natural Republican juices to flow, played off these frustrations. The great silent majority of hardworking Americans, he insisted, were shouldering the burden of wasteful and intrusive social programs which rewarded the indolent while taxing the energetic. Nixon was right; government had grown far more expensive and he was correct that lower-middle-class and middle-class white taxpayers were carrying most of the financial burden, but most of the new expenditures were not, as he implied, being spent on social welfare for black Americans. The bulk of the increase in government spending went, not for Great Society programs to aid the black underclass, but on "providing money for one program which was a generation old and inadequate [Social Security] and in achieving a very limited installment of a proposal [national health insurance] which had first been seriously urged by Harry Truman in 1949." "Between 1960 and 1970, there was a $44.3 billion rise in the funds spent on Social Security and on Medicare." "That was," Michael Harrington points out, "three times as much as all the increased expenditures on public assistance (welfare, Medicaid, food stamps, housing subsidies, and student aid), for the innovative programs of the Great Society."

McGovern, cut off from the pulse of American life, campaigned for more government programs even as government was being discredited. Watching the 1972 campaign commercials, a viewer was likely to conclude that Nixon, whose ads attacked government, was the challenger and McGovern, whose ads proposed new programs, was the incumbent. The sitting President succeeded in depicting himself as the "underdog" running against the permanent "establishment" of big government and Washington liberalism. "Elect me," promised Richard Nixon, "and I will save you from that fellow who created a $33 billion deficit. Elect me and I will protect you from my Justice Department's past support of busing." "Elect me and I will save you from [racial] quotas imposed by my Department of Health, Education, and Welfare." Such chutzpah could never have succeeded had George McGovern not been, despite his earnest efforts, so impervious to the basic sentiments of American life. Richard Nixon never penetrated the hearts of Americans, but his knowledge of surfaces sufficed in a campaign against a man whose promise to crawl to Hanoi to promote a Vietnam War settlement undercut support of the very peace he was trying to achieve.

From Nixon's perspective the only clouds on the election horizon were newspaper accounts of a break-in at the Democratic National Committee's offices in the Watergate complex by men connected with CREEP. McGovern tried unsuccessfully to connect the break-in with the illegal bombing of Cambodia and the Administration's broad disregard for democratic practices. But Watergate, said Robert Shogun of the Los Angeles *Times*, seemed another joke on McGovern, an indication of the futility of his campaign. "If McGovern had kept after Watergate," quipped Henry Kissinger, "he would have made wiretapping popular."

Nixon won in a negative landslide with 61 percent of the vote. McGovern carried only Massachusetts and the District of Columbia. It was overwhelmingly a vote against George McGovern by traditional Democrats who deserted the party in droves. Nixon won almost 40 percent of "habitual" democratic voters. His blue-collar vote jumped from 35 percent in 1968 to 52 percent in 1972. His Southern support grew even more decisively, from 38 to 70 percent, and he was also the first Republican to win a majority of the Roman Catholic vote. The election was a rejection of George McGovern and the New Politics; it was not a victory for the Republican Party, which, despite the sweep, remained in a distinct minority in both houses, losing an additional two seats in the Senate. What we have now, concluded George McGovern, "is a country presided over by a President [Nixon] who had married the Republican Party to the Wallace people . . ."

In 1962 Chicago journalist Lawrence Fanning summed up his worries about Kennedy's Camelot and its glorification by the press: "It boils down to government by an intellectual elite, and the policies can only be as good as the members of the elite. What happens if the elite is replaced by a venal, arrogant or power-mad cabal?" Fanning's question was answered in the winter of 1972 when Richard Nixon became the nation's first activist right-of-center President surrounded by an "elite" of ad men and apparatchiks.

Returned to office with an overwhelming majority, Nixon was freed from the pragmatic demands of his first term. In 1969 Daniel Patrick Moynihan had warned Nixon: "All the Great Society activist constituencies are lying out there in wait, poised to get you if you try to come after them: the professional welfarists, the urban planners, the day-carers, the social workers, the public housers. Frankly, I'm terrified at the thought of cutting back too fast." But as early as September 1972 Nixon knew he would no longer have to hold back. He told White House Counsel John Dean: "We have not used the power in these four years, as you know. We have never used it. We have not used the Bureau and we have not used the Justice Department" against our enemies, "but things are going to change now . . . ."

Nixon's "mandate," as he liked to refer to his 1972 election victory, reinforced the President's sense of himself as the lonely embattled leader, the true representative of all the people, who could not allow himself to be shackled by his bureaucratic and congressional enemies, who, truthfully enough, were representatives of "special interests." It was in the name of this plebiscitary view of the presidency that Nixon followed through on his Huston plan to wage political war on his enemies. In the name of "national security" and a coherent foreign policy, he would apply the tactics of the Cold War to domestic politics.

♦ The first item on Nixon's new agenda was an all-out assault on the Great Society. The day after the election, he told a newspaper interviewer that during the 1960s the upper class had gone soft; it became permissive, he said, and began "throwing money at problems." This in turn, he claimed, led to social breakdown. It was time to restore order by replacing the governmentalism of the Great Society with the old virtues of discipline and hard work. ◊ But before Nixon could take on such a formidable task, the highly divisive matter of Vietnam had to be cleared away.

Kissinger described Nixon to the Soviets as being "direct, honest, strong, fatalistic . . . [and] not affected one iota by public opinion." Yet Kissinger admits in his memoirs that public pressure finally pushed the United States out of Vietnam. As Theodore

Draper put it: "To obey the will of the people went against the [Nixon] grain; to resist indefinitely was, however, impossible. The defense of 'honor' and 'prestige' could only permit a delaying rearguard action." Kissinger, for instance, acknowledged the necessity of withdrawal from the day he took office. The problem was to negotiate a conclusion to the conflict that didn't threaten American credibility by appearing to be a defeat. For four years and 19,000 lost American lives the United States had negotiated with the North Vietnamese in the lingering hope of achieving better terms. But for all that time, the talks remained deadlocked because the North Vietnamese refused a settlement which required them to remove their troops from the South. The talks were stalemated, said Kissinger, because Hanoi "would be satisfied only with victory." And victory is what Hanoi got, not because the military situation had changed in its favor, but because, as Kissinger puts it, the President was "determined not to have his second term tormented like the first by our national trauma." In the early years of his presidency LBJ downplayed the war in order to pass his Great Society legislation. Nixon wanted to put the war aside in part to terminate the Great Society.

Instead of the "Peace with Honor" that the Administration set as its goal, the Paris Peace Accords signed on January 27, 1973, were a cease-fire in place similar to what had been proposed in 1968 by the Johnson administration. In return for North Vietnam's release of all captured Americans, the United States agreed to withdraw the remaining American ground forces within sixty days without requiring a corresponding withdrawal of North Vietnamese troops. A toothless international control commission was to patrol the cease-fire. The accords agreed in principle to a unified Vietnam created by "free and democratic general elections." But electoral rhetoric aside, the reality was that the United States abandoned South Vietnam's Thieu government. The likely outcome, after what Kissinger called a "decent interval," was a complete North Vietnamese military victory. Neither Vietnam nor the Vietnamese people had ever been intrinsically important to the United States. The "experiment" in counterinsurgency having failed beyond a shadow of a doubt, after 56,000 American deaths and 300,000 casualties and $140 billion in war costs, we left the South Vietnamese to their fate.

The Paris Peace Accords, signed just a week after the start of his second term, freed Nixon to concentrate on the limited government/free market themes he had laid out in his inaugural address. Within two weeks after the start of his second term, he had announced plans to eliminate 112 Great Society programs, while cutting the budgets of those that remained. Congressman Carl Perkins of Kentucky described it as an "ill-concealed effort to repeal the nineteen-sixties."

Nixon's stated rationale was to turn the nation "away from the condescending policies of paternalism." He insisted that his reforms were aimed, not at punishing the poor, but at freeing them from the fetters of a government-imposed infantilization. In fact, Nixon cared little about the poor one way or the other. The real target was his political enemies, the liberal bureaucrats and social engineers. "Too much," he insisted, "had been going to those who were supposed to help the needy and too little to the needy themselves." Referring to social welfare programs for American Indians, he asserted that "the bureaucracy feeds on itself, defends itself and fights for the status quo."

If the special interests in Congress persisted in funding their allies among the welfare bureaucrats, Nixon promised to veto their appropriations. And if they passed those appropriations over his veto, then he claimed the constitutionally questionable right to impound (that is, refuse to disburse) authorized monies. If Congress objected and called upon members of the Administration to appear before congressional committees, then, insisted Attorney General Richard Kleindienst, the presidential right of "executive privilege" (that is, immunity from congressional questioning, previously reserved for the President and his cabinet officers) would be extended to all two and a half million employees of the executive branch. "If the senators objected," said the Attorney General, "they could impeach the President." Senator Sam Ervin, later of Watergate committee fame, asked Kleindienst how evidence for impeachment could be gathered if witnesses were not allowed to testify. "No evidence is needed," replied the nation's chief law enforcement officer, "only the vote of the Senate and the House." "The Attorney General's turn of mind was breathtaking. He dismissed evidence and spoke of power."

The Democrats in Congress, angered less by Nixon's disdain

for the rule of law than by his contempt for their power and prestige, struck back in February by appointing a Select Committee on Presidential Campaign Abuses, headed by that "plain country lawyer," constitutional expert Senator Sam Ervin of North Carolina. Ervin, a thoroughgoing conservative on social issues, shared Nixon's distaste for the Great Society, but he could not abide the President's abuse of the Senate. The ammunition Ervin needed for his inquiry came from another conservative, "Maximum" John Sirica, the kind of no-nonsense law-and-order judge Nixon admired, who was hearing the case of the Watergate burglars.

The men put on trial for the break-in at the Democratic National Committee headquarters were veterans of the Cold War. Four of the seven had taken part in the Bay of Pigs fiasco. One of the four, E. Howard Hunt, a writer of popular spy novels, explained their role in the burglary as an act of patriotism. "The election of McGovern," claimed Hunt, "would be the beginning of a trend that would lead to socialism or Communism or whatever you want to call it." The trial revealed little except that the burglars had received money from the Committee to Re-Elect the President. Still loyal to Nixon and their own version of anti-Communism, all the burglars but one agreed to plead guilty in order to curtail any further investigation. The exception, former CIA man James McCord, unnerved by Sirica's threat of harsh punishment, told the judge that the defendants had "stonewalled" as part of an arrangement with the White House. McCord revealed that Nixon's campaign manager, former Attorney General John Mitchell, and White House aides John Dean and Jeb Magruder had helped plan the break-in. The stage was set for Nixon's enemies to counterattack.

Through February and March into April 1973, the Washington *Post*, fed information by bureaucratic dissenters within the government, kept up a drumbeat of accusations about campaign payoffs and a secret White House enemies list, most of which proved to be accurate. On April 17 presidential press spokesman Ron Ziegler announced that new evidence made all previous White House statements on Watergate "inoperative." On April 30 Nixon went on national TV to announce the resignation of his closest advisers, H. R. Haldeman and John Ehrlichman, as well as White

House Counsel John Dean and Attorney General Kleindienst. The "Berlin Wall" had crumbled, but the President himself was largely untouched when the men who resigned were called up before the Ervin committee in mid-May.

If you want to understand the hearings, "keep your eye on the trail of the long green," advised a veteran reporter, as the committee uncovered a web of corruption reaching far beyond the dirty tricks played on Democratic candidates for President. The revelation that giant ITT had promised $400,000 to the White House in return for the quashing of an antitrust suit was sensational. But corruption was not new to Washington. What was startling, as Henry Fairlie put it, was the directness of the bargain struck. It had been "government by stickup," in which corporations not only could buy policy but were told they had to make under-the-table cash "contributions" to the Nixon campaign or face the consequences. The hearings revealed that the old restraints had eroded, not just in the counterculture, but in the marketplace of politics. They were replaced by the naked personal ambition of the cash nexus.

The payoffs by the milk producers' lobby to get an increase in federal milk price supports was one of the lesser stories coming out of the hearings. But the milk price scandal had a big impact because the drama of Watergate was being played out against a rising tide of inflation. As part of his campaign to return to the time-honored principles of limited government, Nixon lifted the wage and price controls of his New Economic Policy. In an increasingly internationalized American economy, worldwide crop shortages and growing Soviet wheat purchases placed strong upward pressures on American prices. When controls were lifted, in February 1973, "the cost of meat, poultry and fish jumped an astonishing 5 percent. . . . By March, the cost of living had increased to an annual rate of 9.6 percent, the highest since the Korean War." By April, when the White House's previous statements on Watergate were declared inoperative, there were attempts to organize a nationwide boycott of meat to protest the price rises.

Prices received an even greater shock in October 1973 when Syria and Egypt's Yom Kippur attack on Israel provided the occasion for an Arab oil boycott which sent prices skyrocketing from $1.40 to $10.50 per barrel. The oil cartel, OPEC, then institutionalized the higher prices through an agreement to limit production. Because oil is used not only for power but in a wide range of chemicals and plastics, the price rise rippled through the already inflated economy. The damage done by OPEC could have been foreseen. There was plenty of warning that an oil shortage and a price hike were on the way. In 1960 Americans imported 19 percent of their oil; by 1970 imports were up to 24 percent; in 1972 we set an all-time record for oil consumption and imports topped 30 percent of oil consumed. Already in the winter of 1972–73 spot shortages had shut schools and factories in Colorado, Louisiana, and Alabama, and the American Ambassador to Saudi Arabia, James Aikens, had issued repeated public warnings about an imminent OPEC price boost. Nixon and Kissinger, however, did little to respond. Eschewing conservation, they welcomed the pre-boycott rise of prices as an inducement to conservation.

Caught unprepared by the October 1973 oil embargo, Nixon responded by wining and dining the Saudi oil minister while bestowing an unprecedented supply of high-technology arms on the Shah of Iran.

Nixon and Kissinger were not so accommodating elsewhere. In September 1973 they helped overthrow President Salvador Allende of Chile after his freely elected Marxist government threatened American-owned copper interests. Asked to justify his actions, Kissinger replied in the manner of the Grand Inquisitor: "I don't see why we have to let a country go Marxist just because its people are irresponsible . . ." By contrast, the far more serious OPEC threat to American economic interests was accepted and even welcomed by a significant section of the American banking and foreign policy establishment led by George Ball and John J. McCloy. Ball asserted that the OPEC price hike was a boon in disguise. America, he said, was suffering from a "capital shortage" created by the high ratio of consumption to investment. The money pulled out of the consumers' pockets by the oil producers, he went on, would be "recycled" into American banks, which would then finance new American industrial investment. OPEC did act as a tax on consumers, but very little of the OPEC money was put into American investment, which continued to lag behind Europe's and Japan's.

One of the admirers of the Saudi regime, Vice-President Spiro T. Agnew, had been, before Watergate, the odds-on choice to win the presidency in 1976. On October 10, 1973, while the nation's attention was focused on the Arab-Israeli war, Agnew, under investigation for accepting bribes and kickbacks from contractors while governor of Maryland, resigned. The prospects of an Agnew presidency had subdued calls for Nixon's impeachment, but Agnew's resignation stripped the President of his "insurance policy." Agnew was replaced as Vice-President by the House Minority Leader, Gerald R. Ford. A self-described "team player" and "middle American," Ford, for twenty-five years the congressman from Grand Rapids, Michigan, was an economic and social conservative who had helped block House inquiries into the Watergate affair.

Nixon clung to office for another ten months as more and more disclosures of misconduct eroded his power. It was, said a congressman, referring to all the relevations, like waiting for the other shoe to drop—on a centipede. Nixon, it was discovered, had failed to report a capital gain on property he sold, had improperly written off business expenses from his income tax, and, most damaging of all, had had elaborate repair work done on his San Clemente home at taxpayers' expense. Nixon justified the repairs in the name of "national security." The President's "monarchical lifestyle," wrote *Fortune*, mocked "the typical homeowner's need to economize."

Through all the investigations, only indirect evidence could be found linking Nixon to the burglary and its cover-up. Finally, in early August 1974, the "smoking gun" of irrefutable presidential involvement was uncovered in the form of taped conversations between Nixon and Haldeman about how to hide White House involvement in the crime. On August 8, 1974, with impeachment looming, a disgraced Richard Nixon became the first American President to resign from office.

There was a good deal of hypocrisy in the criticism of the deposed President. Politicians who had known for years how the policy of containment empowered the Chief Executive to wage permanent war in pursuit of permanent peace professed shock at the misdeeds Nixon committed in the name of national security. Similarly, liberal politicians and newspapers like the Washington

Post, enthusiastic supporters of John Kennedy's escalation of American involvement in Vietnam, used Watergate to shift blame for the conflict solely onto Nixon's shoulders.

It is no defense of Nixon's crimes to point out that both the Bay of Pigs and the Gulf of Tonkin affair involved impeachable behavior. As columnist Nicholas von Hoffman put it: "It was not that Nixon opened other people's mail"—earlier Presidents had done that. "It was whose mail he opened." Nixon, like Joe McCarthy, scabrously exploited the deep rift in American life between populist resentment of elites and the liberal establishment. Like McCarthy, he was smashed in the process.

The Democrats were the short-term winners in the aftermath of the Watergate affair. In the 1974 elections they gained 49 seats in the House and 5 in the Senate. But in the long run, it was the Democrats, as the "party of government," who were the losers. Watergate returned the Democrats to power in 1976 without requiring the party to reconcile its warring factions. The large profits that oil companies made from the OPEC cartel produced a cynical attitude toward big business, already excoriated as the polluter of the environment. But Watergate, as the Democrats were to learn with difficulty, produced an even more pervasive distrust of government, the only means of regulating private power. In a final ironic twist, Richard Nixon succeeded, despite himself, in his second-term goal of discrediting big government.

13

Jimmy Carter, Ronald Reagan, and the Legacy of George Wallace

I hardly know which is the greater pest to society, a paternal government . . . which intrudes itself into every part of human life, and which thinks it can do everything for everybody better than anybody can do anything for himself; or a careless lounging government, which suffers grievances such as it could at once remove, to grow and multiply, and which to all complaint and remonstrance has only one answer: "We must let things take their own course; we must let things find their own level."
—THOMAS BABINGTON MACAULEY

IT WAS LEFT TO NIXON'S SUCCESSOR, Gerald Ford, to oversee the fall of Saigon and the continuing rise in prices. Ford's presidency was initially greeted with hope and relief after "the long dark night of Watergate." But within a month of entering office on August 9, 1974, Ford frittered away a good deal of support by granting Nixon, who had been facing criminal prosecution, a full pardon. Overnight Ford's standing plunged from 71 to 50 percent in the approval polls. Ford then alienated the Republican right by appointing the bête noire of American conservatism, Nelson Rockefeller, Vice-President.

Unelected and unsure of himself, Ford accepted the advice of Henry Kissinger and watched passively in April 1975 as a North Vietnamese offensive conquered South Vietnam. The predictions of a loud outcry at the war's end failed to materialize. Most Americans greeted the end of the war they neither desired not understood with quiet relief. Ford was similarly passive in the face of runaway inflation. Other than distributing WIN (Whip Inflation Now) buttons, he was content to let rising unemployment slow the rise in prices.

With Ford operating as little more than a caretaker, the political leaders of both parties focused their attention on the 1976 election and on George Wallace, whose political popularity had risen dramatically since 1972. Between 1973 and 1976, when Wallace was creating a New Right *avant la lettre* by bringing fund raiser Richard Viguerie and Baptist clergyman Jerry Falwell into his fold, everyone from Ted Kennedy to Tom Eagleton among Democrats and Nelson Rockefeller to Gerald Ford among Republicans tried to curry favor with the Alabama threat. "Brooding over all the activities of all the other Democratic candidates" for President in 1976, said journalist Arthur Hadley, ". . . loomed the Alabama dragon George Wallace." Hadley goes on: "Birch Bayh was in trouble with liberals because he had said in '74, 'I can see circumstances where . . . I would support [Wallace] for Vice-President.' Morris Udall was making a campaign issue out of the fact that he would not have any part of a Wallace ticket. Carter and Sanford were saying they were going to beat Wallace in his backyard. . . . Bayh, who now wouldn't support Wallace, vowed to lacerate the governor of Alabama. Scoop Jackson was merely saying he would defeat Wallace in the primaries. . . . Fred Harris was claiming he was the only candidate besides Wallace who could reach the Wallace constituency . . ." and so on. After criticizing Wallace, Udall felt compelled to back off a bit. Wallace, said Udall, was "asking the right questions, but didn't have any answers." This idea, said Julius Witcover, "that Wallace had put his finger on the causes of national discontent, but wasn't equipped to do anything about them, soon became a litany for other candidates." But the two candidates for whom this litany became an opportunity rather than a threat were Jimmy Carter and Ronald Reagan, two men who hoped to displace Wallace rather than just placate him.

Carter wasn't above using racist appeals to win a term as governor of Georgia, but by 1974 he was reaching out to Georgia blacks in order to position himself nationally as a more moderate alternative to the vituperative Alabamian. Then, at a time when many pros feared Wallace would be able to broker the 1976 Democratic convention by coming in with 30 or 40 percent of the delegates, Carter offered himself to Northern liberals as a stopper. Wallace votes, he told a New York audience, "cannot be transferred to a more liberal candidate." Meanwhile he was presenting himself to Southerners as a man who could carry on the Wallace legacy of standing up for Dixie by cutting down the federal government. He even promised to go one better. Wallace, he said, had told the South "to send them a message," but now Carter gave them the chance "to send them a President."

On the Republican side, Reagan was playing his own cat-and-mouse game with the Wallaceites. A group of self-styled counterrevolutionaries, populists of the right including Richard Viguerie, Kevin Phillips, Pat Buchanan, and Paul Weyrich, hoped to preempt Gerald Ford and what they saw as a dying and hopelessly soft Republican Party with a Reagan-Wallace dream ticket of bipartisan reaction. Reagan resisted, fearing the racist tag that might come with openly courting the Wallaceites.

But, as it turned out, Reagan didn't have to mar his reputation by courting them. They came to him. After Wallace's defeat by Carter in the Florida Democratic primary, Reagan inherited many of the anti-busing and Christian school groups who supported the governor. Thanks to the Wallace cross-over voters in Texas and Indiana, Reagan came very close to defeating Ford in the Republican primaries. Reagan failed to win the nomination but discovered that a sizable portion of the Democratic vote, particularly in the South, was his for the taking. Well before there was such a thing as the Moral Majority, Reagan, who was still considered something of a joke by the major columnists, had quietly absorbed a good part of the Wallace constituency.

The 1980 collapse of the Democratic Party was foreshadowed in its pyrrhic 1976 presidential victory. The Democrats, relatively unified, faced a shattered Republican Party burdened by the greatest political scandal in American history and a badly slumping economy. The Republican candidate, Gerald Ford, troubled by insurgency within his own party, was so dull that, as Walter Goodman has put it, "he was a figure destined to afflict schoolchildren yet unborn with the problem of whether it was he or Martin Van Buren who started the French and Indian Wars." Yet the Democrats barely managed to eke out a victory and then only because their candidate was a Southerner who had mastered the art of straddling. It was a measure of just how conservative politics had become that on the hustings the campaign themes of both parties—God, major tax reductions, a balanced budget, and a strong defense at the expense of social programs if need be—anticipated Reaganism.

Carter's victory, which seemed to hail the recrudescence of class-based New Deal voting patterns, gave off a tubercular glow. There was no winning coalition, merely an aggregation of groups, some of them increasingly conservative, unwilling to vote for Ford and the Republicans. The 46 freshmen congressmen who came in with Carter were, including the Democrats, "more conservative on social and economic issues than any other class." The Democrats among them were fiercely independent, ambassadors from independent and often suburban kingdoms who neither owed Carter their allegiance (he ran behind 272 of the 292 Democrats elected to the House) nor shared common goals. The product, as journalist Thomas Edsall has pointed out, of the same wave of middle-class reforms that had denuded the party organization and made Carter's consensusless nomination possible, they were generally representatives of the burgeoning power of suburban and Sun Belt constituencies.

With the national Democratic Party in shambles and Congress reduced to a collection of independent fiefdoms, it was left to Jimmy Carter to forge a working alliance among the disparate groups who had rejected Ford. Even if the economy had not continued to falter it would have been an impossible task. Sensitive to the growing conservative mood in the country, Carter was caught between the demands of increasingly activist constituencies, ranging from farmers to feminists, and the declining social surplus which had fueled all the Keynesian-based Democratic reforms from the 1940s onward. He tried to reconcile the tension with phraseology. "Waste and inefficiency," he intoned, "never fed a hungry child." But what Carter or any other Democratic President would have faced was not only the end of postwar growth but the limits of liberal social reform as well.

By the mid-1970s the underpinnings of the racial reformation, a belief in the efficacy of social science, the moral pageantry of the civil rights movement, and a sense of debt to people unjustly oppressed had largely dissolved. The frightening growth of street crime, the replacement of the civil rights mystique with bureaucratic muscle, and the decline of public institutions ranging from prisons to schools, after a quarter century of social engineering, left reformers and radicals alike on the defensive. In the 1960s the black movement had benefited from the radical cultural criticism which challenged established institutions, but by the late 1970s the genuine and even awesome successes of the Great Society in reducing poverty were increasingly overshadowed by the social pathology which spread in the wake of "the Age of Aquarius."

The simultaneous expansion of a black middle class and a desperate underclass apparently beyond redemption ripped away the arguments for social reform at both ends. The visible success of well-to-do college-educated blacks seemed to belie the need for government protections, while the fear of lumpen criminals undercut feelings of sympathy for the plight of the worst off. Or as cartoonist Jules Feiffer sarcastically put it: "We need a better class of victims."

The clear-cut issues of the 1960s were increasingly clouded by the growth of competing groups—women, Hispanics, the handicapped, gays—who also claimed victimized status and the right to government-supported redress. At the same time, the arrival of new immigrants, many of them dark-skinned, who seemed to be prospering relative to the mass of poor blacks, reinforced the old arguments that the poor are so because they choose to be. Black interests were increasingly looked upon as just that, one of a number of bureaucratically protected claims without any exceptional moral quality. A hint of racism began to slip back into the private discussions of middle-class liberals and even former 1960s radicals when they spoke of the black lumpens they had come to fear. And though this was generally accompanied by praise for hardworking black yeomen, it was tinged as well by annoyance with the rhetorical excesses of black leaders who were always calling for the government to do more at a time when the government didn't seem able to carry out its basic functions effectively. The same government which was unable to halt inflation or free the Americans held hostage in Iran or aid the victims of the Love Canal was, by contrast, able to sweep into a school district with a court order to prosecute an all-boys choir or order large-scale busing even if there was little public support for it. This disparity, compounded by the disruptive effects of busing weighed against its limited benefits, was far more than most liberals and middle-of-the-roaders affected were willing to bear.

In once liberal areas of Los Angeles and Maryland, attitudes shifted rightward with the protracted conflict over court-ordered busing. But even areas not touched directly were affected. "The frightening difference between a court action and a political action," said Richard Neely in his engaging defense of judicial activism, *How Courts Govern America*, is that the courts give no warning. A federal ruling on violent teenagers made in bucolic Idaho can be applied suddenly by a judge in embattled Cleveland or Canarsie.

Carter was almost a helpless bystander, beleaguered by the issues that had brought him to power. Where once as governor he had agitated against busing he was now being singed by the fires he had stoked. Watergate, though a short-term boon, had in the long run only fueled the fires of discontent with a government which seemed alternately a rogue elephant wandering loose across the countryside and a passive bystander in the midst of the great events affecting the country. On matters of grave national importance such as oil, the Iranian revolution, and the seizure of American hostages, Carter's administration turned in circles like a giant ship whose rudder was stuck. But however feeble it was in dealing with the sheiks, it managed to summon up the energy necessary to threaten Iowa's enormously popular six-women basketball teams with the possibility of a sex discrimination suit, thereby undercutting both itself and women's rights. The result was a sharp drop in the already low estimate held of 1960s programs. As political scientist Kathleen Frankovic points out, between January 1978 and November 1980 the percentage describing 1960s programs as having made things worse jumped from 14 to 20 percent, so that fully 62 percent of those surveyed thought that the programs had either had no effect or made things worse, while only 30 percent of all races thought they had made things better.

It was Hubert Humphrey, not George Wallace, who warned Carter that there had been a total breakdown of the bureaucracy. "The federal regional offices," he told the President, "are zilch." "The best thing to do would be to get rid of all these people." And it was HEW Secretary Joseph Califano, a self-described bureaucratic child of the 1960s, who sounded like a neo-conservative when he complained: "Intricate federal regulations . . . encourage even lengthier and more specific rules as state, local and private institutions scramble to comply. . . . People trying to help each other feel suffocated, frustrated . . . as their freedom to act on matters they face each day is increasingly circumscribed." Stuart Eizenstat, Carter's chief domestic adviser, was as troubled as Califano. Most public contact with government, he said, comes through the post office, Social Security, and the IRS; "if these agencies foul up, it has grave and widespread public repercussions." And, he concluded sadly, foul up they did. If key liberals felt this way, is it any wonder that Reagan was able to convince so many of his listeners that if they looked down their gunsights they would see all the domestic problems along a single line, labeled "big government."

The all too obvious contrast between the good life in official Washington and the decay of our older cities and suburbs made it all the easier for Reagan's 1980 presidential campaign to appeal to the worst instincts of the workaday citizen paying for Washington's froth and folly. Taxes, as journalist Bob Kutner and others have noted, have become increasingly regressive. The gradual elimination of the corporate income tax, ever-burgeoning Social Security taxes, the huge mortgage deductions of the wealthy, and the growth of sales taxes shifted the burden of government revenue raising onto the backs of salaried and often union workers unable to dodge the tax man. It was middle-income earners like the UAW tax revolters in Flint, Michigan, who through the effects of bracket creep were being asked by the Democratic Congress to finance a government they felt to be increasingly remote from their interests and unable or unwilling to come to grips with the inflation that was taking money from their pockets. The Republicans played on the widespread anger over taxes, so that throughout the country, but particularly in the Northeast, Reagan's major gains over Ford came from middle-income families with salaries between $15,000 and $24,000 a year.

It was the declining economy which weakened blue-collar support for the Democrats, but it was the yawning gap between the oversold promises of social reform and the day-to-day dystopian functioning of the courts and the schools which gave the Republicans their political opportunity.

The race issue never appeared on the surface of the 1980 campaign because Reagan was able to quietly reap what Wallace and Agnew had sown. He stood on the undivisive rhetorical high ground, campaigning in favor of economic growth, a strong family, and a strong defense. Moreover, he covered himself against accusations of racism by campaigning among blacks, less to secure their votes than not to lose white moderate ones.

Ever since the 1930s shrewd conservatives dreamed of uniting social and economic conservatives under one tent. They failed, in part, because of the religious and ethnic divisions between the small towns and the city slums, Protestants and Catholics. But as these older antipathies subsided and racial justice became the storm center of American politics, a hitherto impossible unity was achieved in the common response of both Main Street and street-corner conservatives to black advances and the government power behind those advances. It was Reagan's political genius to take advantage of that new unity, to piggyback a program of obeisance to business on the often racially based social issues which agitated conservatives of all stripes. As New Right leader Paul Weyrich put it bluntly: "We talk about issues that people care about, like gun control, abortion, taxes, and crime. Yes, they're emotional issues, but that's better than talking about capital formation."

Another emotional issue that bound the Reagan coalition together was foreign policy. Reagan's loud and consistent anti-Communism stood in sharp contrast to the vacillations of the Carter administration. Carter entered office promising to reduce nuclear arms, end "America's inordinate fear of Communism," and replace military aid to the Third World with economic and social support. But plans for a better relationship with the Third World were sidetracked in early 1979 when the Islamic revolution in Iran overthrew the longtime American client, the Shah of Iran. The Iranian revolution, responded Carter, made it clear that America had to take the "world as it is" and maintain her military strength. The President's attitude toward "Communism" took a similar turn in late 1979 after the Soviet invasion of neighboring Afghanistan. Carter announced that the invasion revealed the true nature of the Soviet regime. The naïveté of Carter's response dismayed his dovish admirers without winning the support of hawks. Finally, Carter responded to the growing buildup of Soviet ICBMs by changing direction on nuclear weaponry to support the building of the giant MX missile. While Carter twisted and turned to meet the complexities of the world situation, Reagan's unabashed calls for U.S. military supremacy appealed to American national sentiments bruised by the Vietnam War.

When Reagan denounced the Soviet Union, his nationalist message was unequivocal, but when he again and again talked about "getting the government off our backs," his message meant different things to different audiences. Sixty-five percent of voters thought there was too much business regulation; only a small percentage of them were businessmen. For a manufacturer Reagan's call may have meant an end to the Occupational Health and Safety Agency, but for many mainstream white Democrats it meant an end to busing or quotas.

Reagan won a smashing victory. He captured 43.3 million popular votes, 44 states, and 488 electoral votes; Carter received 35 million votes, picking up 6 states and 49 electoral votes, while 5.6 million voters cast their ballots for John Anderson's independent candidacy. A great many workers and middle-income whites didn't believe Reagan's rhetoric but still couldn't bring themselves to vote for Carter. A third of Carter's 1976 supporters switched to Reagan, but as political scientist William Schneider points out, the Democrats lost more voters to abstention than to Reagan and third-party candidate Anderson combined. "Former Carter voters were four times more likely than Ford voters to sit out the campaign." In sum, Carter managed to retain only a little more than a third of his 1976 supporters. The 1980 election, then, was an extraordinary vote of no-confidence, a Democratic debacle rather than a Republican triumph.

The End of

American Exceptionalism

What happens when the work ethic runs out of work?
—HANNAH ARENDT

THE DIFFERENCES BETWEEN Europe and America couldn't have seemed greater on that mid-August night in 1971 when Richard Nixon and John Connally scuttled the 1944 Bretton Woods International Monetary Agreement. "European reporters sprinted out of the White House to tell stunned Europeans that the dollar had been dethroned." The American journalists were impassive. Some of the American journalists, reporters from the London *Economist* explained, simply didn't know what Bretton Woods represented; others knew but realized that the foundations of American prosperity were so taken for granted that the fall of the gold standard simply wasn't a big story. We've since been Europeanized.

For three decades after World War II real income grew steadily for most Americans. That growth was accompanied and underwritten by a tripartite consensus which assumed:

—That although the United States engaged in substantial international trade, exchange with other countries would remain marginal to the huge American economy, which would remain uniquely independent of international pressures because of the vast North American mass market.

—That labor and management had come to a social contract in which high wages for mass-production factory workers enabled those same workers to be an essential part of the market for goods produced by American industry.

—That while rising prosperity was dependent on technological change, the pace of that change would be neither so fast nor destabilizing as to outweigh the benefits of new production methods.

All three pillars of the consensus were undermined in the 1970s.

This transformation was not reflected in the 1980 election, which can best be understood as the last election of the 1960s. In the months before the 1980 presidential contest, when voters were asked what the number one issue was, they replied inflation and the economy. When they were asked what should be done about inflation and the economy, about half supported the balanced-budget proposals of incumbent Jimmy Carter, a little less than a third endorsed Edward Kennedy's proposals for wage and price controls, and only one in seven supported the supply-side proposals of the man who went on to a landslide victory. Reagan triumphed as the candidate of traditional American values. The Reagan campaign had two themes—one was cultural conservatism, the other the virtues of unfettered capitalist dynamism. The problem, as George Will has pointed out, is that the latter dissolves the former.

While the nation's political life focused on the *Kulturkampf* at home and Communism abroad, capitalist dynamism, what Joseph Schumpeter called "creative destruction," undermined the postwar consensus. Before the mid-1960s foreign trade was only a small part of our economy, but between 1965 and 1980 the American economy was internationalized. In 1970 a little more than 9 percent of American-made goods were exported; the percentage more than doubled by 1980. But even more significantly, by 1980, as Robert Reich points out, more than 70 percent of the goods produced in the United States were actively competing with foreign-made goods. For the first time, American workers were in direct competition not only with Europe but with the often low-wage labor of Asia and Latin America.

Since 1960 American trade with other countries has grown at roughly twice the rate of the American economy. Investment abroad has risen even more rapidly, as intense foreign competition for what former West German Chancellor Helmut Schmidt calls "the world product" forced U.S. companies to produce and market around the globe. With customers worldwide, high-wage American labor was no longer the essential consumer for the goods produced by American manufacturers. Moreover, high-wage American labor came under increasing competition from low-wage foreign labor employed in plants built by American corporate investments. In many cases, American unionized jobs were lost or wages and benefits reduced in order to meet the threat from abroad. American labor, particularly hard-hit steel and textile workers, responded to the foreign competition with calls for protective tariffs. This strained the United States' relationship with its European "allies," already tested by the growing trade between the U.S.S.R. and Western Europe and the mild European reaction to the Soviet invasion of Afghanistan and the suppression of Solidarity in Poland. For the first time since World War II the Europeans were looked upon as competitors as much as "allies."

Finally, for a growing segment of the American middle class, the costs of technological change clearly outpaced the benefits. In the 1950s, when automation first came to public attention, the chief victims were unskilled black workers. Temporarily overshadowed by the turmoil of the 1960s, the problem of automation became a public issue again in the late 1970s, when new methods of high-technology production based on the microchip and the high-speed minicomputer displaced increasing numbers of skilled and semiskilled workers. In sum, the old smokestack industrial economy which created a large number of middle-income jobs is being displaced by a new "post-industrial" economy which produces either high- or low-wage jobs.

Between 1970 and 1980 the total U.S. labor force grew by only 18 percent while service jobs grew at many times that rate. The number of managers and administrators grew 58 percent, health administrators up 118 percent, public officials increased by 76 percent, bankers 83 percent, systems analysts 83 percent, computer operators 346 percent, lawyers over 100 percent. At the other end of the wage scale, in an employment category called "eating and drinking places," comprised largely of waiters, waitresses, busboys, cashiers, and dishwashers, the increase in employment between 1973 and 1980 was greater than the total employment in the dying automobile and steel industries. The middle is dropping out of the American job structure.

As the United States becomes the university center, bookkeeper, and technician for the world, America is becoming a sharply divided two-tiered society. On one level are the highly paid and highly skilled lawyers, computer analysts, and upper-level managers, people who can write their own ticket in life and whose "superiority" will be meritocratically affirmed by the credentials required for their prestigious jobs. On the other level there are the "left-behinds," the restaurant and cafeteria workers, mechanics, medical technicians, and day-care workers, the people who serve the affluent. These divisions are most visible in the nation's cosmopolitan cities, such as New York, Washington, Boston, San Francisco, and Los Angeles, where restaurants catering to upper-middle-class, often childless, two-career professional couples, with considerable disposable income, flourished in the midst of the late 1970s recession, a recession which devastated many of the older industries hard hit by foreign competition. "What is passing is the traditional American promise, fulfilled particularly after World War II [for whites], that someone whose only credential was a willingness to work long and hard with his hands could earn a good wage."

The creation of a dual society also spells an end to the cultural civil war of the past forty years. The economic and social forces which threw up the New Class cultural challenge to middle America in the 1960s began in the 1970s to undermine not only the social standing but the jobs which had made the American middle-class lifestyle possible.

Bibliography

THERE IS AN ENORMOUS LITERATURE on recent American history. The brief listings I provide are not meant to be exhaustive. The books and articles I have listed are only those which proved the most valuable for a particular chapter.

PREFACE

Dennis Wrong, "The Rhythm of Democratic Politics," *Dissent* (1974).

1. THE CRUCIBLE OF WORLD WAR II

For the development of isolationism, see Manfred Jonas, *Isolationism in America, 1935-41* (1966), and Selig Adler, *The Isolationism Impulse* (1957). Discussions of wartime popular sentiment and politics include John L. Gaddis, *The United States and the Origins of the Cold War* (1972); Robert Darilek, *The Loyal Opposition in Time of War: The Republican Party and the Politics of Foreign Policy from Pearl Harbor to Yalta* (1976); Robert Divine, *Foreign Policy and U.S. Presidential Elections*, vol. I (1974); George Q. Flynn, *Roosevelt and Romanism: Catholics and American Diplomacy, 1937-45* (1976); Ralph Levering, *American Opinion and the Russian Alliance* (1976); and Richard Steele, "American Popular Opinion and the War against Germany," *Journal of American History* (1978). The wartime strategies of the Allies are examined in Herbert Feis, *Churchill, Roosevelt, Stalin: The War They Fought, the Peace They Sought* (1957); Gabriel Kolko, *The Politics of War: The World and United States Foreign Policy, 1943-5* (1968); John Lukacs, *1945: The Year Zero* (1979); Michael Balfour, *The Adversaries: America, Russia and the Open World, 1941-62* (1981); Vojtech Mastny, *Russia's Road to the Cold War* (1979); and Robert Dallek, *Franklin Roosevelt and American Foreign Policy, 1932-45* (1979).

Bibliography

2. 1946: The Crucial Year

For a useful overview of the Truman presidency, see Robert Donovan, *Conflict and Crisis: The Presidency of Harry S. Truman* (1977). Robert Griffith's insightful sketch of Truman's personality, "Harry S. Truman and the Burden of Modernity," was published in *Reviews in American History* (1981). On Truman's personality, see also Robert H. Ferrell, ed., *Off the Record: The Private Papers of Harry S. Truman* (1980). Insights into the origins of the Cold War are found in Franz Schurman, *The Logic of World Power* (1974), and William Taubman, *Stalin's American Policy* (1982). The events of 1946 are described in Lloyd C. Gardner *Architects of Illusion: Men and Ideas in American Foreign Policy, 1941–1949* (1970), John L. Gaddis, *The United States and the Origins of the Cold War* (1972), and Robert Messer, "Paths Not Taken," *Diplomatic History* (1977). George Kennan describes his own role in his *Memoirs, 1925–1950* (1967), and Kennan is discussed in Donald Harrington, "Kennan, Bohlen and the Riga Axioms," *Diplomatic History* (1978), and Thomas G. Patterson, "The Search for Meaning: George F. Kennan and American Foreign Policy," in Frank Merli, ed., *Makers of American Diplomacy* (1974). American policy toward Eastern Europe is discussed in Lynn E. Davis, *The Cold War Begins: Soviet-American Conflict over Eastern Europe* (1974), and Eduard Mark, "American Policy Toward Eastern Europe," *Journal of American History* (1981). For the shift in public attitudes, see Peter Boyle, "The British Foreign Office View of Soviet-American Relations, 1945–6," *Diplomatic History* (1979), and Samuel Lubell, *The Future of American Politics* (1952). The development of the Cold War is treated from a European Perspective in Terry H. Anderson, *The United States, Great Britain, and the Cold War* (1981), Victor Rothwell, *Britain and the Cold War, 1941–1947* (1982), and D. C. Watt, "Rethinking the Cold War," *Political Quarterly* (1978).

3. Isolationist Revenge

Party politics and the legacy of the New Deal are discussed in Arthur Ekrich, Jr., *Ideologies and Utopia: The Impact of the New Deal on American Thought* (1969); Arthur M. Schlesinger, Jr., *The Vital Center* (1949); H. Bradford Westerfield, *Foreign Policy and Party Politics: Pearl Harbor to Korea* (1955); Robert Garson, *The Democratic Party and the Politics of Sectionalism* (1974); Herbert Parmet, *The Democrats: The Years After FDR* (1975); Henry Fairlie, *The Parties: Republicans and Democrats in This Century* (1978); Michael Miles, *The Odyssey of the*

Bibliography

American Right (1980); James T. Patterson, *Mr. Republican: A Biography of Robert A. Taft* (1972); Alonzo Hamby, *Beyond the New Deal: Harry S. Truman and American Liberalism* (1973); and Barton J. Bernstein, ed., *Politics and Policies of the Truman Administration.* The Truman Doctrine and American foreign policy are analyzed in Walter LaFeber, *America, Russia and the Cold War, 1945–1975* (1976); Henry Pachter, "Revisionist Historians and the Cold War," *Dissent* (1968); Joseph Jones, *The Fifteen Weeks* (1955); Gaddis Smith, *Dean Acheson* (1972); and Walter Lippmann, *The Cold War* (1947). For participants recounting their role in American foreign policy, see Dean Acheson, *Present at the Creation* (1969); Arthur Vandenberg, Jr., ed., *The Private Papers of Senator Vandenberg* (1952); and George Kennan, *Memoirs, 1925–1950* (1967); and on Kennan, Henry Pachter, "The Intellectual as Diplomat," *Dissent* (1968). American policy in Asia is discussed by Lewis Purifoy, *Harry Truman's China Policy: McCarthyism and the Diplomacy of Hysteria* (1976); Akira Iriye, *The Cold War in Asia* (1974); Michael Schaller, *The United States and China in the Twentieth Century* (1979); and William Whitney Stueck, Jr., *The Road to Confrontation: American Policy Toward China and Korea, 1947–1950* (1981). The Hiss case is the subject of John Chabot Smith, *Alger Hiss: The True Story* (1977); Allen Weinstein, *Perjury: The Hiss-Chambers Case* (1978); Victor Navasky, "Allen Weinstein's 'Perjury': The Case Not Proved Against Alger Hiss," *The Nation* (1978); and Whittaker Chambers, *Witness* (1952). There are numerous studies of the "witch-hunts" and American Communism; these include Robert Griffith and Athan Theoharis, eds., *The Specter: Original Essays on the Cold War and the Origins of McCarthyism* (1974); Richard Freeland, *The Truman Doctrine and the Origins of McCarthyism: Foreign Policy, Domestic Politics and Internal Security* (1972); Earl Latham, *The Communist Controversy in Washington: From the New Deal to McCarthy* (1966); Victor Navasky, *Naming Names* (1980); Stanley Kutler, *The American Inquisition* (1982); Thomas Reeves, *The Life and Times of Joe McCarthy* (1982); I. F. Stone, *The Truman Era* (1953); Leslie Fiedler, *An End to Innocence* (1952); Richard Rovere, *Senator Joe McCarthy* (1959); William F. Buckley and L. Brent Bozell, *McCarthy and His Enemies* (1954); Joseph Starobin, *American Communism in Crisis, 1943–1957* (1972); Walter Goodman, *The Committee* (1968); and Murray Kempton, *Part of Our Time: Some Monuments and Ruins of the Thirties* (1967). Korea and the Truman-MacArthur controversy are discussed in Adam Ulam, *The Rivals* (1971); John Spanier, *The Truman-MacArthur Controversy and the Korean War* (1965); Francis Heller, ed., *The Korean War: A 25 Year Perspective* (1977); and Richard Rovere and Arthur M. Schlesinger, Jr., *The Truman-MacArthur Controversy* (1951).

Bibliography

4. TRUMAN, EISENHOWER, AND THE POLITICS OF PROSPERITY

For a description of changes in the popular culture during the late 1940s and early 1950s, see Joseph C. Goulden, *The Best Years* (1976); Eric F. Goldman, *The Crucial Decade and After: America 1945–1960* (1960); Geoffrey Perret, *A Dream of Greatness: The American People 1945–1963* (1979); and James Gilbert, *Another Chance: Postwar America, 1945–1968* (1981). Changes in the American economy are discussed in John Kenneth Galbraith, *American Capitalism: The Concept of Countervailing Power* (1952); Daniel Bell, *The End of Ideology* (1960); John Diebold, *Automation: The Advent of the Automatic Factory* (1952); and Richard Barber, *The American Corporation: Its Power, Its Money, Its Politics* (1970). Eisenhower and Stevenson are discussed by Herbert Parmet, *Eisenhower and the American Crusades* (1972); Richard Rovere, *The Eisenhower Years* (1956); Samuel Lubell, *Revolt of the Moderates* (1956); Richard M. Nixon, *Six Crises* (1962); Peter Lyons, *Eisenhower: Portrait of the Hero* (1974); Robert Griffith, "Dwight D. Eisenhower and the Corporate Commonwealth: An Interpretation of the President and His Presidency," *American Historical Review* (1982); Irving Howe, *Steady Work: Essays in the Politics of Democratic Radicalism, 1953–1966* (1966); Joseph Epstein, *Ambition* (1980); Robert Ferrell, ed., *The Eisenhower Diaries* (1981); and John B. Martin, *Adlai Stevenson of Illinois* (1976).

5. FROM UTOPIA TO DYSTOPIA

General works on the 1950s include Charles Alexander, *Holding the Line: The Eisenhower Era, 1952–1961* (1957), and Douglas T. Miller and Marion Nowak, *The Fifties* (1977). Among the more perceptive discussions of changes in work and culture are David Riesman et al., *The Lonely Crowd* (1950); C. Wright Mills, *White Collar* (1956); Andrew Hacker, *The End of the American Era* (1970); Richard Chase, *Democratic Vistas: A Dialogue on Life and Letters in Contemporary America;* Henry Fairlie, *The Spoiled Child of the Western World* (1976); and Russell Lynes, *A Surfeit of Honey* (1957). Changes in child rearing are discussed in Martha Wolfstein, "The Emergence of Fun Morality," in Eric Larrabee and Rolf Meyerson, eds., *Mass Leisure* (1958); and Eric Larrabee, *The Self-Conscious Society* (1960). The suburbs are the subject of Herbert Gans, *The Levittowners* (1967), and John Seeley, *Crestwood Heights* (1956). The "beats" are discussed by Lawrence Lipton, *The Holy Barbarians* (1959); Norman Podhoretz, *Doings and Undoings: The Fifties and After in American Writing* (1964); and John Clellon Holmes, "The Philosophy of the Beat Generation," *Esquire*

Bibliography

(1958). For conservative reactions to the 1950s, see George Nash, *The Conservative Intellectual Movement in America Since 1945* (1976). The impact of Galbraith is analyzed in Charles Hession, *John Kenneth Galbraith and His Critics* (1972), and Ernest Van Den Haag, "Affluence, Galbraith, the Democrats," *Commentary* (1960).

6. THE SPUTNIK YEARS

On the Eisenhower presidency, the most valuable studies include William Bragg Ewald, Jr., *Eisenhower the President: Crucial Days, 1951–1960* (1980); Samuel Huntington, *The Common Defense: Strategic Problems in National Politics* (1961); Maxwell Taylor, *The Uncertain Trumpet* (1959); Fred Greenstein, "Eisenhower as an Activist President: A Look at New Evidence," *Political Science Quarterly* (1979–80); Robert Divine, *Eisenhower and the Cold War* (1981); Edmund Stillman and William Pfaff, *Power and Impotence: The Failure of American Foreign Policy* (1966); Gary Wills, *Nixon Agonistes* (1970); Townsend Hoopes, *The Devil and John Foster Dulles* (1973); and Eisenhower's memoirs, *Mandate for Change, 1953–1956* (1963) and *Waging Peace* (1965). For European reactions to American foreign policy, see Alfred Grosser, *The Western Alliance: European-American Relations Since 1945* (1980). The Kennedy family and John F. Kennedy's pre-presidential years are discussed in Herbert Parmet, *Jack: The Struggles of John F. Kennedy* (1980); Gary Wills, *The Kennedy Imprisonment* (1982); Theodore Sorensen, *Kennedy* (1965); and Richard J. Whalen, *The Founding Father: The Story of Joseph P. Kennedy* (1962) and *Taking Sides: A Personal View of America from Kennedy to Nixon to Kennedy* (1974). For the revival of political activism, see James L. Sundquist, *Politics and Policy: The Eisenhower, Kennedy and Johnson Years* (1968); Karl Meyer, "Triumph of the Smooth Deal," *Commentary* (1958); John Jeffries, "The 'Quest for National Purpose' of 1960," *American Quarterly* (1978); and Milton Viorst, *Fire in the Streets* (1979).

7. THE NEW FRONTIER IN POWER

For discussions of the Kennedy administration, see Henry Fairlie, *The Kennedy Promise* (1972); Bruce Miroff, *Pragmatic Illusions* (1976); Harris Wofford, *Of Kennedys and Kings: Making Sense of the Sixties* (1980); Jim Heath, *Decade of Disillusionment: The Kennedy-Johnson Years* (1975); Richard Walton, *Cold War and Counter-Revolution: The Foreign Policy of John F. Kennedy* (1972); David Halberstam, *The Best and the Brightest*

(1972); Hans Morgenthau, *Truth and Power* (1970); Elie Abel, *The Missile Crisis* (1966); Robert Slusser, *The Berlin Crisis of 1961* (1973); and Victor Navasky, *Kennedy Justice* (1971). Martin Luther King and the rise of the civil rights movement are discussed in Anthony Lewis, *Portrait of a Decade* (1965); Richard Dalfiume, "The Forgotten Years of the Civil Rights Movement," *Journal of American History* (1968); Penina Glazer, "From the Old Left to the New," *American Quarterly* (1972); David Lewis, *King: A Critical Biography* (1970); C. Eric Lincoln, ed., *Martin Luther King, Jr.* (1970); David Garrow, *The FBI and Martin Luther King, Jr.: From "Solo" to Memphis* (1982); August Meier, "On the Role of Martin Luther King," *New Politics* (1965); Jack Newfield, *A Prophetic Minority* (1966); Lerone Bennett, Jr., *Confrontation: Black and White* (1965); and Howell Raines, *My Soul Is Rested: Movement Days in the Deep South Remembered* (1977).

8. FROM THE GREAT SOCIETY TO BLACK POWER

Lyndon Johnson and the Great Society are discussed in Eric F. Goldman, *The Tragedy of Lyndon Johnson* (1969); Louis Heren, *No Hail, No Farewell* (1970); Marvin Gettleman and David Merlestein, eds., *The Great Society Reader* (1967); Hobart Rowen, *The Free Enterprisers: Kennedy, Johnson and the Business Establishment* (1967); James Sundquist, *Politics and Policy: The Eisenhower, Kennedy and Johnson Years* (1968); David Broder, *The Party's Over* (1972); Paul Goodman, "The Great Society," *New York Review of Books* (1965); Daniel P. Moynihan, *Maximum Feasible Misunderstanding* (1970); Rowland Evans and Robert Novak, *Lyndon B. Johnson: The Exercise of Power* (1966); Henry Fairlie, "Johnson and the Intellectuals," *Commentary* (1966); Eli Ginzberg and Robert Solow, *The Great Society: Lessons for the Future* (1974); Robert Caro, *The Path to Power: The Years of Lyndon Johnson*, vol. I (1982); and H. Brand, "U.S. Economic Policy from F.D.R. to L.B.J.," *Dissent* (1967). For Goldwater and the 1964 campaign, see John Kessel, *The Goldwater Coalition: Republican Strategies in 1964* (1968); Theodore White, *The Making of the President 1964* (1965); David Danzig, "Conservatism After Goldwater," *Commentary* (1965); Richard Rovere, *The Goldwater Caper* (1965); and Richard Hofstadter, *The Paranoid Style in American Politics and Other Essays* (1979). Black Power and the transition from civil rights to black nationalism are treated in Theodore Draper, *The Rediscovery of Black Nationalism* (1969); Stokely Carmichael and Charles Hamilton, *Black Power: The Politics of Liberation in America* (1967); Vincent Harding, "Black Radicalism: The Road from Montgomery," in Alfred Young, ed., *Dissent: Explorations in the History of American Radicalism* (1968); Bayard

Rustin, "The Negro Revolution: Where Shall It Go Now?" *Dissent* (1964); Harold Cruse, *The Crisis of the Negro Intellectual* (1967); James Baldwin, *The Fire Next Time* (1963); and Ronald Berman, *America in the Sixties: An Intellectual History* (1968).

9. VIETNAM AT HOME AND ABROAD

For Lyndon Johnson and the Vietnam War, see Larry Berman, *Planning a Tragedy* (1982); Philip Geyelin, *Lyndon Johnson and the World* (1966); Townsend Hoopes, *The Limits of Intervention* (1969); Lyndon Johnson, *The Vantage Point: Perspectives of the Presidency* (1971); George Herring, *America's Longest War* (1979); Don Oberdorfer, *Tet!* (1971); Peter Braestrup, *Big Story: How the American Press Reported and Interpreted the Crisis of Tet 1968 in Vietnam and Washington* (1982); Col. Harry G. Summers, Jr., *On Strategy: A Critical Analysis of the Vietnam War* (1982); and Herbert Y. Schandler, *The Unmaking of a President* (1977). To understand the "cultural revolution" of the 1960s, consult Richard King, *The Party of Eros: Radical Social Thought and the Realm of Freedom* (1972); Christopher Lasch, *The Agony of the American Left* (1969); Daniel Boorstin, *The Image* (1978); Lionel Trilling, *Sincerity and Authenticity* (1973); Harold Rosenberg, *The Tradition of the New* (1965); Peter Clecak, "The 'Movement' and Its Legacy," *Social Research* (1982); Paul Goodman, *Growing Up Absurd* (1956); Tom Wolfe, *Radical Chic and Mau-Mauing the Flak Catchers* (1970); Godfrey Hodgson, *America in Our Time* (1978); and Joseph Conlin, *The Troubles* (1982). The 1968 primary campaign and the Chicago disturbances are discussed in Lewis Chester, ed., *An American Melodrama: The Presidential Campaign of 1968* (1969); Andrew Hacker, "The McCarthy Candidacy," *Commentary* (1968); Abigail McCarthy, "The McCarthy Campaign," *Atlantic* (1970); Jason Epstein, *The Great Conspiracy Trial* (1970); Eugene McCarthy, *The Year of the People* (1969); Jack Newfield, *Robert Kennedy: A Memoir* (1969); and Theodore White, *The Making of the President 1968* (1969).

10. KULTURKAMPF

For discussions of class and ethnic conflict on civil rights and Vietnam, see Samuel Lubell, *The Hidden Crisis in American Politics* (1970); Louise Kapp Howe, ed., *The White Majority: Between Poverty and Affluence* (1970); Michael Wenk, ed., *Pieces of a Dream: The Ethnic Worker's Crisis with America* (1972); Michael Novak, *The Unmeltable Ethnics* (1971);

Bibliography

Irving Howe, ed., *The World of the Blue Collar Worker* (1972); Jason Epstein, "Black Power in the Schools," *New York Review of Books* (1968); Mario Cuomo, *Forest Hills Diary* (1974); Howard Schuman, "Two Sources of Anti-war Sentiment in America," *American Journal of Sociology* (1972); William Schneider, "Public Opinion: The Beginning of Ideology?" *Foreign Policy* (1974-75); and Nelson Polsby, "Public Opinion and the War in Vietnam," *American Political Science Review* (1967). The 1968 election and the beginning of the Nixon administration are analyzed in Richard J. Whalen, *Catch the Falling Flag* (1972); Kevin P. Phillips, *The Emerging Republican Majority* (1969); Leon Panetta and Peter Gall, *Bring Us Together* (1971); John Osborne, *The Nixon Watch* (1970); and Rowland Evans, Jr., and Robert D. Novak, *Nixon in the White House* (1971). The feminist, population reform, environmentalist, and consumer movements are discussed in Robin Morgan, ed., *Sisterhood Is Powerful* (1970); Sara Evans, *Personal Politics* (1979); Carl Degler, *At Odds* (1980); Joan Didion, "The Women's Movement," *New York Times Book Review* (1972); Vivian Gornick and Barbara Moran, eds., *Women in Sexist Society* (1970); Lawrence Lader, *Abortion II: Making the Revolution* (1973); Paul Ehrlich, *The Population Bomb* (1968); Barry Commoner, *The Closing Circle* (1971); Frank Graham, Jr., *Since Silent Spring* (1970); John Maddox, *The Doomsday Syndrome* (1972); William Tucker, *Progress and Privilege* (1982); Samuel McCracken, "The Population Controllers," *Commentary* (1972); Gene Lyons, "Politics in the Woods," *Harper's* (1978); Mary Douglas and Aaron Wildavsky, *Risk and Culture: An Essay on the Selection of Technological and Environmental Dangers* (1983); Peter Passell and Leonard Ross, *Retreat from Riches: Affluence and Its Enemies* (1973); and Charles McCarry, *Citizen Nader* (1975).

11. Nixon and Kissinger: Deception, Dollars, and Détente

For the Nixon-Kissinger foreign policy, see James Chace, *A World Elsewhere: The New American Foreign Policy* (1973); Lloyd Gardner, *The Great Nixon Turnaround* (1973); Jonathan Schell, *The Time of Illusion* (1975); John Stoessinger, *Henry Kissinger* (1976); Roger Morris, *Uncertain Greatness: Henry Kissinger and American Foreign Policy* (1977); Adam Ulam, *Dangerous Relations: The Soviet Union in World Politics, 1970-1982* (1983); Henry Kissinger, *White House Years* (1979); Stanley Hoffman, *Primacy or World Order* (1978); Robert W. Tucker, *The New Isolationism* (1972); N. Gordon Levin, "Nixon, the Senate and the War," *Commentary* (1970); and John L. Gaddis, *Strategies of Containment* (1982). Nixon economic policy is discussed in Leonard Silk, *Nixonomics* (1972); Michael Harrington, *Decade of Decision* (1980); David Calleo, *The Im-*

perious Economy (1982); Alfred E. Eckes, Jr., *A Search for Solvency: Bretton Woods and the International Monetary System, 1941–1971* (1975); Edward P. Tufte, *Political Control of the Economy* (1978); and Richard J. Whalen, *Taking Sides* (1974). For the 1970 election and the importance of Spiro T. Agnew, see Jules Witcover, *White Knight: The Rise of Spiro Agnew* (1972); Jim G. Lucas, *Agnew: Profile in Conflict* (1970); Peter Schrag, *The Decline of the Wasp* (1971); and John Coyne, *Fall In and Cheer* (1979).

12. Coup and Counter-coup

The 1972 presidential campaign is discussed in Michael Novak, *Choosing Our King* (1974); Hunter Thompson, *Fear and Loathing on the Campaign Trail* (1973); John G. Stewart, *One Last Chance: The Democratic Party 1974–1976* (1974); Theodore White, *The Making of the President 1972* (1973); Gary Hart, *Right from the Start: A Chronicle of the McGovern Campaign* (1973); George McGovern, *Grassroots: The Autobiography of George McGovern* (1978); and Jody Carlson, *George Wallace and the Politics of Powerlessness* (1981). Nixon's second-term foreign policy is treated in Tad Szulc, *The Illusion of Peace* (1978); Frank Snepp, *Decent Interval* (1977); James Aikens, "The Oil Crisis: This Time the Wolf Is Here," *Foreign Affairs* (1973); Henry Pachter, "Détente: Myth and Reality," *Dissent* (1974); Edward Friedland, Paul Seabury, and Aaron Wildavsky, *The Great Détente Disaster: Oil and the Decline of American Foreign Policy* (1975); Henry Kissinger, *Years of Upheaval* (1982); and Theodore Draper, "Kissinger's Apologia," *Dissent* (1980). Watergate and Nixon's attempt to assert control over the federal bureaucracy are discussed in James Reichley, *Conservatives in an Age of Change: The Nixon and Ford Administrations* (1981); Theodore Lowi, *The End of Liberalism: The Second Republic of the United States* (2nd ed., 1979); J. Anthony Lukas, *Nightmare: The Underside of the Nixon Years* (1976); Nicholas von Hoffman, *Make-Believe Presidents* (1978); Henry Fairlie, "Lessons of Watergate: An Essay on the Possibility of Morality in Politics," *Encounter* (1974); Kevin Phillips, *Post-Conservative America* (1982); Dan Rather and Gary Paul Gates, *The Palace Guard* (1974); Seymour Martin Lipset and Earl Raab, "An Appointment with Watergate," *Commentary* (1973); Seymour Hersh, "The Pardon: Nixon, Ford, Haig and the Transfer of Power," *Atlantic* (1983); Richard P. Nathan, *The Plot That Failed* (1975); Aaron Wildavsky, "Government and the People," *Commentary* (1973); Hugh Heclo, *A Government of Strangers: Executive Politics in Washington* (1977); and Richard Nixon, *RN: The Memoirs of Richard Nixon* (1978).

13. JIMMY CARTER, RONALD REAGAN, AND THE
LEGACY OF GEORGE WALLACE *and*
EPILOGUE. THE END OF AMERICAN EXCEPTIONALISM

For the Carter years, see Betty Glad, *Jimmy Carter: In Search of the Great White House* (1980); Jules Witcover, *Marathon: The Pursuit of the Presidency, 1972–1976* (1977); Haynes Johnson, *In the Absence of Power* (1980); Joseph Califano, *Governing America* (1981); Jimmy Carter, *Keeping Faith* (1982); Fred Siegel, "Race: The Missing Issue of 1980," *Dissent* (1982); Robert Kutner, *The Revolt of the Haves: Tax Revolts and Hard Times* (1980); Austin Ranney, *The American Elections of 1980* (1981); Gerald Pomper, ed., *The Election of 1980* (1981); Kevin Phillips, *Post-Conservative America* (1982); Edmund Fawcett and Tony Thomas, *The American Condition* (1982); Michael Harrington, "A Path for America," *Dissent* (1982); Robert Reich, *The Next American Frontier* (1983).

Cox, Eugene, 67
Crangle, Joe, 248
Cronkite, Walter, 187

Daley, Richard J., 130, 192, 195, 197, 248
Darlan, Jean, 9
Davies, John Patton, 46, 47
Davies, Joseph E., 13, 29, 30, 37, 57
de Gaulle, Charles, 53, 62, 118, 119, 137
Dean, James, 111
Dean, John, 253, 256, 257
Dellinger, Dave, 176
Dewey, Thomas E., 13, 14, 65, 66, 69, 70, 96, 98
Diem, Ngo Dinh, 139, 141
Dingell, John, 17
Djilas, Milovan, 53
Dobrynin, Anatoly, 237
Doenitz, Karl, 23
Dole, Robert, 223
Douglas, Helen Gahagan, 62
Douglas, Paul, 170
Douglas, William O., 39, 214
Draper, Theodore, 253–54
Dulles, Allen, 51
Dulles, John Foster, 31, 117, 118
Durkin, Martin, 102

Eagleton, Tom, 262
Eastman, Max, 13
Edsall, Thomas, 264
Ehrlich, Paul, 210
Ehrlichman, John, 225, 226, 243, 249, 256
Eisenhower, Dwight D., 23, 35, 64, 76, 84, 92, 96–105 *passim*, 113, 116, 117, 118, 120, 125, 126, 128, 131, 132, 134, 143 146, 202, 203, 212, 217, 231
Eizenstat, Stuart, 267
Eliot, T. S., 178
Ellsberg, Daniel, 228
Ervin, Joe, 67, 143
Ervin, Sam, 67, 255, 256, 257
Evers, Medgar, 149

Fairlie, Henry, 134, 257
Falwell, Jerry, 262
Fanning, Lawrence, 252
Farmer, James, 143, 147
Faubus, Orville, 146
Feiffer, Jules, 265
Fiedler, Leslie, 72, 75
Finch, Robert, 225
Firestone, Shulamith, 209

Ford, Gerald R., 170, 259, 261, 262, 263, 264, 267, 269
Ford, Henry J., 221
Forrestal, James, 37, 46, 63
Franco, Francisco, 127
Frankovic, Kathleen, 266
Frazier, E. Franklin, 142
Freud, Sigmund, 110, 209
Friedan, Betty, 207
Friedman, Milton, 234
Fulbright, J. William, 26, 54, 220, 221

Gaither, H. Rowan Jr., 121
Galbraith, John Kenneth, 88, 89, 113, 114–15, 116, 127, 128, 140, 181, 215, 240
Gass, Oscar, 151, 159
Gates, Thomas, 126
Gelb, Leslie, 227
George II, King of Greece, 55
Gesell, Arnold, 109
Ginsberg, Allen, 112, 182, 244
Goebbels, Joseph Paul, 23, 42
Goldberg, Arthur, 154
Goldman, Eric, 70
Goldwater, Barry, 156, 157, 158, 159, 160, 169, 171, 175, 203, 204
Goodman, Walter, 263
Goodwin, Richard, 211, 212
Gornick, Vivian, 208
Grant, Ulysses S., 66
Greeley, Andrew, 198
Gregory, Dick, 181
Griffin, Robert, 223
Gruening, Ernest, 177

Hacker, Andrew, 106
Hadley, Arthur, 262
Halberstam, David, 177
Haldeman, H. R., 217, 225, 226, 249, 256, 259
Hardwick, Elizabeth, 200
Harlan, John Marshall, 144
Harrigan, Anthony, 113
Harriman, W. Averell, 15, 27, 28, 29, 31, 32, 34, 121, 191
Harrington, Michael, 155, 231, 251
Harris, Fred, 262
Harsh, Joseph, 80
Hartke, Vance, 221
Hatfield, Mark, 222, 223
Hayek, Friedrich von, 88
Hays, Wayne, 248
Heath, Jim, 161
Hegel, Georg, 178
Heineman, Ben, 249
Hersey, John, 123

Index of Names

Acheson, Dean, 22, 40, 51, 56, 59, 60, 72, 73, 74, 76, 78, 79, 80, 81, 82, 84, 100, 117, 135, 136, 191
Adamic, Louis, 195
Adams, Henry, 99
Agee, James, 13
Agnew, Spiro T., 203, 225, 228, 229, 230, 259, 268
Aikens, James, 258
Allende, Salvador, 258
Alsop, Joseph, 158
Anderson, John, 269
Arendt, Hannah, 240
Arvid, Inga, 123
Attlee, Clement, 82

Baldwin, James, 166
Ball, George, 191, 258
Barnes, Harry Elmer, 7
Baruch, Bernard, 26
Batista, Fulgencio, 133, 134
Bayh, Birch, 262
Bazelon, David, 182, 207
Beard, Charles, 222
Beecher, William, 219
Bell, Daniel, 99
Bellow, Saul, 110
Bennett, Lerone, 145
Bentham, Jeremy, 114
Berger, Bennett, 107
Berlin, Isaiah, 16
Bickel, Alexander, 144
Bilbo, Theodore, 67
Birch, John, 71
Bismarck, Otto von, 53
Bohlen, Charles E., 40, 45
Bond, Julian, 147
Boorstin, Daniel, 178, 180, 182
Brezhnev, Leonid, 239, 242
Bricker, John, 14
Brown, H. Rap, 167, 218
Brown, Jerry, 68
Brownmiller, Susan, 209
Bruce, Lenny, 181, 182

Buchan, John, 122, 125
Buchanan, Pat, 263
Buckley, William F. Jr., 126, 157, 249
Bundy, McGeorge, 132, 173, 191
Bundy, William, 191
Burger, Warren, 245
Burke, Edmund, 203, 205, 228
Burns, Arthur, 232, 236
Butler, Hugh, 73
Byrnes, James, 37, 38, 40, 41, 55

Cadell, Pat, 246, 247
Califano, Joseph, 267
Camus, Albert, 86, 177
Cantril, Hadley, 15
Capehart, Homer, 37
Carmichael, Stokely, 166, 167, 207
Carnegie, Dale, 24
Carson, Rachel, 210
Carter, Jimmy, 262, 263, 264, 266, 267, 268, 269, 272
Castro, Fidel, 125, 131, 133, 134, 135, 158, 179, 181, 190
Chamberlain, Neville, 37–38
Chambers, Whittaker, 74, 75, 196
Chessman, Caryl, 181, 182
Chesterton, G. K., 49
Chiang Kai-shek, 32, 38, 40, 47, 53, 59, 70, 71, 72, 73, 74, 77, 79, 82
Chisholm, Shirley, 193
Chu Teh, 71
Church, Frank, 222
Churchill, Winston, 14, 15, 16, 18, 19, 30, 32, 41, 42, 137
Clark, Joseph, 121
Clark, Kenneth, 167
Clay, Lucius D., 63
Cleaver, Eldridge, 182
Cleveland, Grover, 99
Clifford, Clark, 23, 46, 69, 185, 191
Commoner, Barry, 215
Connally, John, 232, 234, 235, 271
Connor, Eugene "Bull," 67, 143, 148
Cooper, John Sherman, 222

·285·

Index

Hickel, Walter, 225
Hilliard, David, 218
Hillman, Sidney, 14
Hiss, Alger, 70, 72, 73, 74, 75, 100, 124, 128, 196, 226
Hitler, Adolf, 3, 5–14 passim, 16, 23, 25, 29, 32, 34, 38, 45, 46, 51, 57, 58, 61, 63, 69, 123, 142, 179, 180, 186
Ho Chi Minh, 138, 139, 185, 205
Hobbes, Thomas, 20
Hobby, Oveta Culp, 103
Hodgson, Godfrey, 142, 148, 179
Hoffa, Jimmy, 189, 190
Hoffman, Abbie, 195
Hoffman, Nicholas von, 260
Hoffman, Paul, 102
Hoover, Herbert, 54, 97, 102, 104, 114
Hoover, J. Edgar, 54, 219, 227
Hopkins, Harry, 18, 30, 31, 32, 227
Hottelet, Richard C., 52
Howe, Irving, 100
Hughes, H. Stuart, 64, 98
Hull, Cordell, 15, 31, 137
Humphrey, George, 102
Humphrey, Hubert H., 127, 193, 194, 196, 198, 200, 201, 203, 204, 212, 229, 245, 246, 247, 266
Hunt, E. Howard, 256
Huston, Tom, 227, 228, 253

Ickes, Harold, 12
Innis, Roy, 167

Jackson, Henry, 245, 247, 262
Jackson, Jesse, 248
Jefferson, Thomas, 8
Jenner, William, 81
Johnson, Louis, 79
Johnson, Lyndon B., 117, 127, 130, 152–64 passim, 169, 171, 172–73, 174, 175, 179, 183–94 passim, 196, 201, 202, 203, 205, 217, 223, 225, 231, 234, 235, 237, 241, 245, 249, 254
Jones, LeRoi, 166
Jordan, Vernon, 215

Kahn, Herman, 118
Kazin, Alfred, 154
Kempton, Murray, 173
Kennan, George F., 10, 45, 46, 47, 61
Kennedy, Edward M., 122, 201, 219, 262, 272
Kennedy, Jacqueline, 132
Kennedy, John F., 64, 72, 86, 121–41 passim, 146–52 passim, 154, 156, 171, 172, 173, 175, 179, 190, 202, 206, 212, 231, 252, 260

Kennedy, Joseph P., 10, 122, 123, 124
Kennedy, Robert F., 122, 132, 136, 141, 147, 148, 153, 188–96 passim, 201, 244
Kennedy, Rose Fitzgerald, 122
Kerouac, Jack, 112
Khrushchev, Nikita, 79, 119, 120, 126, 133, 134, 135, 136, 139, 239
Kiker, Douglas, 200
Kim Il Sung, 79, 80, 84
King, Martin Luther Jr., 145, 146, 148, 149, 163, 165, 169, 190, 192, 193, 197, 200, 228
Kirchwey, Freda, 43
Kirk, Russell, 113
Kissinger, Henry, 118, 121, 206, 216, 217, 219, 227, 235–43 passim, 252, 253, 254, 258, 261
Klein, Herbert, 202
Kleindienst, Richard, 255, 257
Kristol, Irving, 228
Krock, Arthur, 123
Kurner, Bob, 267
Kutcher, James, 61
Ky, Nguyen Cao, 174, 186

Laird, Melvin, 236
Lattre de Tassigny, Jean de, 138
Lausche, Frank, 126
Lawrence, T. E., 122
Leahy, William, 17, 38
Lee, Robert E., 66
Lehrman, Hal, 43
Lenin, Vladimir, 13, 46, 57, 58
Lerner, Max, 122
Levin, Gordon, 223
Levitan, Sar, 162
Lewis, Fulton Jr., 88
Lewis, John, 150
Lewis, John L., 54, 90, 94
Lewis, Oscar, 155
Lincoln, Abraham, 5, 56
Lindbergh, Anne Morrow, 57, 58
Lindbergh, Charles, 10, 57, 58
Lindsay, John, 121, 192, 220, 221, 244
Lippmann, Walter, 18, 26, 44, 45, 59, 62, 63, 65, 98, 99, 126, 176
Litvinov, Maxim, 52
Long, Earl, 155
Long, Huey, 121
Lovett, Robert, 59
Lowell, Robert, 188
Lowenstein, Allard, 188, 194
Lubell, Samuel, 76, 203
Luce, Henry, 71, 72, 74, 131, 192
Lynd, Staughton, 177
Lynes, Russell, 111

Index

MacArthur, Douglas, 65, 72, 82, 83, 84, 159
McCarthy, Eugene, 126, 188, 189, 190, 191, 193, 194, 195, 196, 201, 244
McCarthy, Joseph, 13, 48, 75, 76, 77, 78, 81, 82, 92, 99, 100, 124, 143, 157, 189, 205, 228, 260
McCloy, John J., 258
McCord, James, 256
McGovern, George, 196, 214, 221, 222, 223, 244, 245, 246, 247, 248, 251, 252, 256
MacLaine, Shirley, 248
McMahon, Brien, 83
McNamara, Robert, 132, 135, 140, 173, 191
McReynolds, David, 179
MacVeagh, Lincoln, 55
Magruder, Jeb, 256
Mailer, Norman, 127, 128, 178, 179, 183
Malcolm X (Malcolm Little), 164–65
Mao Zedong, 32, 53, 60, 70, 71, 79, 80, 82, 119, 157, 240
Marshall, George, 55, 56, 62, 100
Marx, Karl, 46, 180
Meany, George, 184, 230
Meyner, Robert, 121
Mills, C. Wright, 106
Mills, Wilbur, 161
Mitchell, John, 202, 226, 229, 230, 256
Molotov, Vyacheslav, 29, 37, 62, 69
Morgenthau, Hans, 238
Morse, Wayne, 161, 177
Moses, Robert, 147
Moynihan, Daniel Patrick, 212, 253
Murphy, George, 223
Muskie, Edmund, 245, 246
Mussolini, Benito, 6, 57, 61
Muste, A. J., 143, 176

Nader, Ralph, 212–13, 215
Navasky, Victor, 78
Neely, Richard, 266
Nixon, E. D., 145
Nixon, Richard M., 62, 74, 77, 100, 101, 124, 126, 128, 130, 196, 198, 200–206 passim, 212, 213, 216, 217, 218, 219, 220, 223–32 passim, 234–43 passim, 245, 246, 247, 249–61 passim, 271

Oberdorfer, Don, 187
O'Brien, Larry, 232
Orwell, George, 180, 204

Packard, Vance, 180
Paine, Thomas, 58
Parks, Rosa, 145
Peale, Norman Vincent, 95
Pepper, Claude, 57
Percy, Charles, 121
Perkins, Carl, 255
Pershing, John Joseph, 81
Pétain, Henri Philippe, 61
Phillips, Kevin, 202, 263
Pius XII, Pope, 11
Prendergast, Tom, 21, 34
Presley, Elvis, 111
Protagoras, 214

Randolph, A. Philip, 142, 143, 145, 149, 165
Rankin, John, 40
Rayburn, Sam, 127, 128, 153, 154
Reagan, Ronald, 170, 202, 242, 262, 263, 267, 268, 269, 272
Reich, Charles, 183, 214, 215
Reich, Robert, 272
Reston, James, 8
Reuther, Walter, 90, 158
Rhee, Syngman, 79
Riesman, David, 111, 224
Robeson, Paul, 143
Rockefeller, Nelson, 118, 121, 122, 157, 202, 226, 229, 261, 262
Romney, George, 229
Roosevelt, Franklin D., 4, 6–24 passim, 27, 29, 33, 39, 40, 41, 45, 47, 48, 49, 50, 54, 56, 65, 66, 68, 70, 71, 72, 74, 78, 87, 91, 124, 127, 137, 138, 142, 152, 160, 162, 172, 175, 221, 222, 229, 235, 238, 239
Roosevelt, Theodore, 124, 132
Rosenberg, Harold, 180
Rostow, Walter W., 173, 217
Roszak, Theodore, 215
Rovere, Richard, 77, 193
Royko, Mike, 248
Rubin, Jerry, 195
Rusk, Dean, 136, 184, 240
Russell, Jane, 113
Rustin, Bayard, 143, 145, 149, 165, 176

Sadat, Anwar, 58
Safire, William, 249, 250
Sahl, Mort, 181
Salk, Jonas, 103
Samuelson, Paul, 108
Santayana, George, 114
Saulnier, Raymond J., 112, 113

Index

Schlafly, Phyllis, 158
Schlesinger, Arthur M. Jr., 65*n*., 126, 127, 129, 130, 132
Schmidt, Helmut, 273
Schneider, William, 269
Schumpeter, Joseph, 272
Schuyler, George, 142
Scranton, William W., 229
Sevareid, Eric, 128
Shadeg, Stephen, 157
Shah of Iran (Mohammed Reza Pahlevi), 258, 268
Sherman, William Tecumseh, 66, 79
Shogun, Robert, 252
Sihanouk, Norodom, 219
Sinatra, Frank, 228
Sirica, John, 256
Skinner, B. F., 239
Smiley, Glen, 145
Smith, Adam, 238
Smith, Al, 127, 245
Sontag, Susan, 182
Sorenson, Ted, 124
Spellman, Francis Joseph Cardinal, 12
Spock, Benjamin, 109
Stalin, Joseph, 10–19 *passim*, 21, 24, 28–35 *passim*, 38, 39, 42, 44, 45, 51, 52, 53, 57, 58, 60, 64, 68, 69, 70, 71, 79, 80, 81, 84, 116, 180, 227, 239
Steel, Ronald, 190
Stevenson, Adlai E., 99, 100, 101, 102, 114, 120, 132, 136, 181, 188
Stilwell, "Vinegar Joe," 70, 71
Stimson, Henry, 28, 33, 34, 35, 36, 37
Stone, I. F., 11, 62, 69
Summers, Harry, 185

Taft, Robert A., 4, 10, 50, 54, 65, 70, 71, 78, 82, 84, 89, 91, 96, 97, 98, 99, 121, 122, 157, 158
Taylor, Glenn, 67
Taylor, Maxwell, 140
Thieu, Nguyen Van, 174, 186, 219, 240, 241, 254
Thompson, Hunter, 244
Thurmond, Strom, 202, 204
Tito, Marshal, 52, 60
Tocqueville, Alexis de, 112
TRB (*New Republic* columnist), 18, 28
Trilling, Lionel, 176
Trotsky, Leon, 11, 13, 39, 48, 57, 70
Truman, Harry S., 13, 17, 19, 21, 22, 23, 24, 27, 28, 29, 30, 32, 33, 34, 35, 37, 38, 39, 41, 43, 44, 45, 48–67 *passim*, 69, 70, 71, 72, 73, 79–84 *passim*, 86–91 *passim*, 94, 96, 99, 104, 117, 121, 131, 153, 159, 161, 172, 175, 184, 222, 235, 240, 251
Tydings, Joseph, 81

Udall, Morris, 262
Unruh, Jesse, 211

Van Buren, Martin, 263
Vance, Cyrus, 191
Vandenberg, Arthur, 28, 31, 41, 56, 71
Veblen, Thorstein, 108
Viguerie, Richard, 262, 263
Vishinsky, Andrei, 18, 69

Wallace, George, 148, 158, 160, 198, 200, 201, 202, 203, 204, 245, 246, 247, 252, 262, 263, 266, 268
Wallace, Henry, 7, 8, 13, 14, 21, 24, 43, 44, 57, 62, 67, 68, 69, 87
Walsh, Edmund, 13, 76
Warren, Earl, 143, 144, 146
Washington, George, 5
Wattenberg, Ben, 229, 230
Weber, Max, 189*n*.
Wechsler, James, 61, 135
Weeks, Sinclair, 103
Westmoreland, William, 186, 187
Weyrich, Paul, 263, 268
Whalen, Richard, 154, 158, 235
Wheeler, Burton K., 7, 31, 47
Wherry, Kenneth, 90
Whyte, William, 180
Wicker, Tom, 196–97, 202
Wiley, Alexander, 109
Will, George, 272
Williams, William Appleman, 178
Willing, Martha, 210
Willkie, Wendell, 7, 98
Wilson, Charles, 101, 102, 111
Wilson, Edmund, 50
Wilson, Robert, 182
Wilson, Woodrow, 4, 5, 8, 137, 138
Witcover, Julius, 262
Wolfe, Tom, 151
Wright, Richard, 169
Wrong, Dennis, 97

Xuan Thuy, 227

Zanuck, Darryl, 101
Zhdanov, Andrei, 42
Zhou Enlai, 239
Ziegler, Ron, 256

DATE DUE

DEC 10 1990

HIGHSMITH 45-220